THE
MENTAL HEALTH
ADVANTAGE

How the World's Best Companies
Drive Performance & Wellbeing
Through Proactive Mental Health

STEPHEN SOKOLER

Sam Litany Publishing
New York, New York

ISBN: 979-8-218-59519-7

Cover design by Shena Honey Lagapa Pulido (Yna)
Interior design by Jess LaGreca, Mayfly book design
Writing Contributor: Marjie Shrimpton

Library of Congress Catalog Number: 2025900811
First Printing: 2025

Ita, for your love and light, and for being my soulmate,
in this lifetime and beyond.

Mom, for your love, selflessness, and strength.

David, for your unwavering love, unending support,
and our unbreakable bond.

Sam, for being our beautiful miracle baby and showing me
the magic of pure wonder and joy.

The four of you are my heart, my compass, my love, and my life.

CONTENTS

INTRODUCTION

"Imagine if . . ."

I think this question is how a lot of entrepreneurs start businesses. See a problem → imagine the solution → decide that you should build the solution. That's certainly how I was in my early career. But what I didn't anticipate early on was where that question would lead me. The questions I'd ultimately ask one day would be: **"Imagine if everyone had access to the tools and support to live happier, healthier, and more balanced lives. How much of a difference would that make? What kind of world would we live in?"**

When I started in the corporate world in the late 1990s, mental health was not widely discussed. It was not prominent in our culture, and certainly not in the workplace. It wasn't talked about in classes I took at NYU, whether the liberal arts or the business classes, nor had I personally thought about my own mental health.

At that time, life was still a bit simpler. The internet existed, but it hadn't completely upended our lives just yet. We didn't have a 24-hour news cycle, we couldn't work from home, and we didn't carry around devices designed to constantly grab our attention. Social media wasn't showing us a stream of people living their "best lives," and the pace of life was slower, with more space for real connections and presence. We weren't plugged into everything everywhere all at once.

Now, with mini computers in our pockets, we see headlines from around the world all day long, scroll on social media whenever there is a dull moment, and answer emails at all hours. Remote work has blurred the lines between professional and personal life, and our news feeds reinforce our beliefs, deepening divisions and making us less tolerant of other perspectives. Life has changed—and fast. Some of these changes make our lives better, easier, and more convenient. Some, however, have caused us to avoid building friendships, deepening our relationships, and getting to know ourselves. And our mental health is suffering because of it.

Work, in particular, has taken on an entirely new role in this digital age. It's no longer just a place where we spend our time; it's a constant presence that follows us home, into our weekends, and even our vacations. The expectations to always be on, to produce more in less time, and to navigate endless streams of information have transformed the workplace into a source of chronic stress. We rarely disconnect, and as a result, the lines between work and personal life have all but disappeared. This constant pressure is taking a toll on our wellbeing, leaving little room for balance or recovery.

The changes to our work landscape, and our life in general, aren't slowing down anytime soon. Neither are the effects on our mental health. But most organizations aren't set up to support employees' mental health in a meaningful way. Some companies provide support when a crisis hits, but most are not set up to support preventive, proactive measures aimed to keep our mental health and wellbeing stable or, better yet, help us thrive.

This has to change. In today's day and age, organizations cannot overlook the central role they play in people's lives and the impact they have—and *can* have—on their employees' wellbeing. They need to start implementing proactive mental health programs and building proactive mental health cultures. This is not just about helping people because it's the right thing to do; it's also good for business.

But let's back up. How did I get passionate about proactive mental health in the workplace to begin with?

WHY I'M WRITING THIS BOOK

The realization hit me in my late twenties. I had accomplished what a lot of young entrepreneurs set out to do: I was running my own company, making money, and living in a big New York City apartment with my closest friends. I enjoyed an active social life and, as a passion project, I bought a bar in Greenwich Village with one of my best friends. By all outside measures, things were going really well. And it's true—there were many highs. But the thrill of each accomplishment, vacation, or wild night out only lasted briefly. As soon as one exciting experience ended, I immediately craved the next one, going to extremes to find the thing that would give me that peak feeling again. Some months, I'd go on a super strict diet and work out constantly. The next month, the pendulum would swing, and I'd party like there was no tomorrow and eat anything and everything. It was never enough. I didn't feel whole or complete. Nothing I was doing was making me feel better, and I knew there had to be a better way. I thought there had to be more to life, and I was determined to find it.

I started reading all sorts of books on self-improvement and purpose by some of the great thinkers of our day—Viktor Frankl, Dale Carnegie, Stephen Covey, Eckhart Tolle, and many others. Their teachings helped me to get clear on my purpose and what I wanted: a balanced, fulfilling life, both personally and professionally; meaningful work that helps make people's lives better; and to one day build a family. I developed a list I called "My Recipe for an Amazing Life," consisting of things I wanted to remember and things I wanted to do in a variety of areas in my life—physical, mental, emotional, spiritual, and financial. I read this list daily, updated it frequently, and to this day almost 20 years later, I still review it weekly.

However, it's one thing to identify the kind of life you want to have; it's another thing to actually live it. While my list helped me to gain some clarity, I remained very inconsistent. I couldn't find a way to stop vacillating between full-on gym rat and complete sloth, ultimate saver and total spendthrift. The imbalance left me in a similar place as before: unfulfilled, searching, and longing for something more. That was until 2011.

In 2011, I was running a company that helped organizations celebrate and inspire their employees. We decided to open offices around the world, and when there wasn't anyone available to open our Sydney office, I jumped at the chance. It not only allowed me to move to Australia for a few months, but I also saw it as a chance to start over. Aside from college study abroad, it was the first time I'd lived outside of New York City, and the journey brought me many things—new friends, new adventures, and the single greatest gift I had ever received.

One day, while roaming around a bookstore in Sydney, I came across a book titled *Buddhism for Busy People: Finding Happiness in an Uncertain World* by David Michie. I had always been disillusioned by dogma, but this title promised exactly what I'd been looking for—what I think a lot of us are looking for: happiness in a world that continues to change. From the minute I picked it up, I was hooked. Michie shared how meditation changed his life, and he explained it in such a simple, approachable way. I was so taken with it that I started meditating with no idea that it would turn out to be the missing piece of the puzzle.

The more I meditated, the more grounded I became and the more I discovered about who I was. Not only did I feel more balanced internally, but I also felt more self-assured, confident, and less reactive. I was able to see the things I was doing that were out of line with who I wanted to be. I was able to be more thoughtful in my responses to people and situations, allowing me to build deeper connections, both with friends and family and at work. I stopped oscillating between extreme exercise and dieting behaviors and developed consistent, healthy habits. My meditation practice brought me both the meaning and contentment that I had always sought as well as stability in my mental health and wellbeing.

It's often hard to articulate the impact meditation had on my life. Years prior, I'd lost 85 pounds, and while that physical transformation was empowering, it didn't come close to the depth of change I experienced through meditation. The mental clarity, emotional resilience, and sense of inner peace that came from regular practice fundamentally reshaped how I lived, thought, and connected with the world around me.

A few years later, I sold the business I'd been running for a decade with no idea of what would come next. I started to do some soul-searching and quickly realized I needed to do something that could really help people. After discussions with friends, family, and many people in the business community, it hit me just how much suffering there was, how mental health was still stigmatized and misunderstood, and how many barriers to care there still were in most places. I had benefited so much from the meditation practice I'd begun years prior, and realized I wanted to help others experience the same. So, in February of 2015, I created Journey, a mental health company with the mission of helping *all* people live happier, healthier, less-stressed lives.

Journey began as a business-to-business ("B2B") company bringing live, on-site meditation classes and workshops into organizations. Our first client was Warby Parker, and we quickly found an audience with companies like Time Warner, Facebook, and Google. In 2018, we took all of our learnings from working with companies and expanded the business to consumers. We built a digital platform called Journey LIVE, bringing live, group meditation classes to people everywhere. No matter where you were, where you worked, or what time of day it was, you could join a class from your device. TechCrunch called us "Peloton for meditation." As more users came on board, we added more types of mental wellbeing classes, incorporating things like journaling, breathwork, and positive psychology.

When the COVID-19 pandemic hit in 2020, it exacerbated mental health concerns for nearly everyone. However, it became clear that while group meditation classes were still something people wanted and needed, there were some broader, more fundamental gaps with mental healthcare. The vast majority of organizations weren't set up to support their employees' mental health at a time when they really, really needed to be.

Many organizations were caught off guard, unprepared to meet the mental health needs of their employees in such a critical moment. Mental health had not been woven into the fabric of most work cultures, and for some, support programs barely existed beyond what health insurance provided. When they did offer more, it was typically through an Employee Assistance Program (EAP)—a standard workplace benefit offering confidential support for personal and professional challenges, including mental health, financial, legal, and work-life issues. With traditional EAPs, the data showed that less than 20% of employees were aware of the benefit and only 3% of employees used it, meaning 97% of employees were not getting care. The programs were not only rarely used, they were reactive—meaning, they provided limited support only *after* a mental health issue escalated past a tipping point.

So, our team at Journey decided to help change this and focus all of our efforts on organizations. We expanded Journey LIVE to become the most comprehensive proactive digital mental health platform available. We introduced a wide range of on-demand classes and, because inclusion is part of our DNA, we tackled topics that other companies avoided. For example, we created content on "Breaking Silence on Black Mental Wellness," menopause, neurodivergence, non-suicidal self-injury, gender equity, and more. We also added features like a daily email to provide employees with bite-sized tips and videos to start their morning, calendar integrations to incorporate healthy habits into their day, and a Zoom app to weave mental health support into the days of back-to-back video calls that had become so common.

After several years of providing proactive mental health support to organizations like Walgreens, L'Oréal, and Sony, we realized we needed to do more. We achieved high engagement—30% on average—and helped employees build healthy habits, but the wait time for clinical care through traditional EAPs was still far too long. On average, employees were waiting three weeks for care, and sometimes as long as five or six weeks. This delay was unacceptable when timely support was needed most. We knew we had to take action.

Building upon the success of Journey LIVE, we created an entirely new product: Journey Proactive EAP. Journey Proactive focuses on preventive care to support employees *before* issues escalate, fostering a healthier, more resilient, and higher-performing culture. Through personalized communication strategies and consistent check-ins, we ensure easy access to both clinical and subclinical mental healthcare, providing employees with the right level of support when and where they need it. We integrated daily tips and videos to keep mental health top of mind and personalized reminders to help employees build habits like mindfulness, movement, and journaling. We gently reach out during key life events—promotions, divorce, new children, or even challenging local events—and after employees have viewed sensitive content, such as videos on grief or suicidal ideation. Using predictive analytics, we identify potential risks early, allowing for timely support before issues escalate. Most importantly, we significantly reduced the wait time for care—employees now receive immediate assistance when necessary, with an average time to care of just three days, 10x faster than the industry norm.

After a decade in this space, working with thousands of organizations—from American Express and Becton Dickinson (BD) to Universal Music Group and the Harlem Children's Zone—across 190 countries and in over 100 languages, I believe we've finally cracked the code. The secret lies in shifting from reactive to proactive mental health: supporting employees before issues escalate, fostering resilience, and driving better business outcomes.

This book is a culmination of what I've learned from collaborating with leading experts in mental health, human resources, and digital health, and from countless conversations with people leaders about their challenges and aspirations for employee wellbeing. My goal is to help more organizations adopt this proactive approach, transforming how they support their employees and families while achieving meaningful results, starting *now*.

WHAT TO EXPECT FROM THIS BOOK

This book is meant to focus explicitly on mental health in organizations and how to implement a proactive approach. This is for HR teams, leaders, executives, managers, and consultants who want to help support the mental health of employees all over the world. My hope is that you will leave with an understanding of the following:

- The difference between proactive and reactive mental health approaches
- Why it's so important to support proactive mental health in organizations, especially now

- How to build a proactive mental health culture that supports all employees, regardless of background, race, gender, life stage, sexual orientation, industry, role, location, etc.
- What tips and tools can help support a proactive mental health culture as well as individuals on their own
- How to measure the success of your proactive mental health approach
- Ways that other successful organizations have created proactive mental health cultures and how they've benefited from them

I am not a licensed mental health professional. I work with many of them, have seen them myself over the years, and have consulted with many others on the development of my company's products as well as this book. However, nothing in this book should be taken as medical or psychiatric advice. If you are dealing with an employee mental health emergency, or are actively struggling with your own mental health, please seek care from a mental health professional or your primary care provider. (In the Appendices in the back of the book, you will also find lists of mental health resources and crisis hotlines that may be useful to you.)

I am writing as an experienced business leader in the space, a passionate mental health advocate, and a personal beneficiary of proactive mental health practices who knows firsthand how central a role workplaces have in shaping people's lives and wellbeing. I have seen and helped facilitate incredible transformations in organizations that have employed a proactive mental health approach—both in the lives of their employees and in those organizations' overall productivity and success. My goal with this book is to shed light on how we can create more of those transformations in more organizations, thereby improving the state of workplaces and mental health everywhere.

CHAPTER 1

UNDERSTANDING MENTAL HEALTH TODAY

Rosie woke up in the morning to find three Slack messages from her manager already waiting for her. It was only 7:03 AM. Her workday wasn't supposed to start until 9:30 AM, but the messages were urgent. A major client wanted to make a last-minute change to their ad campaign. Rosie had worked late making other changes for the client, coordinating with two vendors to get everything up to par. Apparently to no avail. Reading her manager's messages, Rosie could feel her heart rate rise, her throat start to close, and her stomach tighten. This was a big client, and they were known for expecting changes, meetings, and responses right away, no matter what time it was. In fact, just last week, Rosie had to hop on a call at 11:15 PM to make another "urgent" change to a deck she'd prepared for them. And this was just one of her clients. She led three big accounts, and management had made it clear that it was Rosie's responsbility to keep all of them satisfied.

Since starting this job, Rosie's health had taken a turn for the worse. She'd started experiencing insomnia and dreaded going to work every day. "Going to work" isn't quite accurate, though. After going fully remote during the pandemic, her company had recently changed to hybrid. Three days a week, she commuted an hour to work just to spend half the day on Zoom. The other two days, her bedroom was her office. She'd roll out of bed, open her laptop, and with emails and messages already piling up, get started right after her alarm went off. With back-to-back meetings that often went through lunchtime, Rosie wasn't eating well. She'd also stopped working out, and multiple times a month, she had to cancel plans with friends and family to attend to a work matter. Her stress and anxiety from work had gotten so bad, she'd had two panic attacks in five weeks, ending up in the emergency room.

Rosie liked her team and the work they did, but she had reached a breaking point and didn't know what to do. Her manager didn't seem to care about mental health or setting guardrails around working from home. She actually feared losing her job if she spoke up, and, truthfully, she didn't have time to look for a new one. She felt stuck.

Rosie's story is, unfortunately, not uncommon these days. In the last few years, the workplace has undergone its most significant transformation ever, bringing equally fantastic and challenging changes. People are now working from home consistently for the first time. We have greater diversity—of race, ethnicity, age, gender, sexual orientation, religion, neurodivergence, (dis)ability, socioeconomic class, etc.—at work, accompanied by differences in perspectives and expectations of workplaces and leaders. Our social and political climate feels more charged than at any other time in modern memory. Artificial intelligence has just taken a big seat at the table, prompting excitement about possibilities for its use as well as questions about job security in many industries. And many are feeling strapped by inflation and rising housing, food, and healthcare costs. We can all feel the effects on us as individuals, not to mention on our teams.

In this fast-paced, high-stress world, people, like Rosie, are experiencing mental health issues at an increasing, alarming rate. Our mental health influences how we think, feel, act, relate to others, and make decisions. So, when our mental health suffers, so too does our ability to function effectively in our daily lives, including, of course, at work. It's crucial, then, for workplaces to take the mental health of their employees seriously, not just when they reach a breaking point, but all the time. We need preventive, *proactive* mental health in workplaces everywhere.

In order to understand proactive mental health in the workplace, though, we need to first understand mental health in general and what it looks like in the workplace today.

WHAT IS MENTAL HEALTH?

The World Health Organization (WHO) defines mental health as . . .

> *A state of mental wellbeing that enables people to cope with the stresses of life, realize their abilities, learn and work well, and contribute to their community.*
>
> *It is an integral component of health and wellbeing that underpins our individual and collective abilities to make decisions, build relationships, and shape the world we live in.*

This definition underscores the fact that mental health is about more than just the absence of mental disorders—a state of *not* having something. Rather, it's about thriving emotionally and psychologically, maintaining a balanced life, and realizing one's potential. It's about having a positive sense and awareness of self. It's also a continuum that looks different for each of us and can change over time.

That change piece is important. Mental health is not some peak state we can achieve once and check off a list as an accomplishment. We don't reach the "height" of mental health and stay there. Instead, over the course of our lives, we constantly move along the continuum, sometimes experiencing better states of wellbeing and sometimes more challenging states.

So, what things can change our mental health? What affects where we sit on the continuum?

Influences on Our Mental Health

Our individual mental health is impacted by many factors. First, **our biology**, such as our genetics, brain chemistry, and physical health. We can't determine our genetics or brain chemistry, though we can influence elements of our physical health and, if needed, use medication to help rebalance certain hormones in our brain chemistry to improve our mental health.

The second major factor affecting our mental health is **our psychology**—our emotional responses, thought patterns, and coping mechanisms. Many of our instinctive responses, thoughts, and coping mechanisms come from what we see and learn in childhood. It can take time, conscious effort, and the help of mental health techniques and/or professionals for many of us to figure out all of those impulses and influences before we're aware of how they affect us.

Lastly, **our social and physical environments** affect our mental health in distinct ways. This includes our relationships and communities as well as the conditions, stability, and safety of our homes, cities, and workplaces. The news that we see and events that happen around us can certainly impact our mental health positively and negatively, too.

Altogether, these elements help determine how we manage stress, interact with others, and make decisions. They impact our capacity to thrive and, conversely, our risk of developing varying degrees of mental health conditions.

Common Mental Health Conditions

There are over 200 different mental health conditions with varying degrees of severity affecting nearly a billion people around the world, and while it's not solely about illness, to understand the need for prevention, we must also understand the most common conditions that affect us today.

Depression, characterized by persistent sadness and self-doubt, and anxiety disorders, characterized by overwhelming worry or fear, top the list of mental health conditions affecting individuals worldwide. Both can manifest physically and impair daily functioning. Burnout, caused by prolonged stress and exhaustion often due to work, is another common condition of our day—one of particular concern for employers and organizations. Bipolar disorder, substance use disorders, post-traumatic stress disorder (PTSD), obsessive-compulsive disorder (OCD), and eating disorders are additionally among the most common mental health conditions, affecting people in every walk of life and region around the world. Because of their prevalence, organizations, leaders, HR teams, and managers should all be aware of these conditions and how they might show up in and affect teams. (For fuller descriptions of each of these conditions, please see Appendix B in the back of the book.)

While cause for concern, thankfully these conditions are also treatable and manageable with access to the right resources. If left undiagnosed or untreated, however, people experiencing these conditions often cannot get the help they need, especially at work—which has not traditionally been a comfortable place for people to broach the subject of mental health, much less seek support.

THE STATE OF MENTAL HEALTH TODAY

Unfortunately, the global mental health landscape presents a sobering picture. Mental health issues are pervasive, affecting people of all ages, backgrounds, and socioeconomic statuses in every country in the world.

According to the WHO, 1 in 8 adults around the world has some form of mental health condition as of 2019, with anxiety disorders affecting over 284 million people globally and depression serving as the leading cause of disability. In the United States, the numbers are more serious. More than 1 in 5 adults in the U.S. have a mental health condition as of 2021, according to the National Institute of Mental Health. More specific data from the U.S. Substance Abuse and Mental Health Services Administration shows that mental illness affects . . .

- 27% of females
- 18% of males
- 34% of young adults between the ages of 18 and 25
- 28% of adults aged 26 to 49, and
- 15% of adults 50 and older.

Furthermore, the COVID-19 pandemic exacerbated mental health challenges, with increased rates of anxiety, depression, and stress reported globally in the years since.

The economic burden of mental health issues is staggering—and growing. The World Economic Forum estimates that these conditions could cost the global economy up to $16 trillion by 2030 due to lost productivity, healthcare costs, and social welfare expenses. These figures underscore the urgent need for comprehensive mental health strategies that not only address existing issues but also prevent new ones from arising.

THE IMPACT OF MENTAL HEALTH

Reading through even the limited list of conditions and data above, it becomes clear just how many aspects of our lives and behaviors our mental health can impact—basically, every aspect. Society tends to prioritize maintaining physical health, but our mental health is closely linked to our physical health and overall wellbeing.

Looking at physical health alone, poor mental health can lead to a range of problems, including heart disease, diabetes, chronic pain, digestive issues, and a weakened immune system. Conversely, taking care of your mental health can enhance your physical health by promoting healthy behaviors, improving immune function, and increasing life expectancy. Moreover, an individuals' mental health also affects their social and economic outcomes. With strong mental health, people are more likely to be productive, maintain stable employment, and build strong relationships, whereas untreated mental health issues can lead to social isolation, unemployment, and financial instability.

When mental health impacts individuals' lives in such significant ways, it's easy to see the potential for exponential impact when considering groups of individuals and communities, including organizations. Employees with strong mental health are more engaged, creative, and productive. They are also better equipped to handle stress and adapt to changing circumstances. Poor mental health, however, can result in increased absenteeism, presenteeism (i.e., working while unwell), and higher turnover rates, leading to significant costs for employers.

Zooming out another level, mental health issues impact communities and society in not just social but also tangible financial and systemic ways. When more people experience mental health issues, it can strain healthcare systems and social services. In the wake of the pandemic, we've seen a great shortage of licensed therapists, which means fewer people are able to get the help they need, much less in ways they can afford.

Addressing mental health proactively can reduce the burden on these systems. Considering the degree of severity the issue presents, it's easy to wonder why we haven't been able to do that up to this point. What is standing in the way?

THE HISTORICAL CONTEXT SURROUNDING MENTAL HEALTH

You can find references to mental health disorders, under various other names, in texts and records from every ancient civilization—Egyptian, Indian, Greek, and Roman. In those days, mental health disorders were regarded as some type of demonic possession. However, Hippocrates and other medical writers of the time seemed to understand that mental disorders were, in fact, physiologically related to the brain. Despite Hippocrates' insight on the matter, for several centuries thereafter, people generally equated mental illness with religious or moral deviance, leading to widespread misunderstanding and stigmatization. People suffering from mental health conditions faced discrimination and marginalization, and were frequently placed in asylums or otherwise isolated from society and given inadequate care.

In the late 19th century, mental healthcare began to improve with the advent of psychotherapy, popularized most widely first by Sigmund Freud and later by Carl Jung, and the development of psychiatric medications. Things shifted further after World War II and the development of behavior therapy in the 1950s. Public awareness campaigns, improved and increased scientific research, and policy changes in the later 20th century began to highlight the prevalence and impact of mental health issues, and the number of psychiatrists in the United States increased from 3,000 in 1939 to over 50,000 in the early 1990s. Despite these shifts, mental health interventions remained largely reactive, focusing on treating symptoms only after they had become severe. Mental health issues continued to be widely misunderstood, rarely discussed, and insufficiently addressed from a preventive standpoint.

Moving into the 21st century, the growth in scientific research broadened our collective awareness and understanding of mental health substantially. There are now more types of treatment, approaches, and professions in mental health than ever before, and culturally, we've seen a significant, positive shift in how people understand mental health and mental illness as well as the need for early intervention and prevention. Research has shown that preventive mental health strategies can significantly improve outcomes and reduce the incidence of severe mental health issues. There is a growing recognition that mental health is an integral part of overall health and wellbeing, and that proactive measures are essential for maintaining mental health in the long term.

Surviving Myths Around Mental Health Affecting the Workplace

That said, while a lot of the stigmas surrounding mental health and mental illness that began centuries ago have morphed over time—thankfully, most people no longer believe mental illness is the result of demonic possession or moral corruption—certain mental health myths still have their hold in many parts of the world, cultures, and communities. These myths are especially deep-rooted when it comes to discussing mental health in the workplace, which disincentivizes employees from seeking help or bringing up concerns.

Myth #1: Mental health issues are rare.

Reality: As you saw in the data mentioned earlier, mental health issues are not rare at all; in fact, they are quite common, affecting nearly a billion people worldwide. The WHO predicts that 1 in 4 people will be affected by mental or neurological disorders at some point in their lives. But the belief that they are rare contributes to people rejecting the idea that they might need or benefit from treatment, or that they could ever develop an acute issue. In the workplace, this detracts from the reality that roughly 20-25% of employees in every single organization are dealing with a mental health issue at any given time and need support.

Myth #2: Only people with severe issues or New Age beliefs go to therapy.

Reality: The first myth works in tandem with the idea that help—whether therapy, medication, or other forms of treatment—is only for "free spirits" or people with severe issues. Therapy can benefit anyone and provide useful tools and strategies for managing stress, emotions, and relationships, regardless of the severity of someone's mental health concerns or community.

In fact, as Marco Diaz, Global Head of Benefits at News Corp., explained to me, "Most people I know who are in therapy didn't start there because of a mental health crisis. They started because they recognized that their mental wellbeing needed attention, just like their physical health." When you look back in time, a lot of health practices started out with niche followings and skepticism from the masses. Even exercise and jogging were viewed as things only "weird" people did in the 1970s. You'd never guess it now.

Myth #3: Only weak people experience mental health problems.

Reality: Mental health issues have nothing to do with weakness. They can affect anyone, regardless of their strength or resilience, depending on a whole mix of factors, including our work environment. People of every background, socioeconomic class, identity group, industry, and role in an organization can and do experience mental health challenges. CEOs, linemen, teachers, plumbers, nurses, ad execs, lawyers, artists, investment bankers, politicians, social workers—everyone.

Myth #4: Mental health issues will go away on their own.

Reality: Mental health issues don't just evaporate after "sufficient" time. They require attention and, often, the help of mental health professionals. Without appropriate intervention, mental health issues can indeed worsen over time. Seeking help early can lead to better outcomes and prevent conditions from escalating.

Myth #5: Discussing mental health makes you vulnerable.

Reality: Sharing your mental health experiences and concerns can feel scary, especially in professional environments where you haven't talked about mental health previously. There are power dynamics at play in the workplace, too, and a lot of people fear that information about their mental health could be used against them in decisions about work assignments and promotions. While those concerns are understandable, sharing your mental health experiences can actually foster a supportive environment and reduce stigma. Open conversations about mental health tend to lead to greater understanding and empathy. Leaders and managers can help dispel this myth by setting an example for their teams and openly discussing mental health themselves.

THE OLD APPROACH ISN'T ENOUGH

Considering the prevalence of these myths, perhaps it's not surprising that up to this point mental health hasn't gotten significant attention in workplaces. Most organizations today place little emphasis on mental health and even less emphasis on preventive action and care. Even when workplaces provide mental health benefits and services, most of those benefits only handle situations when someone is already sick. Only once an employee reaches burnout, *then* they're given medical leave. Only once an employee's substance use rises to an untenable level, *then* they're directed to addiction support services and rehabilitation facilities. Only once an employee's stress and anxiety spikes, *then* they're routed to a psychiatrist for counseling and medication. It's more "sickcare" than healthcare. And to great detriment—both to the individuals affected and the organizations employing them. Playing catch-up with people's mental health needs means that the root causes often go unaddressed.

On another level, when employees only have access to support once they reach significant levels of mental health distress, it not only takes longer for them to achieve a healthy state again but it also costs them and their employers more money as they end up relying more on their health plans. Paying for a stint in rehab is expensive. Losing an employee for medical leave and having to either fill their position or train and pay current employees to take on the extra work is expensive and time-consuming. Having employees use their medical benefits for emergency room visits for stress-induced panic attacks, additional medications to manage their mental health, or clinical therapy to address an acute mental health condition—the list goes on—costs employers much more than providing services to help keep employees' mentally healthy day to day.

According to 2021 research from the National Safety Council and NORC at the University of Chicago, employees with significant mental health concerns use an additional $3,000 worth of healthcare services per year than those in positive states of mental health. The average cost of lost workdays due to mental health issues is $4,783 per employee annually, while the cost of turnover for employees impacted by mental health challenges adds an additional $5,733 per employee per year.

THE NEED FOR PROACTIVE MENTAL HEALTH IN THE WORKPLACE

Given the profound impact of mental health on individuals, society, and organizations, and the urgent need for support today, it's imperative that we shift our focus from merely reacting to mental health crises to actively preventing them. Peter Rutigliano, a partner at the global consultancy Mercer and leader of its behavioral health practice, shares this viewpoint. "Instead of waiting for problems to arise," Rutigliano said, "we should be building mental health programs that anticipate the challenges employees might face." We need to implement an approach through which people are supported every single day and encouraged to take action to support themselves.

Nowhere is better suited to this task than the workplace. Years ago, when we lived among groups and larger families and stayed in one place for the duration of our lives, most of our caretaking and mental and emotional support came through our neighborhoods and communities.

Now, though, we tend to move away from our childhood homes and our parents at younger ages, we move more frequently, we stay single for longer, and we have kids much later. The traditional community support systems have dissipated, and instead, people spend more waking hours at work and with colleagues than with their families or friends. On top of that, work today is particularly stressful and, for many people, all-consuming. To have a successful career, most people have to sacrifice a lot of time they may otherwise spend on hobbies and with loved ones that contribute to their positive wellbeing to be at work instead.

This was all true before the pandemic, but then COVID exacerbated the issue in different ways, creating an even more dire situation for employees. Dr. Randy Martin, the Clinical Director for the CopeNYC Employee Assistance Program at Weill Cornell Medicine, saw this firsthand. "Suddenly, all these people who had been managing okay were overwhelmed by isolation, fear, and uncertainty," Martin said. "It couldn't be ignored anymore. Companies saw the direct impact on their employees—burnout, anxiety, stress—and realized they had to start taking mental health seriously."

With employees giving more of themselves to the organizations they work for, giving up traditional support structures, and going through increasingly difficult circumstances, organizations have a greater obligation to step in and fill the void. "It starts with acknowledging that mental health is a collective responsibility," said Geetika Bhojak, Global Mental Health Lead at the business consulting firm Accenture. "We often talk about individual mental health, but the truth is, it's a shared experience—our mental health is impacted by the people around us, the environments we work in, and the cultures we build."

Aside from the responsibility, supporting employees' wellbeing is good business. "When employees have poor mental health, there's a ripple effect across the entire organization," said Eddie Gammill, Senior Director at the financial services firm Willis Towers Watson (WTW). "If you don't have healthy workers, you can't expect to have a thriving business." If supporting employees' mental health proactively will allow them to think more clearly, make better decisions, collaborate more effectively, and stay healthier (and thus use the health plan less and show up to work more), that's better for business on every level. Instituting a proactive mental health approach makes sense no matter which way you look at it.

The rest of this book is devoted to discussing *how* we do this. By understanding the factors that contribute to mental health and implementing strategies to promote wellbeing, organizations everywhere can create a foundation for a healthier, more resilient population and a future where mental health is prioritized, individuals thrive, and organizations flourish.

EXERCISE

Reflecting on Your Beliefs Around Mental Health

To affect any change in an organization's mental health approach, or our own, it's important to understand what biases and assumptions we carry—which myths we still believe in—so that we know what personal hurdles we may encounter or need to address to drive real change.

Given all of the information you just read about mental health around the world, its history, and the state of support for mental wellbeing in the workplace, take a minute to read the following questions and think about your personal understanding:

- Do you believe that mental health is as important as physical health? Why, or why not?
- Do you currently espouse any of the myths about mental health listed above, or any others you've heard? If yes, what about the myth(s) rings true, and why?
- Do you have different standards around mental healthcare for yourself than you do for others? For example, do you think it's okay for others to go to therapy but resist the notion of going yourself? Why, or why not?
- How have mental health conditions affected your life, whether personally or through loved ones?
- How would your experience at work change if you had access to more proactive mental health resources and more cultural support for mental health? What would it enable you to do more or less of?

CHAPTER 2

THE PROACTIVE APPROACH TO MENTAL HEALTH

Take a minute to think about your physical health. What do you do to take care of your physical body every day? I'm going to guess that, minimally, you eat, sleep, and drink water. You probably do a handful of other, more specific things, too, like brushing your teeth, trying to eat a variety of vegetables, and limiting your sugar intake. Perhaps you stick to the same bedtime every night and turn off your devices early. You may also have an exercise regimen, like working out a few times a week or going on a walk every morning. Now, what about when things go wrong, when you get sick or injured? You probably stay home from work, rest, and drink lots of fluids. At some point, if severe symptoms present or you have an emergency, you likely visit a doctor. The doctor checks you out, prescribes medication, a procedure, or some exercises, and helps you get back to normal.

You can see in these examples that we all have some things we do to *keep* well and some things we do to *get* well. In other words, we have proactive and reactive approaches to our physical health. But what about our mental health? Perhaps we seek out therapy or treatment when we're in a bad place—or our family does it for us. Perhaps we turn to our company's Employee Assistance Program, if we're aware of it. Yet, what are we doing daily to keep our minds in a good place? This is where things tend to fall apart.

Traditional mental healthcare often focuses on treating symptoms and managing crises rather than preventing problems from arising in the first place. While reactive care is essential for those in immediate need, it does little to reduce the overall prevalence of mental health issues. To do that, we need proactive measures. What would a proactive mental health approach look like instead? This chapter will answer that question, and discuss the benefits, challenges, and effects of a proactive vs. reactive mental health approach in organizations.

WHAT IS THE PROACTIVE MENTAL HEALTH APPROACH?

The proactive approach to mental health emphasizes prevention and early intervention. Désirée Pascual, Co-Founder and Chief Strategist at the executive leadership and human resources consultancy Simply Human, and former Physician Human Resources Leader at Kaiser Permanente, describes the proactive approach as "creating the kind of work environments that actively prevent burnout, reduce stress, and promote mental wellbeing before it becomes a crisis. The key is to build environments where people feel safe and where mental health isn't just an afterthought but a priority built into the fabric of the company."

Moreover, it's not just about stopping mental health issues and conditions from arising but also about helping people feel their best and most confident, enabling them to excel in their endeavors and thrive in all areas of their lives. As Dr. Wolfgang Seidl, the Mental Health Consulting Leader at Mercer, explains it, "Proactive mental health is life-affirming. It's about far more than just avoiding problems—it's about enriching lives. If companies see mental health initiatives as a part of life-affirming engagement rather than just a benefit, we start to change the whole relationship people have with their work."

To that end, a proactive approach in organizations relies on six key elements:

1. **Consistent engagement**
2. **Quick, easy access to care**
3. **A wide variety of mental health resources**
4. **A supportive culture that's inclusive of *all* people**
5. **Effective mental health training for leaders and managers**
6. **Systems and procedures to catch issues and intervene early**

What does this mean in practice?

It means creating an environment where mental health is openly discussed and the importance of it is promoted widely and often. It means having leaders and managers who are equipped to handle conversations about employees' mental health issues and concerns. It means having consistent mental health check-ins with employees, encouraging them to build healthy habits and use the support services when needed, providing mental health assessments, and underscoring the importance of employees' personal lives and families. It means backing up the verbal support for employees' mental wellbeing with policies that facilitate it. It means guaranteeing quick, consistent, and easy access to a variety of mental health resources, tools, and techniques, such as clinical therapy and mindfulness practices, and making sure that all employees are aware of where and how to access them.

Mental health is specific and specialized. Just like with physical health, there is no one-size-fits-all experience of or strategy for mental health that helps every single person. Therefore, a proactive mental health approach in the workplace must also be rooted in diversity and inclusion. There must be resources that speak to everyone's identities and experiences as well as spaces where people can speak openly and comfortably. Global companies with employees all over the world additionally should account for the varied cultural attitudes toward mental health that employees may have or encounter in their communities.

They should have engagement strategies and resources that meet people where they are. Furthermore, different industries have different mental health needs based on what jobs in those industries require, so it's also important for organizations to tailor their proactive approaches to support the unique needs of their workforce and their job requirements.

Seidl sees it this way: "Mental health needs to be seen as part of a holistic strategy for wellbeing. It's not about whether we invest or not—it's part of the package. It's about integrating it to create an overall ecosystem that supports wellbeing as a whole to help people bring their best energy to work and their personal lives."

To execute that holistic strategy and integrate mental health into the ecosystem of an organization, culture, engagement, and personalization are the name of the game. It's not enough for organizations to simply offer benefits and resources and send one-size-fits-all reminders to employees to use them every now and then. It's not enough to assume that people will speak up when they're struggling if they aren't provided ample opportunities to understand that it's safe to do so or that there are people and programs there to support them. Organizations should develop proactive, customized engagement strategies to check in and remind employees all the time that their mental health matters. They must create cultures that promote mental health and encourage community and social support surrounding it.

The next chapters will cover how to build each of these things into your organization, but before we get there, let's talk about *why* these elements are so important.

THE BENEFITS OF THE PROACTIVE MENTAL HEALTH APPROACH

The benefits of a proactive approach to mental health are multifaceted and far-reaching, both for organizations and their individual employees. Look at any recent data and you'll see that organizations with proactive mental health and wellbeing strategies see significant impacts across employee wellbeing, productivity, and satisfaction, not to mention considerable cost savings and reduced stigma.

Enhanced Employee Wellbeing

Individuals who have the ability to engage with proactive mental health initiatives, such as consistent check-ins, report feeling less stressed, anxious, and worried, both about work and in general. Specifically, employee respondents to a 2022 study by inZights Consulting reported feeling one-third less stressed after their organization implemented Journey's proactive approach and platform. These findings were backed up by a similar clinical study on Journey conducted by the U.S. health insurance company Humana, in which employee respondents reported feeling . . .

- 56% more confident about their ability to handle personal problems,
- 18% more on top of things,
- 29% less angry when things were outside of their control, and
- 24% less nervous or stressed.

Engaging in mindfulness practices and completing mental health assessments helps people become more aware of their emotions, patterns, and strengths, and as evidenced by the studies above, employees often report increased focus as well as improved self-esteem. Furthermore, when people engage with their mental health proactively, their physical health tends to improve as well. They sleep better and have more energy and, as a result, can show up in more engaged ways as parents, spouses, employees, friends, and community members.

Increased Productivity

The link between enhanced wellbeing and increased productivity is clear: The better your employees feel, the more they're able to show up at their best, the more work gets done, and the better business results the organization can achieve. It goes beyond just boosting attendance; improving productivity requires employees to have clarity and focus, improved decision-making, and better communication. As Lisa Schoenhaus, Benefits and Wellbeing Manager at the global design company Arup, has found in her work, proactive mental health support aids employees on all of these levels. "Mental health is directly tied to productivity. Employees who feel mentally well are more engaged, creative, and productive. Investing in mental health is an investment in the company's success," she said.

Furthermore, by encouraging employees to communicate about their mental health and take action to support it, organizations help them feel valued. And when employees feel valued, they are more likely to care about their work, speak up with ideas and concerns, perform their best, and contribute to better organizational outcomes.

Leaders at Morgan Stanley, a leading global financial services firm, saw the truth of this after implementing their own proactive mental wellness program, spearheaded by Chief Medical Officer David Stark. "The impact of a well workforce on an organization's productivity and profitability is immeasurable," Stark said. "With an emphasis on wellness, employees are more engaged, less absent, less likely to experience burnout, and experience fewer exacerbating mental health conditions. And, in my experience, they're overall more likely to enjoy and feel passionate about a company if they know that their individual wellbeing is of importance from the top level down."

Decreased Absenteeism

Stark brought up a key point: Employees with stronger mental and overall wellbeing are less absent. When employees are struggling with their mental health—whether for stress, anxiety, burnout, or any other concern—they often need to take time off from work. In recent years, the average employee missed 10 to 12 days of work per year due to mental health, which, estimates show, costs businesses up to $10 billion per year. But studies have shown that proactive mental health initiatives in the workplace significantly reduce absenteeism, which results in substantial cost savings. In fact, research from Deloitte indicates that businesses receive a return on investment of $1.62 for every dollar spent on mental health programs. The WHO cites as much as $4 ROI for every dollar spent. Both numbers represent significant returns for businesses, and decreased absenteeism is a driving factor behind them.

Early Detection and Intervention Before Concerns Develop

The focus on prevention and consistent check-ins in the proactive mental health approach also allows managers to identify early warning signs of distress and raise a red flag when interventions might be necessary. Erika Loperbey found this to be true at an American multinational IT services company with over 100,000 employees. As a Human Resources Manager of Employee Well-being and Talent Management, Loperbey said, "Making the cultural shift from reactive to proactive mental health strategies by normalizing mental health check-ins in our day-to-day has been a game-changer. It allows us to intervene early before issues escalate."

Early intervention can prevent mental health conditions from progressing or becoming more serious and ultimately lead to more effective treatment. It also helps give managers and mental health professionals more time to tailor their support to better meet the needs of the employee, thereby increasing the likelihood of successful outcomes.

Reduced Healthcare Costs

All of this leads to one of the most significant benefits to organizations: reduced healthcare costs. Healthcare is expensive, and the more employees use it, the more it costs businesses. When employees have greater mental health, however, their overall health improves and the need for emergency care and high-cost treatments drops dramatically. Medical claims and prescription costs can all be reduced by proactive mental health in the workplace, providing even greater savings to organizations on the whole.

The numbers bear this out. Having traditional EAPs and limited mental health programs may seem cheaper at face value. After all, they typically cost less up front per employee per year. Yet, they also tend to be far less effective, and ineffective EAPs are very expensive. The costs associated with crisis intervention and acute mental healthcare are significantly greater than they are for proactive programs, so when employees only use services *after* they've developed an acute issue, the costs immediately become acute as well. Companies investing in robust, proactive EAPs spend about $30 per employee annually—twice the cost of traditional EAPs—however, when you account for the additional healthcare expenses associated with traditional EAPs, proactive solutions save nearly $400 per employee per year in total care costs. It's clear: spending a little more upfront on proactive care can save significantly in overall costs while improving employee wellbeing.

And that doesn't even account for the cost of medical insurance and premiums, which, according to recent reporting by management consulting firm PwC, are already projected to rise by 8% year over year for group plans and by 7.5% year over year for individual plans in 2025, driven by behavioral health as well as inflation and prescription drug costs. All told, when employees don't engage with their mental health benefits until they've entered crisis mode, it can increase companies' medical spending by as much as 300%. The overall savings garnered from funding proactive programs, therefore, are considerable.

Improved Employee Satisfaction, Reduced Turnover, Better Talent

Beyond the bottom line, fostering a culture of mental wellness significantly enhances employee retention and loyalty, leading to greater job satisfaction. It goes back to feeling valued. As found in a recent Culture-Monkey survey, employees who feel supported and see a clear path for growth are more likely to stay committed to their organization, which both improves overall morale and reduces turnover.

That's no small thing. Turnover has hit businesses hard in recent years as employees have started to expect more from their workplaces. They've made it clear that when their organization doesn't seem to value them highly enough, support them as whole people, or uphold values they believe in, they'll find another one that will. As several studies in recent years have shown, this means that organizations with proactive mental health approaches and integrated social initiatives have a near-automatic leg up in hiring and attracting top talent, particularly among younger workers who value corporate social responsibility.

Reduced Stigma

Finally, promoting proactive mental health and creating cultures that support it help normalize conversations about mental health, which reduces stigma and encourages individuals to seek help when needed. Just ask Christine Pfeiffer, Director of WorkLife and Well-being at Memorial Sloan Kettering Cancer Center, who spoke with me about what's worked at MSKCC. "One of the most effective mental health strategies we've found," she said, "is creating a culture where employees feel supported, without the stigma attached to seeking help."

Clinical Director for Weill Cornell Medicine's EAP Dr. Randy Martin realized how much of a driving factor stigma was when he worked at Humana. "Especially during COVID, we got flooded with calls. There were so many people suddenly seeking therapy; it became clear how much stigma around mental health had been preventing people from getting help sooner," he said. As the pandemic wore on, he noticed things shift; people started to open up more about their struggles. "It created this opportunity to break down some of those barriers," Dr. Martin said. "It's a challenge, but we need to keep pushing to normalize mental healthcare as part of everyday wellbeing."

The more people feel comfortable speaking about mental health, the more others respect and prioritize it. This is important for all communities but can be particularly impactful for employees who don't have mental health support outside the workplace. Engagement campaigns and mental health training within the workplace can further reduce stigma and promote a culture of acceptance and support.

THE CHALLENGES TO IMPLEMENTING PROACTIVE MENTAL HEALTH

While the benefits of proactive mental health are clear, implementing such strategies can be challenging. Organizations and individuals may face several barriers to adopting a proactive approach, including stigma and the general lack of awareness and expertise about mental health in most settings. Even though ideas surrounding mental health have greatly improved since the start of the 21st century, a lot of stigma remains, and changing organizational culture—not to mention individual attitudes and ideas—requires time and effort. Organizations will need to take deliberate steps to combat the myths, provide mental health education, encourage participation in mental health programs, and change the understanding of mental health for their employees.

Implementing comprehensive proactive mental health programs also requires resources, including funding, personnel, and time. Organizations may struggle with allocating sufficient resources to support mental health initiatives, particularly if they face budget constraints or competing priorities.

Barbara Wachsman is a Managing Director at The Walt Disney Company. With an organization that sizable and multifaceted, you can imagine the level of complexity involved in implementing a large, proactive mental health program. To Wachsman, part of the initial challenge for companies in this position, and specifically HR teams trying to get leadership on board, is marrying the business case to the beneficial health outcomes. "It's not enough to just offer mental health services; companies need to make mental health a priority within their HR strategy," she said. "It's about setting standards for how mental health is addressed and ensuring it is seen as a business case rather than just a nice-to-have."

There are two things to remember here: (1) You can always start small and gradually expand your mental health programs as resources become available; and (2) communicating about mental health costs nothing. You can still foster a supportive environment, check in with employees, and encourage people to communicate about mental health openly without incurring any cost. If you're not someone with control of the pursestrings, keep making the business case to the people that are. Point to the data showing cost savings and improved business outcomes, and persistently advocate for your proposal.

EXERCISE
Reflecting on the Challenges of Implementing a Proactive Mental Health in Your Organization

Organizations face challenges, both large and small, to implementing proactive mental health.

If an organization is a highly profitable venture with social values baked into the culture already, leaders may not struggle to allocate funding or get employees to engage with proactive programming.

On the other hand, if an organization is struggling with profitability and a workforce concentrated in regions whose cultures don't prioritize mental health, HR teams may have a harder time getting a proactive approach off the ground.

Take a few minutes to reflect on the specific circumstances of your organization.

What do you see as the biggest hurdles your organization faces to implementing a proactive mental health approach?

What are the things you could do in your role to help the organization or your team overcome some of these hurdles?

Which benefits of having a proactive mental health approach do you think your organization would stand to gain the most from?

CHAPTER 3

BUILDING A PROACTIVE MENTAL HEALTH CULTURE

Leo Lukenas III was a 35-year-old former Green Beret working as an investment banker at Bank of America in New York City. On May 2, 2024, he died from an acute coronary artery thrombosis, a type of blood clot. It turns out, he'd been working over 100 hours a week for months. Only two months before his death, he had engaged a recruiting firm to help him find a new job—one with a less demanding schedule and better work-life balance. Later in May, Bank of America lost another promising young employee, 25-year-old Adnan Deumic. Deumic, a trader in the BofA London office, was playing soccer at a company charity event when he collapsed and died from a suspected heart attack. Neither Lukenas nor Deumic had acute health concerns prior to their deaths.

These heartbreaking stories are, unfortunately, not unheard of in investment banking. London cardiologist Dr. Arjun Ghosh told Business Insider that, in the last 10 years, he has seen a 10% increase in heart attacks among bankers under 30 years old—not a common age for heart conditions otherwise. But cardiac arrest isn't the only outcome of the intensity of working in finance. Substance abuse is a widely known issue in the industry, with people often turning to substances to relieve stress and anxiety or to stay awake during long work days.

In 2021, a group of young analysts from Goldman Sachs conducted an internal "Working Conditions Survey" of their peers and found that, on the whole, they'd been averaging 95-hour work weeks and only five hours of sleep each night. Describing their experience as "workplace abuse," they shared that such conditions were negatively impacting their mental and physical health. Thankfully, Goldman Sachs has heeded their concerns and worked hard to implement proactive mental health organization-wide, including instituting a new, mandated mental health training program for all managers and employees at the vice president level or higher, among several other initiatives.

While other major banks have announced or instituted similar initiatives to start addressing the mental health of their employees, not all financial institutions have done so. Finance is known to be a fast-paced, high-stress world, but whatever monetary benefit these companies presumably gain by maintaining such high-octane cultures comes at a very real human cost. What could have been the outcome for Leo Lukenas and Adnan Deumic had the companies prioritized their health and created a culture promoting prevention and wellbeing instead? To get to the root of the matter, these companies need to build fully proactive mental health cultures.

HOW TO BUILD A PROACTIVE MENTAL HEALTH CULTURE

In my two decades in corporate America, I have seen many companies put together an impressive collection of benefits, but they often struggle to encourage employees to utilize the benefits available to them or prioritizes prevention. Now, as any leader knows, company cultures result from numerous inputs. When you're not intentional about those inputs, it's pretty hard to create an intentional culture.

Between my team's work and research, we've found that **building a proactive mental health culture comes down to espousing three core beliefs:**

1. **Engagement must be inclusive of all employees, especially the hardest to reach.**
2. **Employees need proactive tools that meet them where they are.**
3. **Providing benefits is just the start; the culture must support mental health.**

These beliefs both encapsulate the proactive mental health approach and speak to what's needed to build a wholly supportive mental health culture for employees everywhere.

Building a proactive mental health culture based on these beliefs involves the following key actions: creating a supportive environment, providing access to resources, instituting proactive mental health policies and procedures, establishing support networks within the organization, expanding your internal network of mental health leaders, and providing care to your employees' loved ones and communities.

Create a Supportive Environment

Think about the most supportive relationships in your life. What makes them feel supportive to you? Likely, some combination of the following: good communication, the safety to say what you're feeling and going through, encouragement, regular quality time together, and frequent conversations to check in with each other. When you're creating a supportive work environment, you're essentially creating a relationship between the organization and its employees. The same things that make personal relationships feel supportive make work environments feel supportive, especially when it comes to mental health.

It all starts with promoting open communication.

Promote Open Communication

Explicitly encourage employees to talk about their mental health. Let them know that you—the organization's leaders, managers, and HR personnel—want to hear how they are doing on a real level, consistently, and without judgment.

You can do this in a number of ways. Verbally state it outright—throughout the interview process, on employees' first days of employment, and in meetings. Add language about it to all of the written materials about your company's culture and values, including hiring and onboarding materials as well as internal emails and newsletters. Create channels on Teams or Slack (or whatever digital communication platforms you use) dedicated to mental health discussions. Hold regular meetings specifically to discuss mental health openly in groups, allowing employees to share their experiences and challenges. Share resources for and information about mental health frequently and in many places. Most importantly, set the example for your employees. If you want your employees to feel safe and encouraged to share about their own mental health, you need to show them that you will do it too. You need to build that trust. That means, all leaders, managers, and HR personnel should consistently talk about their mental health in a genuine way as well.

Implement Regular Check-Ins

It's also important to create specific infrastructure to support, and further prompt, conversations about mental health. Implementing regular check-ins gives employees a dedicated time and space to share how they're doing. These could be as simple as having employees share a word to describe how they're feeling that day in a morning huddle. You can also use external tools that ensure anonymity but allow employees to track their own mental state. Within the Journey platform, we've created a tool where people can do a quick pulse-check and select from four different emojis to describe how they're feeling that day. This tool then provides them with a bite-sized mindfulness video based on their mood, tracks their responses—which are kept anonymous from the organization—and if they indicate that they're feeling particularly low two consecutive times, the system will prompt that employee with additional mental health resources such as speaking with a therapist.

While these quick, low-touch interactions are valuable, it's best when check-ins take multiple forms. Richard Thaler and Cass Sunstein wrote a great book called *Nudge* that discusses how many little decisions we make every day and all the ways we can gently nudge people (including ourselves) to make better decisions. When it comes to people taking care of their mental health, they tend to need a lot of nudges. Check-ins in multiple forms are one way of nudging.

Having conversations with employees and having them submit longer surveys are other ways to help ensure employees are encouraged to both think and share about their mental health more frequently and seriously. Some organizations add a verbal mental health check-in to weekly 1-on-1s between managers and team members. Some, including Journey, do a weekly written check-in. We use 5-15s that take no more than five minutes for employees to fill out and no more than 15 minutes for managers to review. This ensures people do a more thorough check-in regularly while not requiring too much time from their workday. Some organizations also do longer surveys quarterly or semi-annually.

A leading American multinational IT services company with over 100,000 employees started integrating mental health check-ins into their weekly meetings and all regular touchpoints. "Now, it's not just about performance metrics but about the person behind those metrics. We ask: 'How are you, *really*?'" said Erika Loperbey, HR Manager of Employee Well-being and Talent Management at the company.

Encourage Work-Life Harmony

No one's mental health (or life) revolves solely around what happens to them at work. We all have personal lives that impact us significantly—and that's a good thing. In the workplace, and especially in certain high-stress professions, we run into issues when leaders and organizations don't recognize the lives people have outside of work, or when the culture is such that employees don't feel they can prioritize anything aside from their job. As exemplified by the stories from investment banking, cultures like this tend to breed burnout—and worse.

Employee mental health is also about something bigger than any one employee. "Mental health isn't just about individuals; it affects people's family and home life, too," said Erin Young, Director, Health & Benefits, at consultancy WTW. "Employers need to recognize that when they support an employee's mental health, they're also supporting their family's wellbeing."

So, to create an environment that supports people's mental health, it's crucial not only to recognize the importance of people's personal lives, but also to encourage work-life balance, or work-life harmony. Acknowledge that employees' families and loved ones come first. Encourage them to take care of personal and family matters when needed. For example, when possible, build in flexibility for people to be able to go to a doctor's appointment during the day or pick up their children from school. Create policies that grant people the agency to take care of things in their personal life, and ensure that leaders and managers communicate their support and exemplify this in their own behaviors.

"Work-life harmony" as an alternative to "work-life balance"

"Work-life balance" came into fashion over a decade ago, and since then, we've heard it touted time and again as the ultimate goal for working people everywhere. But the thing is, it's too hard to achieve balance. By its nature, the word "balance" describes something teetering on a fine point, easily pushed to one side or the other—in this case, between feeling like we're working too hard and not spending enough time with family, or feeling like we're working too little and not accomplishing what we want or need to. Why make "balance" the goal when it's near impossible to maintain?

I advocate for a more integrative line of thought: work-life harmony. "Harmony" allows us to recognize both priorities without them being in conflict with one another. Rather, they coexist, operating with a natural push and pull. Sometimes, work takes priority—for example, a major deadline might call for a few days with longer hours. Sometimes, family takes priority—your partner has a health scare, or you need to move your aging parent out of their home.

Our work lives and personal lives are not separate things; they both contribute to our *full life*. Especially with the rise of remote and hybrid work, for many people the division of work and home is now limited to nonexistent. Organizations can better serve their employees (and the organizations themselves as a result) by acknowledging the fluid mix of people's work and home lives and showing support for all of it.

Champion Inclusion

On a more fundamental level, creating a supportive environment for proactive mental health comes down to fostering trust, community, and inclusion—not just *between* leaders and their teams, but also *among* teams. If team members don't feel comfortable being themselves around each other—if they don't feel welcomed by the group, or they don't trust their colleagues—you can hardly expect them to feel comfortable sharing about their mental health and wellbeing, much less do their best work.

That's not merely an opinion; it's a biological fact. We evolved over thousands of years to operate in groups. It's how we survive. If we don't feel included in the group, it's as if we're under threat; we feel we have to remain vigilant. We may experience additional stress or anxiety. It may take a negative toll on our body and certainly on our focus. Under those circumstances we can't bring our full selves to the table or contribute our best work.

Additionally, several studies, including an often-cited study by Amy Edmondson conducted at Google, have shown that teams that share a sense of what she calls "psychological safety" have improved communication, collaboration, and resilience. Psychological safety is defined as "a shared belief held by members of a team that it's okay to take risks, to express their ideas and concerns, to speak up with questions, and to admit mistakes—all without fear of negative consequences." Basically,

Edmondson says, "it's felt permission for candor." Psychological safety, then, is a supportive environment among a team. It allows for the ease to be yourself, speak your mind, share your ideas, and fail together—and then to be able to figure out how to right the ship together, too. The point being, you're not doing it alone, and because you know that you'll have support, your own wellbeing at work, along with that of the rest of your team, is improved and you can continue to show up at your best.

For this reason, among many others, it's deeply important for organizations to bolster community and institute inclusive practices and policies—something DEI and health equity expert Dr. Shawnte Elbert knows a lot about. "I'd love for everyone to talk more about how we integrate mental health from a culturally competent, inclusive lens for different populations," she said. No matter where your organization is, you have diversity among your ranks—diversity of race, age, experience, ethnicity, gender, religion, sexual orientation, language, culture, values, political leaning—you name it. These identities and factors play a role in organizations small and large, and in global companies especially, they intersect in innumerable ways. "Whether it's socioeconomic status, spirituality, or social determinants of health, incorporating these factors is crucial for creating truly inclusive mental health services," Dr. Elbert said. To help everyone feel welcomed, respected, and valued, leaders must proactively promote diversity, address discrimination, and ensure that community activities and resources are accessible to all.

Part of resources being accessible is making them representative of the people they are for. When building proactive mental health into your organization, make sure your mental health services and platforms incorporate people from all identity groups so that every one of your employees can see themselves and their experience in the conversation. This means having diverse clinicians, counselors, and teachers; providing resources in all the languages of your employees; ensuring visual materials depict diverse groups; and approaching your mental health conversations in a way that fits the cultural context of the employees you're addressing, no matter where they live. We'll discuss each of these actions in greater depth in Chapter 5.

Institute Proactive Mental Health Policies and Procedures

In any organized body, policies function to not only drive increased awareness but more importantly to put your money where your mouth is. It's easy to say you support mental health, but if you don't back up your words with institutional actions, it's also easy for that support to wane or falter right away. You can't create a proactive mental health culture with lip service alone. You need policies to help establish the institutional support and structure to maintain a healthy culture for the long term.

What kind of policies and procedures do that? Policies for vacation, time off, and family and medical leave; flexible work arrangements; workload management; transparent bonus and promotion structures; crisis intervention plans; and consistent feedback solicitation.

Policies for Vacation, Time Off, and Family and Medical Leave

Flexible working arrangements go hand in hand with taking time off. Every organization has policies for taking vacation and time off for illness or other emergencies. But those policies vary widely in time allowance and flexibility, and many organizations, especially in certain regions of the world, don't do enough to encourage employees to actually take the time. In fact, in some industries, time off is almost explicitly discouraged.

Without time away from work, though, people get sick, burn out, and lose important time with loved ones—none of which helps their mental health or the organizations they work for. These issues are easily exacerbated among smaller teams, pointed out Lisa Schoenhaus, Benefits and Wellbeing Manager at Arup. "In smaller teams, mental health support can be challenging, but it's even more important," Schoenhaus said. "When everyone is stretched thin, the risk of burnout increases, so it's crucial to have mental health strategies in place." Implementing proactive mental health in the workplace requires that organizations embrace the value of time off for their employees and institute—or expand—policies accordingly.

To start, consider implementing more generous vacation policies. In the U.S., employees get an average of 10 paid days each year. Across Europe and South America, the average is 30 days. Most of Africa, the

Middle East, Asia, and Oceania fall somewhere in the middle. It's also not uncommon for many organizations to lump all time off into a single allotment of days each year, meaning that employees who are sick have to take vacation days in order to get well, further limiting time they can take off for important holidays, family events, or simply to rest.

Making policies that delineate ample days for various time-off needs can help improve employees' experience and mental wellbeing significantly. Here are some recommendations:

- **Sick Days:** Designate an allotment of days separate from vacation time that employees can take off when they're sick each year—or, better yet, put no limit on sick days. If someone is sick, forcing them to work through it only produces stress and poor work, increases the chances of them staying sicker for longer, and threatens the health of the rest of your team.

- **Mental Health Days:** Allow employees to take specific mental health days, outside of their vacation time, without needing to provide a detailed explanation.

- **Parental and Family Leave:** Institute generous parental and family leave policies to support employees during significant life events.

- **Return-to-Work Programs:** Offer return-to-work programs that support employees transitioning back to work after a period of absence.

By creating a culture where taking time off for mental health is accepted and encouraged, organizations can help employees manage stress and maintain a healthy work-life dynamic.

Flexible Work Arrangements

The pandemic changed the game for work flexibility. Pre-pandemic, some companies had started letting employees work remotely, especially in tech-related industries that were already well-suited to remote work. But once the pandemic hit, it forced numerous other industries to change their policies and infrastructure to support working from home. And they learned, as we all learned, that it was totally possible. Now, post-pandemic, even though many organizations have moved at least partially back into their offices, there's a new understanding that working arrangements can be flexible, especially when it helps employees maintain better work-life harmony and, thus, contribute most effectively. However, some companies are now requiring employees to return to the office full-time, sparking debates about productivity, collaboration, and employee satisfaction.

Organizations can offer remote work options, compressed work weeks, and hybrid schedules to allow some remote days along with required days in the office. Some organizations allow employees to manage their own schedule or encourage employees to take breaks throughout the day. "When you have back-to-back meetings and constant demands, it can be hard to prioritize mental health. That's why it's essential for companies to create opportunities for employees to have protected time," said Jeff Levin-Scherz, WTW's Population Health Leader. As another example, a company might offer a "summer hours" program, allowing employees to work longer hours Monday through Thursday and take Friday afternoons off, providing more time for rest and relaxation. They might also discourage employees from answering emails or messages outside of typical working hours. There are plenty of ways to introduce more flexibility.

Flexible working arrangements also impact the design and functionality of the physical workspace. You want your employees to feel physically set up well to do their jobs healthily. Ask yourself, what do your employees need to work more comfortably? Maybe you need to invest in more ergonomic workstations, or give employees a work-from-home stipend to improve their physical setup for remote work. Maybe that means having healthy food and water stations available throughout the office, or changing the lighting to improve the overall feel of the environment.

Workload Management Policies

It's not just about having a flexible setup, though. No matter how good an employee's work setup is, if they have a completely unmanageable workload, their mental health will suffer. Whether it's intentional or not, many organizations give employees the responsibilities of multiple roles, which makes it impossible for them to complete their work within a standard 40-hour or even 50-hour work week. Having a larger workload for shorter periods—to wrap up a big project, during busy seasons, or during a team transition with incoming or outgoing team members, for example—is to be expected. When short stints balloon into permanent expectations, however, it has negative impacts.

While there's no need to strictly limit everyone to 40-hour work weeks, organizations committed to proactive mental health need clear policies around workload expectations and monitoring, recognizing the difference between temporarily pushing people to stretch vs. constantly demanding unsustainable workloads. Leaders should regularly assess team capacity, redistribute work when needed, and be willing to hire additional staff rather than overtax existing employees. Having these guardrails in place helps prevent burnout and shows employees that their health matters more than squeezing maximum productivity from minimal headcount.

Transparent, Values-Driven Promotion and Bonus Structures

A lot of organizations say they value employee wellbeing but end up rewarding behaviors that undermine it: The employees who skip vacations, answer emails at midnight, and work 80 hours a week—and get testy with colleagues as a result—get promotions and bonuses, while those that maintain more work-life harmony do not. To cultivate a true proactive mental health culture, organizations need to explicitly recognize and reward the employees who model behaviors that align with proactive mental health values instead—those who support team members' work and wellbeing, who model sustainable work practices, and maintain healthy boundaries outside of working hours.

Furthermore, simply having and sharing transparent advancement criteria for all roles with all employees helps support a proactive mental health culture. When leaders aren't clear about how team members can advance in the company, or what actions get rewarded and why, it can cause employees unnecessary anxiety. Laying it all out there up front gives employees the mental clarity to know how and when they can expect to advance.

When the path to promotion is both transparent and rooted in these values, it demonstrates that prioritizing mental health isn't just encouraged, it's actually fundamental to success. Moreover, it creates an authentic culture where employees can thrive personally and professionally without feeling pressured to compromise their wellbeing in order to get ahead.

Crisis Intervention Plans

Developing clear plans for responding to mental health crises, including who to contact and what steps to take, is essential for providing timely and effective support. All employees and managers need to be trained on how to implement these plans so that everyone knows how to respond when necessary. You want to ensure support is available 24/7 for employees experiencing a mental health crisis. There are several mental health crisis hotlines, such as the National Suicide and Crisis Lifeline and the National Sexual Assault Hotline, that employees can call to be connected to immediate support and appropriate interventions. (I have included a list of crisis hotlines in Appendix A in the back of this book.)

Mental Health Assessments

A major goal of the proactive mental health approach is getting people the right help at the right time. Implementing regular mental health assessments at various stages of someone's employment and/or the calendar year helps ensure this happens by monitoring employees' wellbeing and identifying early signs of mental health issues. Joel Axler is a Partner and

National Behavioral Health Leader at the national insurance brokerage Brown & Brown. He's a big advocate for widespread use of mental health assessments. "Early intervention is extremely key, and the best way to detect mental health issues early on is through these assessments," Axler said. "They help employers and employees alike see soft warning signs, which enables individuals to start using other mental health resources to improve their mental state and gives organizations and clinicians the information needed to step in if necessary."

Assessments can sometimes do this better than other kinds of internal check-ins—for instance, when an employee presents as perfectly healthy but is actually struggling and doesn't feel comfortable sharing that (or maybe isn't fully aware, themselves). If that's the case, it's helpful to have multiple ways for people to reflect on their mental health and receive feedback or recommendations for care.

Beyond simple daily check-ins, there are many kinds of assessments as well as many different avenues to conduct them through—surveys, online tools, or 1-on-1s with trained professionals or mental health clinicians. At Journey, we use a clinical assessment called the Outcomes Ratings Scale, a four-question survey that measures the current state of four areas of people's lives: (1) individual wellbeing and personal distress, (2) interpersonal wellbeing and distress in intimate relationships, (3) social wellbeing and distress or satisfaction in relationships outside the home, and (4) overall wellbeing. Other popular assessments include the General Anxiety Disorder-7 (commonly called the GAD-7), which measures the severity of someone's current state of anxiety, and the Patient Health Questionnaire-9 (or PHQ-9), which measures the level and severity of someone's depression.

It should go without saying that assessments must be conducted confidentially, and results should be used to provide support only.

Consistent Feedback Solicitaton

Businesses thrive on data—whether that's sales data, engagement analytics, or survey responses. You can't know how your business is doing without these things. The same goes for your mental health initiatives.

It's hard to know how effective or valuable they are to your employees without touching base and soliciting their feedback.

Conduct annual reviews of mental health policies and procedures to identify areas for improvement and make necessary adjustments. Involve employees in the development and refinement of mental health initiatives to ensure the programs meet their needs and are relevant to their experiences. Send quick surveys after the rollout of a new program to see how it went and learn how it is and isn't serving your team. Ask team members during 1-on-1s and open the floor for feedback during team meetings.

However you do it, solicit feedback frequently. Asking your team regularly how you're doing on mental health initiatives not only gives you the insights necessary to continue to improve, but it also consistently reminds employees to make use of the programs that are there, helps reduce stigma, and further establishes a culture of open communication.

Provide Access to Resources

Organizations can do a lot to create a culture that makes people feel welcome and included; they can communicate openly and establish a strong sense of community—both of which contribute to improved well-being for employees. Yet, for organizations to fully promote proactive mental health, they must provide easy access to effective mental health resources. At the bare minimum, that includes health insurance that covers mental health services. Beyond that, we're talking about Employee Assistance Programs with a preventive focus, proactive digital mental health platforms, counseling services, wellness programs, mental health hotlines, and mental health training and workshops.

Employee Assistance Programs (EAPs)

EAPs are programs providing confidential, short-term counseling, support, and referral services for employees and their families. These programs can address a range of issues, including mental health, substance abuse, grief, crisis intervention, financial concerns, and family difficulties. Many programs offer other services such as family planning and parenting classes, adoption assistance, and career coaching. Traditionally, though, EAPs are set up to *react* to acute issues. In other words, only after issues have escalated and become a big problem do people usually contact their EAP. This is how they were set up at the start.

The first EAPs in the United States were born out of a need to address increasing alcoholism in the workplace in the 1930s and 40s. Drinking at work was a norm at the time, but industrial manufacturing companies began to notice lost productivity and worsening employee performance. Instead of continuing to fire everyone struggling with alcoholism on the job, as they had been doing, they started implementing occupational counseling programs, prompted by the growing Alcoholics Anonymous movement.

Bill Wilson and Bob Smith had started Alcoholics Anonymous informally in 1935, and in 1939, the founders published what is known as the "Big Book," *Alcoholics Anonymous: The Story of How More Than One Hundred Men Have Recovered from Alcoholism*. The book's popularity spread across the country quickly, prompting a wider movement. The first workplace counseling programs came from this movement and were initially informal arrangements pairing struggling employees with other employees who had gotten sober through AA. In the 1950s, corporations such as Consolidated Edison (ConEd) and The Standard Oil Company (now ExxonMobil) expanded their occupational counseling services to offer support for other substance abuse issues. Then, in 1970, Congress passed legislation creating the National Institute on Alcoholism and Alcohol Abuse (NIAAA), whose priority was to research and treat alcoholism as well as giving states grants to hire and train EAP specialists. Education about EAPs, substance abuse treatment, and mental health issues spread over the course of the following decades.

Today, most large companies offer EAPs in some form, however, EAPs have not evolved to meet today's challenges, and unfortunately are no longer providing the value they once did. On average, only 3% of employees use their organization's EAP each year, and healthcare costs for individuals and companies keep rising. Despite growing awareness around the importance of mental health in the workplace, many organizations continue to grapple with outdated, reactive approaches in EAPs. *If* an employee knows that their company has an EAP—and that's a big "if"—they encounter long wait times to get counseling and work-life support. It's not uncommon for employees to have to wait an average of three weeks, and sometimes as many as six to eight weeks, to see a provider—more than enough time for issues to worsen. Traditional EAPs also tend to provide a frustrating and often clunky user experience, limited proactive strategies, and outdated resources that don't reflect the diversity of people and experiences of today's workforce. All of this means that most organizations are constantly playing catch-up with their employees' mental health needs, driving up claims and overall healthcare costs in the process.

Today, organizations need updated, modern, proactive EAPs. These programs should still provide all of the traditional services—therapy and counseling, health plan coordination, medication coordination, specialized care and rehabilitation services, substance abuse and be-havioral health treatment, and crisis support and follow-up—but with improvements in accessibility, inclusivity, and usability. Services should be widely and quickly accessible, ensuring employees can see a provider within days, not weeks. Proactive EAPs must also offer specific, targeted support during crises, guide HR teams on additional support measures, and include resources that help employees improve and maintain their mental health on an ongoing basis.

Here's what that looks like:

- **Consistent engagement campaigns to keep mental health top of mind.** This includes daily emails with mental health tips, videos, and check-ins, as well as helpful reminders to pause, breathe, or take a break throughout the day.

- **Proactive support at crucial life moments.** This includes communications and prompts with resources and courses centered around:
  - › Key life events, such as becoming new parents, going through a divorce, getting a promotion, moving, etc.
  - › Challenging local events, such as natural disasters and community tragedies.

> ›   Particularly sensitive moments and concerns, such as loss and grief, suicidal ideation, self-harm, etc.

- **Additional support during the clinical experience.** This includes personalized content and resource recommendations as well as check-ins to assess the person's progress, level of care and satisfaction with it, and how well they match with their therapist. Minimally, it should also include digital scheduling for fast access to clinical care.

- **Predictive insights to drive early intervention.** This includes incorporating the use of AI-driven analytics to help identify mental health risks for employees based on their check-ins and content consumption—all of which allows for personalized support before issues escalate.

Effective proactive EAPs should offer work-life support, live group coaching classes, and both in-person and virtual therapy for employees and their loved ones. They should have detailed reporting capabilities for organizations to understand both the state of the mental health of their workforce in general and how their EAP is being used. They should additionally offer guidance on engagement strategies for the unique needs of the organization. Finally, a proactive EAP needs to have offerings rooted in diversity and inclusion so that every employee you have can access care unique to them and their needs from wherever they live, and in whatever manner is easiest for them, whether online, in-person, over video, on the phone, via text, or over email.

Digital Mental Health Platforms and Self-Guided Courses

One of the great benefits of having a digital mental health platform is being able to offer a wide variety of one-off classes and longer-term courses that allow people to move at their own pace and seek out the exact support they need, when they need it. Ideally, these should cover a whole range of mental wellness topics, tools, and techniques drawing from cognitive behavioral therapy, positive psychology, neuroscience, mindfulness, and breathwork, all led by licensed clinicians and practitioners. Classes and courses can cover topics as expansive as establishing healthy habits, managing stress, and working with strong emotions, and as specific as finding happiness in uncertain times and rousing energy when you feel tired.

To serve employees best, any proactive digital offering should provide courses that speak to employees' unique experiences as well. For example, having distinct mental wellness courses for all different communities—people with disabilities, women, and the Black, AAPI, LGBTQ+, Indigenous, or neurodivergent communities, for example—gives members of those communities safe spaces to explore and address their specific mental health needs. Courses for the mental wellness of managers, salespeople, nurses, teachers, creatives, or executives, for example, can speak to the challenges people in each of those roles and industries face. As mentioned above, you also want courses addressing specific mental health concerns, such as suicidal ideation, grief and loss, and addiction, as well as courses to help people through new life stages, like menopause or becoming a new parent.

During the pandemic, courses on coping with social isolation and handling organizational change became integral for many employees to help them navigate the drastic changes they experienced in those years. And at the time of this writing, courses on navigating political differences at work and coping with mass tragedies have seen a rise in engagement on the Journey platform because of the current political landscape across the world.

In addition to offering courses on a wide range of mental wellness topics and focuses, it's important to account for the fact that people learn differently. A strong digital program should provide educational materials in a wide range of mediums and styles as well—including video, audio, and written offerings, and the option for solo work and group classes.

If your organization doesn't use a mental health platform, consider providing subscriptions to other mental health apps so that your employees can manage their mental wellbeing consistently on a timeline, in a setting, and to a level of specificity that works best for them. You might also consider offering books or other written resources that employees can easily access whenever they need them.

Wellness Programs

Because mental health and physical health are inextricably linked, implementing a proactive mental health approach involves offering comprehensive wellness programs that incorporate both areas. Some organizations offer gym memberships, onsite fitness classes, subsidies for offsite fitness classes or subscriptions, and nutrition workshops in addition to things like mindfulness apps and seminars on healthy communication and stress management.

For example, Apple and Meta both have state-of-the-art fitness centers on their main campuses for employee use, and Nike and Adobe both offer gym membership reimbursements or stipends for fitness classes and at-home equipment. Intel also has dietitians and nutritionists who provide personalized dietary advice for employees that want it.

Whatever wellness programs you put in place, offering incentives, such as wellness points or rewards, can encourage participation and engagement to ensure your employees get the benefits of the programs you offer.

Mental Health Workshops and Trainings

Just as being promoted to manager doesn't automatically give someone the skills to lead effectively, it also doesn't give them the skills to support a direct report who is, for instance, dealing with the loss of their spouse or experiencing a substance misuse emergency. As Brown & Brown's Joel Axler said, "HR leaders are trained in CPR. But CPR will only help in moments of physical crisis. To be able to effectively recognize warning signs and help with mental health concerns, all HR staff should go through mental health first aid as well."

Broader than HR, managers, and leadership, employees at all levels have a wide range of knowledge, experience, and comfort with mental health as a topic generally; some have little awareness, and some harbor negative assumptions and stigmas. No proactive mental health culture can fully take root without organizations offering the training and education necessary for everyone to be able to understand mental health in more nuanced ways, better manage their own wellbeing, and effectively navigate mental health issues in the workplace.

Training programs can cover numerous topics—such as recognizing signs of mental health issues, having supportive conversations, and providing appropriate resources and referrals. And offering training in various formats, such as live workshops, webinars, and online, self-guided learning modules, ensures that it's accessible to everyone.

Walgreens, a leader among corporations spearheading proactive mental health programs, wanted to extend some of its support to customers and patients, so in 2019, they began offering mental health first aid training to certain pharmacy staff. They have since expanded the program, offering the training to all Walgreens pharmacists chain-wide.

In Chapter 10, we'll look further at all the training and education organizations should consider providing to managers, specifically, as well as how to incorporate it.

Establish Support Networks

We've talked about the need to create a supportive environment, including promoting both open communication and inclusion. Organizations can bolster both efforts in major ways by establishing peer support groups or Employee Resource Groups (ERGs). ERGs are voluntary, employee-led groups dedicated to specific identities or interests, focused on fostering inclusion, supporting employee growth, and advocating for organizational change. Peer support groups tend to be less formally structured and more specifically focused on providing emotional or mental health support, rather than influencing organizational policies. The purpose of both ERGs and peer support groups is to provide resources and support to employees based on their identities and interests, thereby establishing safe spaces and communities within the workplace where employees can express themselves fully and freely in a group they strongly relate to.

These identities and interests can vary widely—including people's identity groups, hobbies, disabilities, locations, or social causes they care about. For instance, you may have ERGs for women, LGBTQ+ employees, accessibility and disability, young professionals, or veterans, while also having peer support groups around grief and loss, chronic illness, caregivers, or substance use recovery. Truly, you can have ERGs or peer support groups around anything that brings people together and fosters a sense of commonality and belonging.

Many organizations with proactive mental health approaches create a peer support group specifically dedicated to mental health that provides resources, organizes events, and offers a space for discussion and understanding around this topic. "Providing safe spaces where employees can openly discuss mental health is essential," said Lauren Goldstein, Senior Director of Human Resources at the management consulting firm Gartner. "Whether it's through peer support groups or professional counseling, the goal is to create an environment of openness and trust."

Google, for instance, offers at least 15 different ERGs focused on different aspects of diversity and inclusion, including one for mental health. A global consulting firm with 125,000 employees in over 70 countries also established a mental health ERG and has seen very positive results. "An important aspect of our ERGs is how they provide a safe space for people to talk about stress and mental health in a community setting," said Michelle Eckert, Director of Human Resources. "This way, it doesn't feel like a top-down directive but rather more of a peer-led initiative, which has been powerful at our company."

Expand the Network of Mental Health Leaders in Your Organization

Speaking of top-down vs. peer-led initiatives, while those at the top of the organization must enable mental health programs and have the ability to adequately lead in this arena, they can't do it alone. Leaders, HR teams, and managers can't be everything to everyone all the time, nor can they be the sole carriers of the mental health message throughout the organization. You need other mental health ambassadors. Training additional groups of employees, including people at various levels, departments, and office locations, in mental health certification programs gives you the ability to build a groundswell of support, advocacy, and action toward mental health within and throughout the organization. It allows people—especially those who are particularly passionate about mental health—to get involved and take ownership of the culture of the company. And it provides increased support for managers and other leaders so that they don't have to carry the torch of mental health on their own. You can all champion mental health together.

Provide Care to Employees' Loved Ones

Incorporating family and loved ones is crucial to building a proactive mental health culture, and many big companies recognize this. US Foods is among them. Joe Toniolo, the company's Senior Director of Health and Welfare Plans, described some of their efforts: "We launched programs for adolescent stress, family support, and mental health to make sure our employees and their families had a network to lean on, especially during tough times," he said. Microsoft, EY, and Johnson & Johnson, for example, all provide access to mental health resources to employees and their immediate families as well.

This is fantastic—and there are more rungs on the ladder to cover. When I talk about incorporating family and loved ones, I'm not just talking about having employees' spouses and dependents on their health insurance plans. I'm talking about providing access to care for *anyone* they love and care about—partners, children, nieces, nephews, close friends, neighbors, etc.

Saying this usually prompts a lot of raised eyebrows. But a person's mental health is not based on themselves alone; it's greatly impacted by what's going on with their friends and loved ones. If you're a parent whose teenager is really struggling with depression and anxiety, that's going to impact your own mental health. If your next-door neighbor, who looks after your elderly father during the day, is struggling, you're likely to be worried about your neighbor *and* your father. If your roommate has just lost their job and no longer has access to their own mental healthcare, that may affect you too.

In any one of these scenarios, being able to give employees' loved ones access to the mental health resources you provide helps bring them more relief and, in turn, prevents greater mental health or other issues from developing that could cause them further stress or harm. Different organizations do this in different ways—for instance, by offering specialized mental health providers for children, teenagers, and families, and allowing employees to give full access to therapy and the mental health platform you use—including countless mental wellness classes—to unlimited loved ones for free. When you support someone's community, you're supporting them too.

THE POWER OF COMMUNITY AND SOCIAL SUPPORT

It's impossible to overstate the power of community and social support for people's mental health. The widely used Gallup Q12 Employee Engagement Survey has people identify whether or not they have a best friend at work. According to data from the survey, someone's answer to that question is a major indicator of their engagement at work. If their answer is yes, it tends to correlate to higher engagement for that employee; if no, lower engagement. It points to the deep truth that having strong social connections helps people feel seen and cared for, which improves their wellbeing and daily performance on the whole. Having a best friend or a whole supportive community at work provides emotional support, reduces stress, and gives people a greater sense of belonging, which in turn helps them feel safe to be themselves and share what's really going on with them, when and if they want to.

There's another important function of community for mental health that often goes unstated: It takes the pressure and burden of maintaining mental health off of individuals alone. Often in the modern discourse, mental health falls into the category of self-help and self-care. By definition, those terms put the onus on the individual person to help and care for themselves, *by* themselves. But our mental health doesn't exist in a vacuum because we as people don't exist completely on our own, off the grid and cut off from all other humans (at least, the vast majority of us don't). We operate in groups and communities, and our mental health is something we can keep up with *in community*, too. In fact, this is precisely the reason we first created our group meditation class app, Journey LIVE: to get people in community with each other for the purpose of keeping up with and maintaining each other's mental health *together*.

Geetika Bhojak, the Global Mental Health Lead at Accenture, summed it up well: "A sense of community has real power in mental health. Often, people feel isolated in their struggles, even when surrounded by colleagues. Building safe spaces where employees can connect, share, and support one another is so important. When you create these kinds of environments, you're not only addressing the immediate needs of mental health but fostering long-term resilience. It's about having open, honest conversations and normalizing the challenges we all face. That's where the impact really starts to take hold."

Thankfully, organizations can intentionally foster social connection among their teams in numerous ways. Establishing ERGs and peer support groups is one. But it can also be as simple as organizing social events, such as team lunches, company outings, or celebrations, or setting up regular team-building activities, like team challenges or group games. Leaders of the Metropolitan Transit Authority (MTA) in New York City host an Employee Appreciation Day every year for their more than 10,000 employees. "Six agencies get together to host the same breakfast for employees in various areas throughout the MTA. You have leadership stopping by on trains to speak to employees and sharing their appreciation, plus swag bags and lines going down the block in Midtown, Battery Park, and Jamaica, Queens," described Yvell Stanford, Deputy Chief of Organizational Design and Development for the MTA People Organization. That is certainly a day for connection and community.

You can foster connection further through celebratory Slack channels or email threads dedicated to, for example, giving a shoutout when team members exemplify the organization's core values or achieve big wins. On an even lighter note, many teams have channels to share funny memes, good music, or movie recommendations. Several companies also give opportunities for employees to lead workshops or give presenta-tions about an expertise or interest of theirs to the rest of the company. At Journey, team members lead weekly workshops on a mental health concept, technique, or tool for the whole organization.

Whatever different ways you want to do it, the idea is to create con-sistent opportunities for interaction—both work-related and not—and encourage broad participation to get more people involved and help strengthen relationships across the board.

EXERCISE
Assess Your Organization's
Mental Health Culture

Creating a supportive mental health culture in the workplace is vital for employee wellbeing and organizational success. This exercise is designed to help you evaluate the current culture around mental health at your workplace and identify strengths and areas for improvement. Use these insights to develop a more comprehensive and effective approach to mental health in your organization.

Rate each statement on a scale of 1 (strongly disagree) to 5 (strongly agree).

Mental health is openly discussed in our workplace. _____

Employees feel comfortable seeking help for mental health issues. _____

Our leadership actively promotes mental health and wellbeing. _____

We have clear policies and procedures related to mental health. _____

Mental health resources are easily accessible to all employees. _____

Managers are trained to recognize and support mental health issues. _____

Work-life balance is encouraged and respected. _____

There are programs in place to prevent burnout and manage stress. _____

Employee feedback on mental health initiatives is regularly sought and acted upon. _____

Our workplace culture promotes inclusivity and psychological safety. _____

Total Score: _____ / 50

Scoring Key:
40–50: Excellent—Your organization has a strong, supportive mental health culture.
30–39: Good—Your organization is on the right track but has room for improvement.
20–29: Fair—Your organization needs significant improvements in its mental health culture
10-19: Poor—Your organization urgently needs to prioritize mental health initiatives.

How does your organization stack up?

Regularly revisiting this assessment can help you track changes, both positive and negative, in your organization's culture and ensure an ongoing commitment to mental health initiatives.

CHAPTER 4

THE ROLE OF LEADERSHIP IN SUPPORTING PROACTIVE MENTAL HEALTH

Say you're building a new house. You clear the area and put up the studs and the crossbeams. Then, you add the pipes, insulation, and drywall. You lay the flooring, add roofing, and even paint the whole thing. But you neglect the most essential part: the foundation. If you skip pouring the foundation, no matter what you do, the house won't stand for long. It may bear weight for a while, but when the wind picks up or a storm comes through, there won't be anything solid to hold the structure in place. No one will be protected; no one will actually be able to live there.

That's what happens when you don't have leadership support for initiatives in organizations, and that's definitely the case for proactive mental health programs. Leaders provide the foundation for the organizational structure. They're the ones setting the tone for the organization, reinforcing its culture and policies, and generally providing the ultimate support for their employees, including HR and the managers carrying out the culture and policies beneath them. HR can try to implement all the programs they want, and even build the framework to facilitate them, but if they don't have the dedicated support of the leaders at the root of it all, the structure simply won't hold. So, leaders, this chapter is for you.

To build a lasting culture of proactive mental health, the leaders at the top levels of the organization—all C-suite executives, plus the heads of each business division, vertical, and department—must get on board. Here's how: lead by example, embed mental health into the company's values, provide budget for proactive mental health initiatives, prioritize mental health in business operations, train leaders in mental health, and act on the mental health data available to you.

LEAD BY EXAMPLE

For all the proactive mental health protocols you can create, they will do only as much good as your willingness to carry them out, embody them, and practice them yourself as the leader. That starts with open communication.

Communicate Openly About Mental Health

As we discussed in Chapter 3, fostering a culture of open communication about mental health can help reduce stigma around mental health, encourage employees to seek help, and solidify the understanding and practice that proactive mental health is a priority for your company. Of course, that means verbalizing your support for proactive mental health, but it also means showing up and actively participating in meetings, forums, and communication channels on the topic of mental health. It means touching on mental health in performance reviews—though only in service of caring and checking in, not ever as a criterion of good performance—and generally building it into the day-to-day conversations around the workplace.

Moreover, it's important to openly communicate about your own mental health. Sharing your own journey shows your employees a level of vulnerability that prompts connection and care, and further encourages them to be vulnerable and prioritize their mental health. Chief Medical Officer David Stark has seen the positive effect of this at Morgan Stanley: "When senior leaders discuss mental health candidly, it sends a powerful message that mental health is viewed like any other health topic," he said. "That de-stigmatization leads to increased awareness and allows people to step into the light and seek help if they need it."

The same has been true at KKR, where Chris Kim, Global Head of Employee Experience, Benefits and Wellness, has seen important cultural shifts come from leaders' willingness to share. "We've focused on the power of storytelling and creating a more inclusive employee experience with senior leaders and employees sharing their own personal health journeys across important topics, including mental health as well as things like cancer," said Kim.

Model Appropriate Work-Life Boundaries

Supporting a proactive mental health culture as a leader is about more than talk. Your words matter, but your behaviors matter just as much—sometimes more. Especially in the case of mental health policies, people need to see your commitment in action, in no small part so that they also have permission to prioritize their mental health.

So, model good work-life boundaries. Don't stay in the office 80 hours a week (or more) every week. Don't consistently answer emails in the middle of the night and on weekends. Schedule your emails to be sent during working hours. Talk about things other than work. Take breaks throughout your day. Eat lunch away from your desk. And definitely take vacations. If you don't ever take time off, no matter how much you encourage your employees to do so, your actions send a different message—one telling employees that, in fact, you value working nonstop above taking breaks and taking care of yourself, and thus, you may value that in them as well. To help your employees know that they can and should take time off to support their mental health and overall wellbeing, set an example and take vacations throughout the year.

And when you do, really *be on vacation*. If leaders go on vacation but then stay on top of email the entire time, chiming in on threads and responding to non-urgent questions or requests, it sets a precedent. Whether or not it's your intention to do so, your employees learn implicitly that they may also be expected to check in with work while they're away. They learn that it may not be professionally safe or prudent to turn off. They may fear that if they do really disconnect, they'll risk reputational damage or, worse, their job. Those fears further contribute to an overarching sense that their mental health and wellbeing are not priorities after all. "It's not just about stress management," said Erika Loperbey, "it's about how we create an environment where people feel empowered to take care of their mental health. From leadership down, everyone needs to model what healthy mental wellbeing looks like."

I have to admit that I personally struggle with this, and it's a work in progress. It always seems like there is so much to do, and I don't mind working long hours, late nights, or weekends, but I also know the impact it has on my team. As I evolve as a leader, I try to be more and more mindful of the way my actions at work affect my team and the culture we've built.

Prioritize Your Own Mental Health

Embracing proactive mental health practices benefits not only your employees but also you as a leader. These practices, policies, and programs are not just for the benefit of your team; they're also for you—and importantly so. If you're struggling with your mental health, not only does that impact your performance and ability to show up at your best, but it will also have downstream effects throughout your organization, impacting the tone of the workplace and your teams' performance as well. "Employees look to leadership for guidance, and when leaders prioritize mental health, it sets the tone for the entire company," said Elisha Engelen, Partner, Human Capital Solutions Client Leader at the financial services company Aon. Make the time to invest in your mental health, make use of the programs your organization offers, and show your employees that it's a priority for you as well as them.

EMBED MENTAL HEALTH INTO THE COMPANY'S VALUES

Unlike broad mission statements or general commitments to wellbeing, explicitly incorporating mental health and employee wellbeing into your organization's core values—the principles that guide behavior and decision-making at every level—signals that supporting mental health isn't just a nice-to-have benefit but a fundamental part of how your organization operates. It gives it staying power beyond any individual program, initiative, or leader themselves.

Amazon's widely known Leadership Principles, for example, include "Earn Trust," "Strive to Be the World's Best Employer," and "Success and Scale Bring Broad Responsibility." The descriptions for these principles spell out the importance of leading with empathy, listening attentively to employees, creating a more just work environment, empowering employees, committing to employees' personal success, and doing and being better for their employees, their communities, and the world at large—all of which speak to creating a more mentally healthy workforce.

Ali Hasan is the Commercial Director at AXA Health, a leading U.K. health insurer. Hasan takes a lot of pride in putting mental health front and center. "Great organizations are committed to making mental health and wellbeing part of their corporate DNA. It's not an afterthought or a temporary initiative. It is essential for maintaining a healthy, productive, and effective workforce, and approaches to build and reinforce good mental health at work should be integrated into every level of organizations."

As Hasan alluded to, making this commitment concrete means going beyond simply adding "we value mental health" to your company statement. It requires thoughtfully integrating language and expectations around mental health into your existing value framework, then ensuring that your behaviors, policies, benefits, and day-to-day operations, align with and reinforce those values.

Many organizations have values that incorporate aspects of mental health and wellbeing. At Journey, one of our core values is "Truth through safety and courage," through which we aim to always make space for people to feel secure sharing their experiences and mental health concerns openly. This value shapes everything from our benefits and policies to our daily operations, ensuring mental wellbeing remains central to how we function.

General Mills, too, has five main commitments, including inclusion, which emphasizes racial equity, and employee wellbeing and safety. The company backs up these commitments through initiatives like "Work with Heart," allowing employees the flexibility to balance in-person and remote work, as well as its "My Well-being" program, which takes a holistic approach to wellness, addressing physical, emotional, financial, and social wellness together. General Mills also offers digital counseling services, parental and caregiver leave, and financial wellness tools, among many other benefits. All of these efforts reflect the company's ongoing investment in employee wellbeing and align with its commitment to creating a safe, inclusive, supportive workplace for all employees.

PROVIDE BUDGET FOR MENTAL HEALTH INITIATIVES

To support the mental health of your employees and create a proactive mental health culture, leaders, you must allocate dedicated budget for mental health initiatives—not as a peripheral expense but as a fundamental investment in organizational success. This means funding not just basic EAP services but also proactive digital resources, mental health training, engagement campaigns, and the other initiatives and programs discussed in the previous chapter. The logic is clear: If you provide budget for programs, they can flourish and make a real difference; if you don't, they can't.

Funding is no small thing, KKR's Chris Kim acknowledged. "Senior leadership support has been at the foundation of everything we've accomplished in the past decade I've been at KKR," he said. "It has enabled the breadth and depth of investments we've made to enhance and introduce new programs as well as broadly and repeatedly message the importance of our employees' (and their families') mental health." Because executives have allocated the necessary funding, Kim's team has been able to expand employee healthcare and programming to cover things like pediatric behavioral health, caregiver support, and family planning, including unlimited IVF cycles, a generous surrogacy and adoption stipend, and global caregiver concierge services, among other things.

Employees have taken note. Kim said, "Employees have expressed deep appreciation for the benefits we provide that make complicated things a little easier to manage." When important aspects of life outside of work become more feasible and less stressful for employees, everyone benefits. And when employees see the organization putting their money where their mouth is, they know the organization's commitment to their wellbeing is real, not just a talking point.

PRIORITIZE MENTAL HEALTH IN BUSINESS OPERATIONS

To truly integrate mental health into your company culture, it's essential to weave it into the fabric of daily business operations. As Désirée Pascual, Co-Founder and Chief Strategist at Simply Human, said one of the biggest challenges to promoting mental health in organizations is getting leaders to understand that it isn't just about providing therapy and reacting to issues with their support. "It's about building sustainable systems that support employees daily and make them feel valued and cared for," she said.

To give that daily support, bolster the larger institutional policies outlined in the previous chapter—vacation, family leave, workload, crisis planning, etc.—with business practices.

Integrate Mental Health into the Organization's Strategic Priorities

Integrating mental health into the organization's strategic priorities starts with identifying clear, measurable goals that align employee well-being with business success. You could also make it a goal to increase the amount of budget or resources allocated to mental health every year up to a certain amount. Whichever measures you choose to target and track, making mental health a part of the organization's bottom-line focus both ensures that it stays top of mind and serves as a consistent reminder of the value that those programs provide.

That reminder and strategic commitment from leaders goes a long way. "There was a period where we had a ton of momentum with mental health programs," said Bayard Russell, Program Manager for gPause at Google, "but I've seen this over and over—it takes consistent reinforcement from leadership to keep mental health a priority in the company."

Staff Your Company with the Right People

This might not sound like it relates to mental health at first, but it does. It goes back to the idea of "right people, right seats"—a tenet leaders in all industries have heard time and again. You want people that have both the appropriate expertise to do the job well *and* the attitudes that align with the team and the culture the organization has or wants to create. This goes for roles at all levels of the company, from other members of the leadership team to assistants and interns—and certainly, as Lee Lewis emphasized, for benefits teams. Lewis is the Chief Strategy Officer and General Manager of Medical Solutions at Health Transformation Alliance. "Support benefits teams and invest in strong talent to run them. Well-resourced and technically diverse benefits teams significantly outperform the status quo and generate enormous value for their organizations," he said, adding, "This is potentially the most overlooked business opportunity in the country to reduce cost and improve business results."

Staffing well is crucial for the business's bottom line, but it's also vital for your team's mental health. When you have the wrong people in the wrong roles, or simply the wrong people, you end up putting other team members in a position to pick up the slack and do more work where their colleagues are falling short, which can lead to frustration, longer hours, and feeling undervalued—none of which make for improved wellbeing or job satisfaction.

On top of that, if you have someone who isn't a team player—they have a poor attitude, they shoot down others' ideas, or they're not welcoming to other team members—that can make other employees feel uncomfortable or ostracized. It leads to poorer communication and collaboration, and can bring down entire teams, both in performance and wellbeing. So, while it might seem unrelated, staffing your team well makes a huge difference in the mental health of your employees and the culture of your workplace.

Set Realistic Deadlines

A lot of businesses have a great bias toward speed, which is not a bad thing in and of itself. Speed is often a competitive advantage, and endeavoring to move quickly can be a great tool, spurring helpful energy and creativity in people's work and motivating us to achieve more than we think we can. Moving fast is, in fact, one of the things that I pride myself on. However, when an organization tries to move *too* fast or push its teams to complete work on impractical or unreasonable timelines all the time, it creates unnecessary stress and anxiety for employees, which can certainly lead to working longer hours, burnout, and poorer mental health, let alone poorer work product and business outcomes.

Bayard Russell spoke to this too. "At Google, it's always a balance between keeping productivity high and ensuring employees have the mental health resources they need. The culture is fast-paced, but we've learned that mental wellbeing plays a critical role in sustaining long-term success."

Setting deadlines that allow employees to do their work well within the normal workday enables them to find a healthier work-life harmony, feel supported by the organization, and, as a result, do better work on the whole. You want the status quo to feel sustainable so that times where you need to prioritize speed can actually be fruitful.

Implement Email Protocols that Reinforce Work-Life Boundaries

Some leaders have also implemented proactive mental health protocols around email. For instance, they've set up systems that pause emails on the weekend. Any email sent to an employee's work email from Friday night to Sunday night is held in the cloud and won't land in the employee's inbox until Monday morning. Companies do similar practices around vacations. In some cases, they hold emails for the full duration of the employee's vacation. In others, they institute a hold in the opposite direction and actually lock employees out of their email so that they aren't tempted to check it. Other companies have settings that delete any emails that get sent to an employee while they're out: An out-of-office auto-reply is sent to the initial sender alerting them that their email will be deleted and that, if it's important, the sender should email the employee when they're back from vacation.

All of these practices encourage employees to truly disengage from work when they're off. In today's day and age, it's a tall order to find many people who actually do this, and it's taking its toll on the workforce. By implementing practices such as these, leaders can encourage and reinforce behaviors that proactively contribute to employees' improved wellbeing and happiness at work.

ACT ON THE MENTAL HEALTH DATA AVAILABLE TO YOU

Considering all of the digital tools available in the mental health landscape now, executives and HR leaders can access essential data that, when thoughtfully analyzed and strategically applied, can significantly enhance organizational wellbeing. Aggregated, anonymous data from sources like

Employee Assistance Program (EAP) usage, mental health assessments, employee surveys, and engagement metrics reveals important patterns, such as departments with higher stress levels, regions needing additional resources, or how seasonal changes impact overall morale.

It's challenging to draw direct cause-and-effect links between mental health initiatives and business outcomes due to the numerous external factors and personal circumstances that affect people's mental health and the work environment. However, tracking trends in absenteeism, healthcare costs, productivity, and turnover in tandem with mental health insights enables leaders to distribute resources effectively and make better, more informed policy and program decisions to support a healthier workplace culture and better business outcomes on the whole. We'll go into more detail on analyzing data and measuring success of mental health outcomes in Chapter 8, but bottom line: Use the data available to you to make decisions that can improve the mental health of your employees.

EXAMPLES OF LEADERS DRIVING MENTAL HEALTH INITIATIVES

In addition to the examples scattered throughout this chapter, several other major organizations have implemented successful mental health initiatives backed by leadership. Take Unilever. Unilever's leadership made mental health a strategic priority by becoming a founding member of the Global Business Collaborative for Better Workplace Mental Health, which aims to advance mental health in the workplace. They further created a Wellbeing Framework for their organization, which they have published on their website for the public, and which includes an explicit commitment from the company's CEO, Hein Schumacher:

> At Unilever, our talented, committed people are vital to business success. A psychologically safe environment where employees are empowered to contribute their best is a key enabler of Unilever's

culture. Dialing up our performance edge includes prioritizing the physical and mental health of our people, unlocking their full potential to drive innovation, execution and business results.

Their Wellbeing Framework includes a range of initiatives, including mental health training for managers, access to a variety of mental health resources, a robust EAP, and regular energy and wellbeing surveys. They have committed to not only treating the health issues of their employees but also preventing them in the first place—a truly proactive approach. Additionally, by making their commitment public, Unilever's leadership has ensured both internal and external accountability. It seems to be paying off: According to a survey the company conducted in 2023, 84% of Unilever's office employees believe that the company cares about their wellbeing.

Employees of the Metropolitan Transit Authority in New York City have shown appreciation for some of the organization's wellbeing initiatives as well. The MTA instituted an Occupational Health and Safety team, with medical facilities to host check-ups and drug tests, as well as a resident EAP team of psychologists. They also invest in events that highlight wellbeing directly. "Our benefits leaders host various wellness events throughout the year that serve thousands of employees. One event lasts all day, with free food, massages, and other wellness products," said Yvell Stanford, the MTA People Organization's Deputy Chief of Organizational Design and Development. "New York City Transit conducts annual surveys, representing 50,000 employees, and it always gets great feedback."

Amy Gilliland, President of the multi-billion-dollar global defense company General Dynamics Information Technology, or GDIT, created a program called "How Are You Really?" to encourage employees company- and industry-wide, with a special emphasis on veterans, to talk more openly about their mental health in the workplace. Salesforce leadership has made mental health a key focus, offering increased access to mental health resources, consistent wellbeing check-ins, and initiatives like the company's Mental Health Awareness Week as well as its Mental Wellness Reimbursement Program, which provides employees with funds to support their wellbeing. And two years ago, leaders of five major American nonprofit corporations—the National League of Cities, American Public Health Association, American Psychological Association, YMCA of the U.S.A., and International City/County Management Association—joined forces to create the "Striving for Mental Health Excellence in the Workplace" campaign, with the sole focus of reshaping the conversation about mental health in work settings to increase awareness and emphasize its importance.

Mental health has also become a priority among leaders of sports organizations. During the pandemic, Andrew Miller, COO of the NFL team the Minnesota Vikings, took the lead in sharing his own experience with depression on a 200-person, organization-wide Zoom call. People responded so positively that others within the Vikings organization started sharing about their struggles with mental health as well. Soon after, they launched an online interview series called "Getting Open" to encourage further discussion and support for mental health among all employees.

Leaders within the National Basketball Association have stepped up, too. In discussing the NBA's mental health initiatives, the organization's Head of Benefits and Well-Being, Danielle Shanes, has said that the NBA created mental health objectives based on what they heard from employees, players, consultants, and healthcare partners. These objectives include ensuring that the NBA is (1) an emotionally healthy place to work, (2) an inclusive environment where it's okay for everyone to acknowledge when they're struggling emotionally, and (3) a supportive workplace with the appropriate resources and access to treatment. "This isn't a benefit; it is culture," Shanes says. "It's what employees experience from the moment they first arrive at the NBA, and what they feel in their daily work and throughout their careers."

BE THE CHANGE

Shanes speaks to a crucial point: Organizations shape what people feel every single day, throughout their *entire* careers. That's a massive impact, and it's heavily influenced by the people at the very top. If leaders don't recognize the outsized role they have in shaping their employees' mental health, they lose the opportunity to help support and improve it. They lose the chance to create an organization where employees remain engaged, healthy, happy, and connected. They lose the ability to see what a workforce that's truly set up to thrive can accomplish.

A final word from Accenture's Geetika Bhojak, "Leaders need to realize that mental health is just as important as any other business outcome. It impacts productivity, engagement, creativity, and ultimately, the success of the organization. When leaders prioritize mental wellbeing, they create an environment where employees feel safe to bring their whole selves to work. This not only improves individual wellbeing but also has a ripple effect on team dynamics and organizational culture. It's time we stop seeing mental health as a side issue and start treating it as a core part of our business strategy."

EXERCISE
Leadership Self-Reflection on Mental Health

Leaders, what is your current approach to mental health? By honestly evaluating your practices, you can become a more effective advocate for mental health in your organization.

This self-reflection exercise will help you assess your approach and identify areas for growth.

- How often do I discuss mental health openly with my team?

  ☐ Never   ☐ Rarely   ☐ Sometimes
  ☐ Often   ☐ Very Often

- Do I model good mental health practices?

  ☐ Yes   ☐ No   ☐ Sometimes

- Have I received training on supporting employee mental health?

  ☐ Yes   ☐ No

- Do I know how to recognize signs of mental health issues in my team?

  ☐ Yes   ☐ No   ☐ Somewhat

- How comfortable am I having conversations about mental health with my team?

  ☐ Very Uncomfortable   ☐ Uncomfortable
  ☐ Neutral   ☐ Comfortable   ☐ Very Comfortable

- What is one area of mental health leadership I can improve on?

- What specific action can I take in the next month to enhance mental health support in my team?

CHAPTER 5

THE IMPORTANCE OF DIVERSITY AND INCLUSION

On International Women's Day in 2018, roughly 14,000 employees of the American multinational investment juggernaut BlackRock met for the final day of a major company gathering. At their seats, they found a data-packed booklet on the power of diversity, prepared by the then–Global Head of Inclusion and Diversity, Jonathan McBride, and his team. Along with relaying other key pieces of information about the importance of diversity in business, the booklet was intended to help everyone understand how fostering a culture of belonging, where employees of every single background feel welcome and included, helps every other employee—and the organization as a whole—thrive. McBride knew at the time that, while the company was on its way toward change, its hiring structures as well as the general awareness around diversity among its workforce weren't fully actualized. Getting the full team to understand diversity and belonging was just one step. As BlackRock continued to build out its efforts, McBride and other leaders realized that to fulfill its commitment to inclusion and shape a culture that nurtured diversity, they needed to invest in stronger mental health programming and ensure it covered the needs of every demographic.

VaynerMedia, a leading global digital marketing agency, faced a slightly different conundrum: their workforce skews younger than most industries, and in the increasingly fast-paced world of modern advertising, their majority Millennial and Gen Z employees were expressing the need for more varied and robust mental health services. These employees wanted more digital services that would be accessible and convenient, no matter the time of day or their location in the world. They also wanted more personal and holistic approaches that could help them manage their stress and wellbeing daily instead of just periodically. Essentially, they wanted mental health to become a bigger focus of VaynerMedia's culture so it mirrored the level of importance their employees' generations give it.

Both of these companies were contending with different sides of the same coin: Their mental health approaches did not adequately include or provide support for the needs of the diverse populations in their workforces. And because of it, the wellbeing of their employees was suffering. When they realized the gap in their services and cultures, the leaders at both BlackRock and VaynerMedia moved into action to find better mental health solutions for *all* employees and increased the focus on mental health in their cultures.

WHY DIVERSITY AND INCLUSION ARE SO IMPORTANT FOR PROACTIVE MENTAL HEALTH

When it comes to mental health in the workplace, diversity and inclusion aren't just added optional bonuses—they're absolute necessities. In fact, no mental health approach can be truly effective if it doesn't account for the diverse experiences, backgrounds, and needs of all employees. The rationale is fairly straightforward: Including people and the diversity of their backgrounds helps them feel seen. When people feel seen, they feel valued. And when they feel valued, their mental health improves as does their ability to show up their best at work and in the rest of their life. But there are more complex reasons as well.

The Mental Health Impact of Discrimination

Research clearly shows that people from different racial, ethnic, cultural, and identity groups face unique, often disproportionate, mental health challenges, both in and out of the workplace. They face discrimination, a lack of representation, and other stressors, all of which can take a significant toll on their psychological wellbeing. For example, a 2020 study found that anxiety and depression symptoms more than tripled among Black and Latino communities in the United States that year, with a notable spike occurring after the murder of George Floyd. The health disparities of the COVID-19 pandemic further compounded these issues, as Black and Latino Americans were three times more likely to become infected and nearly twice as likely to die from the virus compared to White Americans.

Even in the absence of major societal events, day-to-day experiences of discrimination take a profound toll. Microaggressions—subtle insults or slights based on race, gender, sexual orientation, or other aspects of identity—harm people's mental health over time. Employees may face stereotyping, exclusion from important conversations or opportunities, or pressure to conform to dominant cultural norms.

These experiences create what psychologists call "minority stress"—the cumulative impact of chronic prejudice and discrimination. Over time, minority stress is associated with higher rates of anxiety, depression, substance abuse, and other mental health issues.

However, the effects aren't limited to emotional wellbeing. A survey by the National Alliance on Mental Illness found that 40% of employees who experienced workplace discrimination had left a job because of it. Clearly, failing to address discrimination and creating inclusive environments have very real costs for both employees and organizations.

Barriers to Accessing Mental Health Care

On top of facing higher rates of mental health challenges, employees from marginalized groups often struggle to access appropriate care, due to a variety of reasons, including discrimination, cultural stigmas, and lack of culturally competent care. These issues only create additional barriers to getting help—a point underscored by data from the American Psychological Association showing the stark disparities in mental health treatment in the United States: Asian Americans are 51% less likely to use mental health services compared to White Americans, with Latino Americans 25% less likely and Black Americans 21% less likely to use mental health services in comparison.

Multiple factors contribute to these gaps. Cultural stigma around mental health in some communities can discourage people from seeking help. Language barriers and lack of culturally competent providers create obstacles. Economic disparities play a role, as marginalized groups are more likely to be underinsured and live in economically depressed areas.

One major factor contributing to gaps in mental healthcare is that there's a significant lack of diversity among mental health professionals themselves. Black, Latino, and Asian psychologists combined account for less than 20% of psychologists in the U.S. This lack of representation means many patients struggle to find providers who understand their cultural context and experiences. Furthermore, they may encounter providers or referring physicians with biases that affect the healthcare and advice they provide diverse patients. Dr. Shawnte Elbert, a recognized leader in health equity, DEI, and leadership development, described it to me in basic terms as a pipeline issue. By not addressing it, she says, we're missing a big piece of mental healthcare. "We have this expectation that people will receive care from professionals who may not understand their lived experiences or the nuances of their culture," Elbert explained. "How can we expect someone to open up about their mental health when the person on the other side of the table doesn't even see their identity?"

It's not just about the clinicians themselves, either; it's also about the types of care they provide. "For example, we can't keep pushing cognitive behavioral therapy (CBT) as the only solution. It's not effective for every population," Elbert said. "For people of color dealing with bias or discrimination, we need different modalities, but those options aren't always available. We need more diverse clinicians who can approach mental health from a place of true understanding."

These disparities in access to care mean that employees from diverse backgrounds are less likely to get the support they need, even as they face higher rates of work-related stress and trauma. Clearly, any organizational approach to mental health must specifically recognize and address these gaps to ensure they provide an opening to better, more equitable and accessible care, not another barrier to it.

PROACTIVE MENTAL HEALTH CONSIDERATIONS FOR SPECIFIC GROUPS

"Diverse groups" are not a monolith, of course. All identity groups, particularly those who are marginalized, face different challenges and have different mental health considerations. Having a proactive mental health approach means thinking through the distinct needs of each group and offering specialized resources accordingly. Here are some key identity groups—though by no means is this an exhaustive list—and some unique mental health considerations organizations should keep in mind when supporting them.

People of Color

While data show that people of color in the U.S. report lower rates of depression than their White counterparts, the numbers may not accurately reflect the experience of that population because the cultural stigma around mental health in communities of color can often discourage individuals from seeking help. In no small part due to centuries of racism and discrimination, many communities of color emphasize resilience and stoicism, which may prevent open discussions about mental health challenges. However, as Dr. Shawnte Elbert explained, even when they do seek help, the shortage of mental health professionals of color means that people of color often struggle to find professionals and clinicians who understand their cultural contexts. This can lead to a disconnect between patient and provider and, in some cases, a less-than-helpful experience for the person seeking care.

The fuller picture includes the ongoing experience of racial trauma, which—whether through overt discrimination, microaggressions, or systemic racism—often leads to heightened levels of stress, anxiety, and depression. People of color also often face additional socioeconomic barriers, such as lower rates of insurance coverage, greater disparities in pay and wealth, and an increased likelihood of living in areas with fewer healthcare facilities and more public health concerns. These inequalities exacerbate mental health challenges and further reduce the likelihood of communities of color receiving adequate care.

The combined effect of institutional racism, inadequate care and access to care, and cultural stigma is that mental health disorders among people of color often persist for longer periods of time. As Daniel H. Gillison, Jr., CEO of the National Alliance on Mental Illness, has said, "The effect of racism and racial trauma on mental health is real and cannot be ignored. The disparity in access to mental healthcare in communities of color cannot be ignored. The inequality and lack of cultural competency in mental health treatment cannot be ignored."

To restate the point above, though, "people of color" are also not a monolith by any stretch. Black people face different realities and mental health concerns than those of Asian descent, who face different realities than those of Latin American or Arab descent, who face different realities than Indigenous people, who face different realities than people of mixed-race identity—and so on. It's vital to consider each group individually, not just as a categorized whole.

Women

Of the unique mental health challenges facing women, many are tied to societal expectations and traditional gender roles. The pressure to balance work, caregiving, and household responsibilities can lead to chronic stress and anxiety. This is coupled with the disproportionate levels of gender-based violence women experience, including sexual harassment and domestic abuse, which often result in trauma, PTSD, and long-term mental health issues. In fact, whether the result of gender-based violence or not, women are two times more likely to experience anxiety, depression, and PTSD, according to the American Psychiatric Association. Women also make up 86-95% of all diagnoses of anorexia and bulimia nervosa—also a result, in many ways, of societal expectations and messaging about women's bodies.

Reproductive mental health affects women alone, as they experience challenges related to pregnancy, infertility, miscarriage, postpartum depression, and menopause, among others. These experiences can be incredibly taxing emotionally and often require specialized mental healthcare. Importantly, women also continue to face systemic gender bias in the workplace, where pay gaps, limited leadership opportunities, and discrimination can contribute to mental health strain.

Men

While men benefit disproportionately in many facets of life, men do face serious stigmas around their mental and emotional wellbeing. Generally speaking, cultures worldwide have discouraged men from investigating and expressing their emotions, or cultivating support networks wherein they feel safe to explore their emotional lives. As a result, men tend to be less likely than women to discuss their mental health and even less likely to seek help or professional treatment. This is especially true for men of color, who utilize mental health treatment services at significantly lower rates than White men and women in general.

Unfortunately, this all comes with very real and damaging effects. According to Psychology Today, men are at least two times more likely than women to develop substance dependence and misuse, and they account for 75% of suicide victims in the United States, with higher rates of suicide in rural communities. There is still great societal pressure on men to conform to traditional gender roles, to perform and provide, and to keep a "masculine" (a.k.a. strong and unemotional) front. But these pressures and expectations wreak havoc on men's emotional lives and mental wellbeing. For organizations, particularly those in predominantly male industries, combating the stigma associated with men expressing emotions and mental health needs is crucial. The more that leaders, especially male leaders, in these spaces can open up and communicate about their own mental health, the better.

The LGBTQ+ Community

Members of the LGBTQ+ community encounter numerous mental health challenges. The latest data from the American Psychological Association shows that LGBTQ+ individuals are 2 1/2 times more likely to experience anxiety, depression, and substance misuse than heterosexual individuals and more than twice as likely to experience a mental health disorder in general.

The mental health challenges faced by members of the LGBTQ+ community stem in no small part from societal discrimination and rejection. Many individuals encounter prejudice or exclusion from family, peers, or communities because of their identity, which can lead to social isolation, depression, and in some cases, suicidal ideation. The process of coming out and navigating identity acceptance is particularly difficult in unsupportive environments, which can increase people's anxiety and undermine their self-esteem—effects that can last for many years.

Access to inclusive and affirming mental healthcare remains a challenge for LGBTQ+ individuals. Many struggle to find therapists who are knowledgeable about LGBTQ+ issues, especially in areas like gender identity, transitioning, and sexual orientation. Furthermore, LGBTQ+ individuals face higher rates of trauma, including bullying, assault, and hate crimes, all of which contribute to a higher prevalence of mental health issues within the community. These rates increase significantly for LGBTQ+ people of color.

Generational differences play a role as well. LGBTQ+ folks in older generations hold decades of discrimination, silence, and trauma related to their sexuality and sexual orientation within them. They are newer to the notion that speaking publicly about their sexuality and the effects on their mental health could be a good thing and, as a result, tend to take longer before taking part in mental health conversations, particularly in the workplace. Younger generations face less stigma within their peer groups and tend to be more open about mental health concerns in general, however, they still face stigma and discrimination, particularly when navigating differences with older generations inside and especially outside the LGBTQ+ community.

Finally, geographic location has an effect. While the LGBTQ+ community has gained many rights in Western nations, in many parts of the world, LGBTQ+ people have few to zero rights. In certain countries, it's still illegal and even punishable by death to be homosexual. This kind of cultural knowledge is crucial for organizations with employees around the world to have and understand as they provide support.

All of these factors mean that for VaynerMedia's Chief Heart Officer, Claude Silver, "creating a safe and inclusive environment for LGBTQ+ employees is a priority." Over the last few years, as the company shifted its focus to prioritize employee mental health in a major way, Silver and her colleagues established strong anti-discrimination policies and inclusive benefits, including mental health services that address the specific needs of LGBTQ+ individuals like their Pride Colleague Resource Group (CRG). "Our Pride CRG provides a space for connection and advocacy, supported by allies programs and diversity training," she said. These targeted services have helped create a culture of empathy for the LGBTQ+ employees at the company, which, Silver notes, is critical for their mental wellbeing.

Immigrants

Acculturative stress—the pressure to adapt to a new culture while maintaining one's own identity—is often a key component of immigrants' mental health. Navigating this delicate balance can lead to anxiety, stress, and depression. Additionally, immigrants are often separated from their families, communities, and support networks, which can further heighten feelings of loneliness and isolation.

Trauma is a big factor in many immigrants' stories as well. The migration process can be very traumatic—especially for refugees who may have fled violence, war, or persecution—and can lead to PTSD and other severe mental health conditions. In recent years, anti-immigrant sentiments have risen around the world, and we've seen increases in anti-immigrant rhetoric among individuals and politicians in the media as well as anti-immigrant policies and legislation. This has been particularly true across North America and Europe, with immigration featuring heavily as a key issue in elections. The rhetoric and policies have prompted increasingly volatile and even hostile treatment of immigrants in the communities they've migrated to, negatively impacting the mental health of immigrant populations. For instance, in the U.S., where anti-immigrant sentiment has noticeably grown in recent years, the UCLA Center for Policy Research reported in 2023 that rates of serious psychological distress, including depression and anxiety, among surveyed immigrants living in the country for less than five years rose from 5% in 2017 to 12% by 2021. Of this group, two-thirds did not see a mental health professional or healthcare provider between 2019 and 2021, and 77% reported unmet mental health needs.

Language barriers and confusion around social services systems are two of the issues complicating access to mental health services for immigrants, making it difficult for them to communicate their needs or find culturally sensitive providers. These challenges can deepen feelings of alienation and further hinder their mental healthcare journey. Organizations can ameliorate such challenges by ramping up mental health programs for all employees.

Veterans

Research shows that veterans are more likely to experience mental health disorders and traumatic brain injury than nonveterans. In the U.S. alone, data from 2017 from the National Institute of Mental Health shows that 1 in 5 veterans has a mental health condition, and 1 in 10 struggles with multiple conditions simultaneously. Veterans' unique mental health challenges stem in large part from their experiences in combat, which result in prolonged exposure to violence, death, and loss as well as life-altering physical injury and pain. Reintegrating into civilian life also presents challenges, as many veterans struggle to find purpose, fit into societal norms, or rebuild their identities after military service.

Whether in or out of active duty, many veterans experience anxiety, depression, and PTSD. In fact, as much as 7% of veterans have PTSD, according to data from the U.S. Department of Veterans Affairs (the VA). Deployment increases the risk of PTSD by as much as 300%. To cope with the trauma and pain, many veterans turn to alcohol or drugs. Self-medication in this way can lead to substance use disorder, which affects roughly 12% of the veteran population, according to the Substance Abuse and Mental Health Services Administration, and often exacerbates other mental health struggles.

While veterans' services exist, access to mental healthcare can be difficult due to long wait times, bureaucratic complexities, and the enduring stigma surrounding mental health within military culture. Unfortunately, many veterans go untreated or under-treated, causing long-term consequences for their wellbeing—sometimes tragically long-term: In 2022, the VA reported that an average of 17 veterans die by suicide in America every day. Providing mental health programs and creating strong mental health–focused cultures in organizations helps combat issues around access and stigma and encourages more veterans to get the care they need.

People with Disabilities

Because the focus tends to fall on the physical or readily apparent conditions for people with disabilities—both for physical and developmental disabilities—members of this community often find that their mental health needs get overlooked. Yet, their needs are not insignificant. The stress of managing a disability, coupled with frequent social isolation and discrimination, can lead to depression and anxiety. Individuals with disabilities often face reduced opportunities for employment or social engagement, which further contributes to feelings of alienation and low self-esteem.

Data from the Centers for Disease Control and Prevention (CDC) highlights the severity of the issue: In 2018, the public health organization reported that nearly 33% of American adults with disabilities experienced frequent mental distress—defined as having 14 or more mentally unhealthy days over the past 30-day period. That's over 4 1/2 times more than adults without disabilities. In fact, the report confirmed that adults with disabilities generally report symptoms of depression and anxiety and limited access to care than adults without disabilities.

The physical conditions, of course, play a role here, too. Chronic pain or fatigue associated with many disabilities also takes a distinct toll on people's mental health. Despite the clear need for psychological support, access to mental health services is often limited due to physical accessibility issues or the lack of accommodations in mental healthcare settings, which creates additional barriers and makes it even more difficult for individuals with disabilities to receive adequate mental health support.

It's important to note the effect disability has on loved ones as well. Dr. Randy Martin shared his own experience with disability with me. "I have a sister who has an intellectual disability, and growing up, I saw firsthand how much therapy and support she needed, but also how much my family needed. It really opened my eyes to the fact that mental health challenges aren't just isolated to the individual—there's a ripple effect that impacts the entire family." He's also worked with a lot of children and families dealing with intellectual and developmental disabilities throughout his career, and early on, he noticed beyond his personal family experience how often siblings of children with disabilities are overlooked despite needing support just as much as the sibling with a disability. "That's when I realized that mental health needs to be addressed in a more comprehensive and inclusive way, supporting not just the person in therapy but their whole support system," Dr. Martin said. When you have employees with disabilities, they need tailored mental health support, and employees who have family members with disabilities need it, too.

The Neurodivergent Community

Despite comprising an estimated 15-20% of the global population, neurodivergent individuals, such as those with attention-deficit/hyperactivity disorder (ADHD), autism, or dyslexia, face significant societal misunderstanding and stigma. As some neurodivergent people, whose brains simply work differently than those of neurotypical people, struggle to conform to traditional social norms, they can feel that they don't fit in, which can lead to (or come from) social isolation. These experiences can result in anxiety, depression, and low self-esteem.

According to research published in 2020, as much as 81% of adults with autism spectrum disorder and two-thirds of those with ADHD have one or more mental health conditions. Roughly 25% of adults with ADHD also experience mood disorders, like depression, and almost 50% have an anxiety disorder.

The clear mental health concerns of this population can be either exacerbated or helped by environmental factors. More prone to sensory overload, neurodivergent individuals often have difficulty in busier environments. In certain highly stimulating workspaces, or even daily commutes, experiencing sensory overload can lead to heightened states of stress and anxiety. Creating designated zones for quiet, focused work can help reduce stress for neurodivergent employees and give them spaces where they know they can go to regulate in these moments.

As you might expect, neurodivergent individuals often require mental health therapies that are specifically tailored to their cognitive processes. Unfortunately, such therapies are not always readily available, or they may require additional resources or expense, leaving many without appropriate support for their mental health needs. Organizations that account for that need and provide access to tailored care can help meaningfully improve mental health outcomes for their neurodivergent employees.

Different Generations

While not an identity group that automatically comes to mind, people's age and generation affect both their experience of and approach to mental health and the workplace in definite ways.

In the beginning of this chapter, I shared how the leaders of Vayner-Media increasingly heard from younger employees that they needed better mental health benefits and services at the company. VaynerMedia is not alone here—companies across industries, particularly those whose workforces skew younger, are having similar conversations with their employees. The daily working experience of employees has shifted over recent decades as technology has changed our modes of work, causing burnout and work-related mental health issues to rise. Even aside from work, numerous studies from recent years have reported that young people are experiencing higher rates of anxiety, depression, and other mental health conditions than in decades past. Financial realities are different for the younger generations as well; at similar ages, members of older generations had greater financial outlooks than many Gen Z and Millennials do today. At the same time, younger generations are more open to discussing mental health issues and are pushing employers, and society at large, to put mental health front and center—right where it should be, on par with physical health. These changes contribute to vastly different experiences and approaches to mental health between generations.

MindShare Partners' 2021 Mental Health at Work Report found that Gen Z and Millennial employees have a higher likelihood of experiencing nearly every mental health disorder compared with Baby Boomers. In their findings, Millennials were 3 1/2 times more likely than Baby Boomers to say work contributed to their mental health conditions. It also showed that more than 50% of Millennial and 75% of Gen Z employees had left jobs because of mental health concerns. Only 10% of Baby Boomers said the same. In general, comfort discussing mental health is a new phenomenon, especially at work. For most Baby Boomers, it's a full paradigm shift. Add in the increasing use of new technology and digital support tools and a lot of Baby Boomers find themselves feeling even more out of the loop. As organizations increase the prevalence of mental health conversations, services, and support, the different comfort levels and needs of all generations—including how technology is used as a support tool—must be taken into account.

VaynerMedia tried to do just that. "Navigating generational differences around mental health in the workplace can be tricky," Claude Silver admitted, but the company found success through education, inclusive communication, and tailored support. "We launched workshops that addressed specific generational concerns and created communication strategies around those concerns that included email newsletters, social media updates, and face-to-face meetings. The key was offering flexible support options, from in-person counseling to teletherapy, through our Journey Proactive EAP, ensuring that everyone, regardless of age, could access the help they needed." Ultimately, with the company's dedication to going fully proactive, its EAP engagement increased 16-fold, from a mere 2% to 32%.

Life Stages and Transitions

Age brings another factor worth planning for in proactive mental health: big life stages and transitions, such as becoming new parents, transitioning roles at work, moving cities or homes, approaching menopause or retirement, etc. All of these transitions carry emotional and mental weight to them, not to mention expectations and cultural significance. They may also require significant time and attention. Joe Toniolo, Senior Director of Health and Welfare Plans at US Foods, realized this when he went through major transitions in his own life. "I got married later in life, and shortly after had my first child. It's been a big shift and can be mentally exhausting," he told me. "I've learned that you need to make time for your mental health as a parent, even if it's just finding small moments for yourself, like a quick coffee break or a day trip with just you and your partner." My wife and I also just had our first child last year, and I can attest to Joe's advice. My personal mental health practices are harder to get to now but more important than ever. They help me maintain my wellbeing so that I can be present and healthy as a parent and partner.

A proactive approach to mental health incorporates resources that distinctly deal with each of these big life moments. Mercer's behavior health leader, Peter Rutigliano, PhD agrees: "Workplaces need to be more flexible in supporting employees through major life events, whether it's dealing with divorce or the loss of a loved one. Mental health support should adapt to these moments." Many digital mental health platforms and EAPs have special classes dedicated to helping people navigate these stages as well; these are great resources to direct people to so they can engage with them at will. Better yet, if and when managers, leaders, or HR personnel learn of employees' impending changes, you can anticipate some of their mental health needs by providing resources in advance or gently reaching out during a transition.

Marco Diaz, News Corp.'s Global Head of Benefits, made sure News Corp. included these offerings in its mental health program. To him, it's important that their program covers every aspect of wellbeing and offers the right kinds of support, at the right times. "Mental health is a broad spectrum, and people need different types of support depending on what they're going through," he said. "We want to make sure that no matter where someone is on that spectrum, they have the resources and tools they need to manage their mental health effectively." Diaz acknowledged that it's not an easy task. "But," he said, "it's necessary if we're going to really improve people's lives."

ACCOUNTING FOR INTERSECTIONALITY

Each identity group deals with its own set of mental health considerations and concerns based on the various levels of inclusion and discrimination they face. When someone is a member of more than one identity group that faces inequities and disparate treatment, though, those considerations can overlap in unique ways or even multiply—an issue characterized by the term "intersectionality."

Columbia Law School and UCLA professor Kimberlé Crenshaw, a scholar on civil rights, racism and the law, and feminist legal theory, initially coined the term "intersectionality" in 1989 to describe the complexity of oppression that race and gender put on Black women in the United States; not only do African-American women contend with racial prejudice, they also deal with gender bias, and the two identities combine to affect their experiences and how they're treated in society. In other words, it's not just one axis of social inequality that affects them; it's multiple.

The term's meaning has expanded over the years to consider how anyone with multiple marginalized identities—for example, a gay East Asian man or a Latina immigrant with disability—may be affected, depending on the societal perception and treatment of people with each of those identities. In general, intersectionality acknowledges that people possess multiple interconnected identities that shape their experiences and access to resources.

In mental health, the concept of intersectionality illuminates how various social categories intersect to specifically influence a person's mental wellbeing and their ability to seek and receive care. People may, and often do, have unique mental health needs based on how their identities intersect, and in many parts of the world, they may encounter unique barriers to treatment based on certain identities. In fact, research shows that people with intersecting marginalized identities often face higher rates of mental health issues and greater obstacles to accessing quality care. One study published in 2017, for instance, found that subjects with mental health issues had an average of six stigmatized conditions or identities.

To create truly inclusive and effective mental health cultures at work, employers must be aware of intersectionality and incorporate an intersectional lens into their approach to mental health. How? Ensure diverse representation in mental health resource groups and decision-making processes, for one. Additionally, provide culturally competent mental health resources that address the unique challenges faced by different intersectional groups, and finally, offer training to managers and HR professionals on intersectionality and its impact on mental health.

By embracing an intersectional approach, employers can create a more equitable and supportive mental health environment for all employees, recognizing that each individual's mental health journey is shaped by their unique combination of identities and experiences.

WHAT A DIVERSE AND INCLUSIVE APPROACH TO MENTAL HEALTH LOOKS LIKE

Given these realities, there are several things organizations can do to make their mental health approaches genuinely equitable and inclusive.

Ensure Diverse Representation

Make sure that the mental healthcare professionals and services you provide employees have appropriate representation of a wide range of backgrounds and identities. This is crucial for all employees to be able to see themselves in their care and feel that they will be understood and treated with respect. And, as Dr. Shawnte Elbert has seen time and again in her work with organizations and universities, it pays off. "As someone who's fought for more diverse clinicians, I've seen firsthand the positive outcomes. When we hire clinicians who reflect the diversity of our communities, we see better engagement with our mental health programs and higher satisfaction from those receiving care."

The effect of diverse representation doesn't just stop with mental healthcare services, however. Having increased diversity among people in leadership and managerial roles in your organization also improves the overall psychological safety and sense of inclusion that employees in marginalized groups feel day to day.

Accommodate Multiple Languages

Extend representation another layer to languages. All employees need to be able to access care in the language that is most comfortable for them. That means ensuring every employee has access to local mental health clinicians and/or clinicians available through telehealth who speak their primary language. It means providing all written mental health resources and materials in all primary languages claimed by your employees. As much as possible, it also means using digital resources—whether a digital EAP, other mental health platform, or mindfulness apps—that are available in as many languages as possible.

Let's not forget about sign language and the needs of the deaf community. There are over 300 different sign languages around the world. If you have deaf or hard-of-hearing employees, make sure they get support in the sign language they know best. Blind and visually impaired employees will also need resources available to them in their preferred mode of accessibility, whether Braille or audio recording.

Ideally, no employee should have to hunt for the resources in their language. Knowing your employees' primary language, make sure that HR and employees' managers proactively point them in the direction of the resources in their preferred language from the start.

Address Discrimination Directly

Implement clear policies against discrimination, and provide training on unconscious bias and inclusive behaviors. For employees to feel truly safe at work, both generally and in the context of sharing their mental health concerns, they need to know that their organization will not tolerate acts of discrimination toward them at any point in time. It's important for these measures to have associated accountability mechanisms as well, both so you can adequately address issues when they arise and so that employees know that there are enforcement measures in place.

Ensure Cultural Competence

Make sure that your mental health benefits and EAP providers offer culturally responsive care. Minimally, this means having diverse providers available and offering services in multiple languages, as previously mentioned. It also means providing training for managers and team members on cultural competence, which comes into play in a big way for global organizations with employees in multiple countries. I address this further in the next chapter on employing a global perspective.

Fulfill Pay Equity

According to 2022 data from the Pew Research Center, White women in the United States make 83 cents for every one dollar a man makes, on average. That's 17% less—a gap that has decreased by only 3% in the last two decades despite significant efforts and cultural conversation to highlight and address the issue. The numbers are even more stark for Black and Hispanic women, who make 70 cents and 65 cents to a man's dollar. Asian women fare better at 93 cents on the dollar, but the average woman, no matter her race, still makes less than the average man.

Pay disparities based on gender, race, ethnicity, age, or other classification have broad effects, including, in the case of gender, on women's mental health. If and when employees make less than their counterparts for the same work, it often makes them feel undervalued, which can lead to a sense that their ideas and contributions are either unwanted or not taken seriously. Pay gaps can also increase financial strain on affected employees and, over the long term, lead to significant loss of income. All of these things contribute to increased stress and anxiety. By actively working to eliminate gender and race-based pay gaps, organizations demonstrate their commitment to fairness and equality, which in turn fosters a more inclusive and psychologically safe work environment for women and people of color, thereby enabling them to do better work and contribute more meaningfully to the organization.

To achieve pay equity, organizations should conduct regular pay audits to identify and rectify any discrepancies between pay to employees of different genders, races, ethnicities, etc. Implementing transparent salary structures and promotion criteria to ensure equitable opportunities for advancement helps fix gaps. It's also important to provide training for managers on recognizing and mitigating unconscious biases in compensation decisions. By openly communicating about pay equity efforts and inviting employee feedback, organizations can build trust and show that they value all employees equally.

Leverage Peer Support Groups

Peer support groups and ERGs can play a powerful role in shaping mental health strategies and promoting awareness of available resources, leveraging their unique insights and expertise to foster a supportive environment. ERGs can provide valuable insights into the needs of specific communities, particularly when certain communities aren't represented on the leadership team and/or when more perspectives are needed to provide adequate care.

This was one solution that BlackRock implemented as part of the company's expansion of mental health services. To shape its programming for Mental Health Awareness Month and World Mental Health Day, the company partnered with its internal employee networks to incorporate pertinent materials and information from each identity group and network.

Measure Impact on Diverse Groups

When evaluating your mental health initiatives, look at outcomes specifically for different demographic groups. This helps identify any disparities in effectiveness. If you notice certain groups are experiencing worse outcomes than others, look deeper into the data you have and actively seek out additional feedback to determine what's causing the disparities and how you should change your approach and improve support for these groups.

Provide Education on Diverse Experiences

Offer training and resources to help all employees understand the mental health challenges faced by marginalized groups. Chapter 10 covers different kinds of training organizations should provide to managers, including anti-bias and diversity and inclusion training. However, trainings of this nature, as well as those specifically covering the mental health challenges that come as a result of bias and discrimination, are important for everyone in the organization, not just managers. When more people in the organization understand the experiences of people who are different from them, it builds empathy and creates a more supportive culture overall.

THE PATH FORWARD

All told, creating truly inclusive mental health support requires sustained effort and commitment from leadership. It means critically examining organizational culture, policies, and practices through a lens of diversity and inclusion. It requires investing in new resources and training. And perhaps most importantly, it demands ongoing dialogue with employees from diverse backgrounds at all levels of the organization to best understand their needs and experiences, not just now, but as things continue to evolve and change into the future as well.

EXERCISE

Evaluate Your Organization's Diversity and Inclusion Practices Around Mental Health

In this exercise, think about how your organization approaches diversity and inclusion and the mental wellbeing of all of its employees. Evaluate the current state of diversity and inclusion around mental health at your workplace and identify strengths or areas for improvement.

Rate each statement below on a scale of 1 (strongly disagree) to 5 (strongly agree).

1. Our organization prioritizes diversity and inclusion in its culture. _____
2. Our organization prioritizes diversity and inclusion in its current mental health programming. _____
3. Our organization has support networks in place for employees of all identity groups. _____
4. Our organization recognizes the distinct wellbeing concerns and experiences of employees from all backgrounds and identity groups, and actively promotes measures to ameliorate and support them. _____
5. Our organization provides education opportunities and training on anti-bias, diversity and inclusion, and/or the experiences of people in different groups. _____
6. Our organization has transparent pay and promotion structures. _____
7. Our organization addresses discrimination directly and supports employees in speaking up. _____

Review your answers. For the items you rated with a 3 or less, do you have the ability to directly change this in your organization? If so, what can you do right away to make improvements? If not, consider bringing up your concerns with someone who can.

CHAPTER 6

EMPLOYING A GLOBAL PERSPECTIVE

Alorica is one of the largest providers of business process and customer experience solutions for companies around the world. Headquartered in California, the organization has over 100,000 employees spread across 20 countries between North America, Latin America, Europe, Africa, and Asia, which means their workforce is not only large but also incredibly diverse, with many different cultures and healthcare infrastructures at play.

A few years ago, Alorica's executives and HR leaders started reevaluating the mental health benefits they had in place across all 20 countries. They quickly saw that each country presented unique challenges. "In the U.S. and Canada, utilization rates hovered at or below 3%—hardly enough to resonate with our employees," said Marcela Villamar, Director of Global Benefits at the company. "In Latin America, while our branches in five out of nine countries boasted onsite psychologists, the offices in two countries in the region relied on a rudimentary EAP, with the remaining Latin American countries lacking any support. Europe, Africa, and the Middle East faced a similar void in mental health resources." There were, Villamar and her colleagues realized, whole groups of employees whose mental health needs were simply not being met.

Countries and regions around the world view mental health in significantly different ways. The culture around mental health in the U.S. is different than it is in Japan, which is different than in South Africa.

Culture also influences policy, and governments around the world have very different approaches and levels of commitment to mental health from a policy and public health perspective. Naturally, each of the 20 countries in which Alorica has employees has its own culture and sub-cultures, as well as its own government, laws, and systemic approach to mental healthcare.

All of these components—culture, government, local and regional healthcare infrastructure—play massive roles in people's mental health, from their understanding of what mental health is to the kinds of treatment they can receive, to the level of stigma they face. That presents a challenge for global companies, asserts Barbara Wachsman, Managing Director of The Walt Disney Company, to create a standard for mental health that can be applied equally across different regions. "HR must take into account cultural sensitivities while promoting mental wellbeing in a way that resonates with local employees and aligns with global business goals," Wachsman said.

For companies with a global workforce, like Alorica and The Walt Disney Company, or those looking to expand into new regions, under-standing these cultural differences is crucial for developing effective, culturally competent mental health strategies and providing adequate, proactive care for your employees everywhere. This chapter explores some of the perceptions and provisions surrounding mental health in the major regions of the world today that organizations will need to consider.

NORTH AMERICA: PROGRESS AMID PERSISTENT DISPARITIES

North America has a diverse approach to mental health, with varying levels of access to care, awareness, and recognition of its importance. Both the United States and Canada have made strides in promoting mental health, but stigma and healthcare disparities persist.

The U.S. has seen increased awareness and investment in mental healthcare in recent years. Initiatives like the Affordable Care Act have expanded access to mental health services, and the public conversation about mental health has become increasingly positive. A lot of public figures and celebrities have helped with that by speaking more openly about their mental health—from top athletes like Serena Williams, Michael Phelps, and Simone Biles, to celebrities like Dwayne "The Rock" Johnson, Demi Lovato, Ryan Reynolds, and Lady Gaga, to public and political figures like Oprah and U.S. Senator John Fetterman. Along with the rise in personal mental health stories coming to light, we have also seen a rise in popularity of mental health apps, like Headspace and Calm, which have brought meditation to more and more people, as well as more podcasts, media, and influencers discussing mental health. Thankfully, these lists continue to grow, and as they do, the stigma around mental health in North America continues to shrink.

Additionally, businesses are playing a more significant role in supporting mental health through enhanced EAPs and wellness initiatives. However, access to care remains uneven, with disparities largely based on socioeconomic status and geographic location. For example, the Mental Health Parity and Addiction Equity Act requires insurance plans to cover mental health services on par with physical health services, but access to care is often still limited in rural and underserved urban areas. The reality is, this tends to affect more marginalized groups and communities of color, who can also suffer more mental health concerns due to the effects of institutional racism and discrimination. Furthermore, despite some businesses taking up the mantle, the general tenor of the conversation around mental health in the U.S. still leans toward mental health being the personal responsibility of each individual rather than something to concern collective society.

Canada has a different approach. Whereas in the U.S. the culture around mental health has expanded in large part due to the help of individuals furthering the national discourse, Canada's government has played a larger role, institutionalizing mental healthcare to a greater degree and emphasizing public awareness and community-based care. In 2007, the Canadian government created the Mental Health Commission of Canada, with the express purpose of studying mental health, developing a national mental health strategy and a campaign to reduce stigma, and creating a knowledge center to share mental health resources. In 2012, the Commission published its Mental Health Strategy for Canada, which aims "to help improve the mental health and wellbeing of all people living in Canada, and to create a mental health system that can truly meet the needs of people living with mental health problems and illnesses and their families." Canada's private companies have stepped up to the plate as well. In 2011, the Canadian telecommunications company Bell Canada created and funded the "Bell Let's Talk" campaign, which has raised over $100 million for mental health initiatives and research. Even with greater public and institutional support and focus on mental health in the country—including publicly funded mental health services—access can still vary by province, especially in broad swaths of rural Canada.

As companies look to approach mental health initiatives in the U.S. and Canada, they benefit from reduced stigma, some institutional precedent, and a growing cultural acceptance of mental health broadly. However, the stigma is not gone, and in certain parts of each country, especially within specific industries, leaders, and organizations will need to do more to address enduring assumptions and stigma.

Moreover, both countries are incredibly ethnically and racially diverse. As of the 2020 census, over 40% of the U.S. population identified as people of color, with 18.7% identifying as Hispanic or Latino, 12.1% identifying as Black or African American, and 11.4% identifying as Asian, American Indian, Alaska Native, Native Hawaiian, Pacific Islander, or two or more races. In Canada, according to data from its 2021 census, 26.5% of the population identified as people of color, with the largest groups being South Asian at 7.1%, Chinese at 4.7%, and Black at 4.3%. Within these populations are a wide range of languages, cultural contexts, and, importantly, experiences with discrimination and migration.

All of these factors play a big role in the mental health of individuals of color, and it's important for organizations addressing mental health to account for that in their approach, ensuring they provide adequate resources, support groups, and widely accessible care according to each group's needs.

LATIN AMERICA: PREVAILING STIGMA AND AN OVERWHELMING TREATMENT GAP

At first glance, Latin Americans generally seem to have a positive outlook on life, rating high on the happiness scale according to the World Happiness Report. The region has also made significant progress in addressing mental health through community-based care and public awareness initiatives in recent years. However, a closer look reveals a more complex picture when it comes to mental healthcare in the region.

In South America, Brazil stands out with its publicly funded, universal healthcare system called the Sistema Único de Saúde (SUS), which provides free services, including mental healthcare, to nearly the entire population. In 2011, the country implemented the Psychosocial Care Network, or Rede de Atenção Psicossocial (RAPS), which expanded public mental health services to community centers, outpatient clinics, and hospitals. Additionally, the country's "Open Door" program provides community-based mental health services and support to individuals with severe mental health conditions, helping to promote recovery and social inclusion.

Argentina and Chile have also implemented important mental health initiatives and campaigns in recent years. In 2010, Argentina passed the National Mental Health Law, which instituted the integration of mental health services into primary care. They now offer free mental health services through public health clinics and have launched initiatives to train healthcare workers in mental healthcare. Chile, too, provides mental health services through its public health system and has implemented policies to promote mental health in schools and workplaces, reduce stigma, and promote early intervention and prevention.

Despite these positive developments, regional happiness scores and select national initiatives don't paint the whole picture. Mental health is still largely a taboo topic, and there remains significant stigma associated with mental health disorders across Latin America. This is, in part, due to prevailing cultural beliefs and practices. Family and religion lay at the heart of many Latin American cultures. Strong family bonds and shared faith can certainly positively influence people's mental health by providing a deep sense of community, mutual caretaking, and greater purpose. Yet, some studies have found that, in Latin communities where mental health disorders already carry stigma, people are more likely to keep concerns about their mental health quiet for fear of disgracing their family or being ostracized or met with skepticism. Furthermore, with religion at the center, some communities hold to the belief that mental health conditions result from moral failing or a lack of faith—ideas which, you may recall, originated centuries ago.

That's not to dismiss or blame religion. As a cultural pillar not just in Latin America but around the entire world, faith, spirituality, and religion all factor strongly into people's mental health understanding and maintenance. Public health and wellbeing expert Dr. Shawnte Elbert sees it as a major missing piece of the conversation, in fact. "You can't separate spirituality from people's lives if that's a core part of who they are," she said. "We need mental health services that acknowledge the whole person, including their faith and beliefs. And until we address these nuances, we're only scratching the surface of what it means to be culturally competent." Considering the strength of religion in Latin America, Elbert's point is certainly pertinent for companies developing employee mental health programs there.

Regardless of the source, however, the impact of prevailing stigma is real. According to the Pan American Health Organization, mental healthcare in Latin American countries receives an average of only 2% of national health budgets, most of which goes toward psychiatric hospitals. By contrast, the average European and North American country allocates between 6% and 12% of their health budgets to mental health. With institutions concentrated in cities and more populated areas, rural communities get left behind. As a result, well over 70% of people in Latin America who need mental healthcare do not receive it—and the need is definitely there. The Global Burden of Disease Study in 2019 showed that, across Latin America and the Caribbean, over 16% of adults reported experiencing depression and over 25% reported experiencing anxiety. Those numbers don't include the 16 million kids ages 10 to 19 living with a mental health disorder in the region, nor do they account for the suicide rate among adolescents, which increased by 6% between 2000 and 2019.

While the statistics and government provisions for mental health-care vary between countries across the region, it's crucial for companies with employees in Latin America to be aware of the prevailing stigma against mental health, the cultural barriers to speaking openly about it, and the great gap in available treatment, depending on employees' specific locations. Organizations may need to increase efforts to disman-tle stigma, encourage open communication, and reinforce the safety of sharing about one's mental health at work. By doing so, companies can play a vital role in bridging the treatment gap and fostering a more sup-portive environment for employees in Latin America.

ASIA: ADDRESSING STIGMA AND EXPANDING SERVICES

The Americas aren't alone in their regions' increased prevalence of mental health conditions in recent years; Asia has also experienced a dramatic rise in mental health challenges over the past three decades. From 1990 to 2019, the number of people affected by mental disorders across Asia increased by nearly 60%, rising from about 378 million to 555 million individuals. Some of this increase can be attributed to both a growing and an aging population, rather than a higher prevalence of mental health issues exclusively. But whatever the cause, the increase has had a distinct impact on public health. In 1990, mental disorders ranked as the 13th most impactful health issue in the region; by 2019, they had climbed to 8th place, highlighting the growing importance of addressing mental health across Asia.

Across Asia, varying cultural attitudes, limited resources, and stigma pose significant challenges to mental healthcare access and effectiveness, as they do in many regions, and mental illness is often seen as a sign of weakness or shame. Despite efforts to reduce stigma and expand services in many countries, progress varies widely. In Japan, for instance, stigma remains a major barrier. However, the country has implemented policies to improve mental health services, such as integrating mental health into primary care and expanding access to counseling. Japan's government has also focused explicitly on workplace mental health, instituting policies to limit overtime work and encourage employees to take paid leave. Both efforts aim to reduce stress and promote work-life harmony among the Japanese workforce.

South Korea faces a high prevalence of mental health issues, particularly among young people. The South Korean government has launched public awareness campaigns to address the issue and expanded mental health services in schools. The country also provides free mental health counseling through community health centers and has implemented suicide prevention programs, including its "Mind Health 2030" initiative, aimed at reducing the suicide rate and improving mental health services by increasing funding and expanding access to care.

China, home to an estimated 170 million people suffering from mental disorders, faces challenges with many cases remaining undiagnosed or untreated. The country has made efforts to expand mental health services, but stigma and a shortage of mental health professionals continue to be major obstacles.

In India, significant challenges persist due to limited resources, widespread stigma, and a vast, diverse population. About 10% of adults in India suffer from common mental disorders, with treatment gaps exceeding 80% for conditions like depression. In 2017, the Indian government introduced the National Mental Health Programme and the Mental Healthcare Act to improve access to services and protect the rights of individuals with mental health conditions. Community-based initiatives like the "Atmiyata" program, which trains community volunteers to provide mental health support in rural areas, are also helping to bridge care gaps, though with only 0.75 psychiatrists per 100,000 people, provider shortages are acute. While some large companies offer mental health support, the majority of India's workforce in the informal sector lacks access. Multinational companies operating in India should develop culturally sensitive, accessible mental health strategies that address deep-rooted stigma and diverse socioeconomic needs.

Generally speaking, many Asian countries, including some of those listed above, lack adequate mental health policies, laws, and funding, and mental health services are often inadequately integrated into primary healthcare and social welfare systems. The number of mental health professionals is far below recommended levels per capita, leading to significant workforce shortages. Altogether, this leads to serious treatment gaps as well as low awareness and utilization of the mental health resources that are available.

For multinational companies operating in Asia, it's crucial to recognize the diverse mental health landscapes across countries and tailor approaches accordingly. This may include providing culturally sensitive mental health education and resources, offering confidential counseling services that align with local norms and preferences, training managers to recognize signs of mental health issues and support employees appropriately, implementing workplace policies that promote work-life harmony and stress reduction, and collaborating with local mental health organizations to support community initiatives. By addressing mental health proactively and sensitively, companies can contribute to reducing stigma, improving access to care, and supporting the overall wellbeing of their employees across the region.

EUROPE: ADDRESSING MENTAL HEALTH AS A SHARED, PUBLIC HEALTH PRIORITY

Europe has seen a growing focus on mental health in recent years, with both the European Union and individual countries integrating mental health into public health systems and implementing initiatives to improve care and reduce stigma. Many European countries prioritize mental health through comprehensive policies, widespread public awareness campaigns, and robust support systems.

The United Kingdom, Germany, and Sweden have shown particular commitment. In the U.K., for instance, the National Health Service offers free mental health services, including therapy and counseling, to all residents, and the government has launched initiatives to provide mental health first aid training in schools and workplaces. From 2007 to 2021, the U.K. government also funded a national "Time to Change" campaign, which aimed to reduce stigma and discrimination related to mental health.

Germany's mental healthcare system places a strong emphasis on community-based care, with numerous designated mental health centers across the country providing counseling, therapy, and support groups to the public. Germany also offers generous mental health–related sick leave policies for workers, allowing employees to take up to six weeks of paid leave at their full salary if they cannot work due to a mental health condition, with additional support available if needed.

Sweden, too, provides comprehensive mental health services through its public health system and has implemented policies to promote work-life harmony, such as flexible working hours and generous parental leave. The country strongly emphasizes youth mental health as well. Across the country, children and adolescents have access to free mental health services, and they've implemented school-based programs designed to identify and support students experiencing mental health challenges.

The scale of mental health issues in Europe is significant. Prior to the COVID-19 pandemic, approximately 84 million people (1 in 6) across the EU experienced mental health problems, with an estimated economic cost of over €600 billion per year, or more than 4% of GDP. The pandemic further exacerbated these challenges, with an 2023 Eurobarometer survey showing that 46% of Europeans experienced emotional or psychosocial problems, such as feeling depressed or anxious, in the previous 12 months. Furthermore, one out of every two individuals dealing with a mental health issue did not seek professional assistance.

Recognizing the urgency of the situation, the EU has taken significant steps to prioritize mental health. In June 2023, the European Commission adopted a Communication on a comprehensive approach to mental health, allocating €1.23 billion to support Member States and stakeholders in addressing mental health challenges. This initiative aims to put mental health on par with physical health and recognizes the cross-sectoral nature of mental wellbeing, involving areas such as employment, education, research, and urban planning—something I wholeheartedly support and believe all countries, regions, and organizations should do.

Additionally, several EU countries have implemented innovative programs to improve mental healthcare. For instance, Belgium has undertaken a mental health system reform focusing on strengthening client-centered, community-based services, and Austria has implemented a multi-level suicide prevention program. Initiatives like these are being rolled out across 21 Member States through the Joint Action ImpleMENTAL, supported by €5.4 million in EU funding.

To combat stigma and improve access to care, particularly for young people, the EU has launched projects like iFightDepression, a tool for self-management of mild to moderate depression, as well as initiatives specifically targeting children and adolescents, such as Icehearts Europe and Let's Talk About Children. The EU has also put €9 million behind the EU-PROMENS project, offering multi-disciplinary training on mental health for health professionals, teachers, educators, and social workers.

The EU's approach also emphasizes the importance of workplace mental health. With 27% of employees reporting work-related stress, depression, or anxiety in 2022, initiatives are underway to address these issues and reduce their economic impact. The European Commission is working on developing EU guidance on stigma and discrimination related to mental health, collaborating closely with the World Health Organization, stakeholders, and people with lived experience.

For all the promising efforts across the continent, access to mental healthcare in Europe remains uneven, with disparities based on socioeconomic status and geographic location. The pandemic only further exacerbated existing inequalities, and the rising demand strained services.

For companies operating in Europe, it's crucial to recognize the diverse mental health landscapes across countries while also leveraging EU-wide initiatives. Organizations can contribute to improving employee mental health by implementing workplace policies that align with EU guidelines on mental health and work-life harmony, and collaborate with local and EU-wide mental health organizations to support community initiatives. By taking a proactive and culturally sensitive approach to mental health, companies can play a vital role in supporting the wellbeing of their employees across Europe, complementing governmental efforts and contributing to a more mentally healthy society.

AFRICA: TACKLING FORMIDABLE CHALLENGES WITH LIMITED RESOURCES

Africa faces some of the most significant mental health challenges of any region in the world, with a high burden of mental health conditions and extremely limited resources to address them.

According to the World Health Organization, over 116 million people in Africa were estimated to be living with mental health conditions even before the COVID-19 pandemic. Despite this high prevalence and substantial burden, the vast majority of people living with a mental health condition in Africa do not access or receive the treatment they need. In South Africa, which has one of the more developed mental healthcare systems on the continent, an estimated 75% of people with common mental disorders like depression and anxiety do not receive treatment. In other countries, the gap is even wider. In Sierra Leone, for example, it's estimated that 99% of those needing treatment don't receive it.

A key factor driving the treatment gap is the severe shortage of mental health professionals and services across the continent. The most recent data from UNICEF and the WHO show that African countries, on average, have just one mental health worker per 100,000 people, compared to a global average of nine per 100,000. This shortage greatly affects access to care. While the global annual rate of visits to mental health outpatient facilities is 1,051 per 100,000 people, in Africa the rate is just 14 visits per 100,000 people. Because mental health services in most African countries are concentrated in urban areas, inpatient facilities, and at specialized hospitals, the majority of the population, especially in rural areas, has little to no access to mental healthcare.

Funding for mental health services, or the lack of it, also affects care shortages. In 2020, Africa spent less than $1 USD per capita on mental health—half the WHO's recommended spending of $2 USD per capita for low-income countries. The reality is, many African countries don't allocate much of their national health budgets toward mental health—less than 1%, in fact, according to the WHO.

Cultural attitudes and stigma pose additional barriers; in fact, they're strongly connected to how African nations fund and approach mental health on the whole. Mental health conditions are often still viewed through the lens of traditional beliefs about spiritual causes, leading some to seek help from traditional or religious healers rather than medical professionals. A systematic review of studies in Africa found that, of patients with mental health concerns, approximately 17% contacted a traditional healer and 26% contacted a religious advisor before seeking formal mental health services. While these community-based healers can play an important role, reliance on them alone may delay access to evidence-based treatments. However, there are also arguments that advocate for non-Western approaches to mental health in Africa. They contend that the cultural understanding of mental health on the continent is so different that it warrants having completely different approaches—approaches that integrate trusted local institutions and spiritual traditions, rather than dismiss them in favor of an exclusively Western model.

Thankfully, community-based approaches that work with existing cultural frameworks are showing promise. In Zimbabwe, the Friendship Bench program trains community health workers to deliver brief psychological interventions. Having seen positive results, this model has now been adopted in several other African countries.

There are additional measures of progress and innovative approaches emerging across the continent, too. In 2012, Ghana became the first African country to pass legislation emphasizing the rights of people with mental illness and promoting community-based care. The following year, South Africa created a National Mental Health Policy Framework and Strategic Plan to integrate mental health into primary care and increase community-based services. Several other countries followed suit.

To help address access issues and the shortage of mental health specialists, some countries have implemented task-sharing models, such as the Mental Health Gap Action Programme from the WHO, where non-specialist health workers are trained to deliver basic mental health interventions. They've also used technology in key ways. During the pandemic, several countries rapidly scaled up telehealth services and mobile health interventions for mental health. The Mentally Aware Nigeria Initiative, for instance, saw a 60% increase in demand for its online counseling services. Finally, research capacity for mental health is growing, with initiatives like the African Mental Health Research Initiative (AMARI) working to build a critical mass of mental health researchers across the continent to help develop locally relevant, evidence-based interventions.

Multinational companies operating in Africa must recognize the significant mental health needs of the workforce there as well as the limited resources available in many countries. Organizations may need to play a more active role in providing mental health support, services, and training to employees than they might in other regions, while, importantly, maintaining awareness and sensitivity to the cultural attitudes at play. Given the shortage of specialists, companies might consider training peer support networks or implementing more robust digital mental health solutions for those in the region to expand access to resources.

THE MIDDLE EAST: RECONCILING TRADITIONAL VIEWS WITH MODERN CARE

Rates of mental health conditions in the Middle East and North Africa (MENA) region have remained relatively stable over the past two decades. However, they have increased significantly as a share of the total disease burden. The global average rate for mental health conditions as a proportion of the total disease burden is 5%, yet in countries like Jordan, Oman, Kuwait, and Qatar, that rate is more than doubled, with Qatar's rate coming in highest at 13.7%. Collectively, the MENA region is the global hotspot for mental disorders as a proportion of total disease burden.

Despite this substantial burden, accurate diagnosis statistics remain difficult to determine, as mental health tends to be under-studied, under-reported, and under-diagnosed across the region due to stigma and low levels of awareness. For example, while global data suggest relatively moderate prevalence rates, local studies often reveal a higher burden. A 2018 national survey by Egypt's Ministry of Health found that 25% of Egyptians suffer from mental health issues.

Similar to Latin America, religion and cultural beliefs shape attitudes toward mental health here in complex ways that are both beneficial and counterproductive. On the one hand, the overarching faith and cultural beliefs tend to drive strong family bonds and valuable community support. At the same time, some beliefs sustain ideas that mental health challenges are moral failings, spiritual weaknesses, or supernatural causes rather than treatable medical conditions. Culturally, these "failings" reflect poorly on not just an individual but also their whole family. Studies have illustrated this point, showing that in many Middle Eastern communities, people are more likely to keep mental health concerns private for fear of bringing shame to their families or facing social ostracism. Furthermore, one 2018 study examining attitudes toward mental illness among Arab populations found that many prefer seeking support from faith healers or turning to religious practices as their first approach to addressing mental health concerns.

All of these ideas perpetuate stigma about mental health conditions. Studies have found that 80-90% of people with mental health disorders globally report experiencing stigma and discrimination, but the impact is particularly pronounced in the Middle East, where both self-stigma (individuals believing they are lesser people for having mental health conditions) and public stigma (common societal attitudes that devalue those with mental health conditions) create significant barriers to help-seeking behavior. These attitudes, combined with inadequate mental health literacy, make many reluctant to seek professional care.

One result of the prevailing stigma is that it keeps access to care severely limited. The number of mental health professionals across the Middle East has actually declined in recent years and remains lower than global averages. In high-income countries worldwide, the median number of mental health workers per 100,000 is 62.2, but Kuwait, Qatar, Oman, and Saudi Arabia all have less than half this number. Jordan, with

4.13 mental health workers per 100,000, falls well below the average of 14.7 for upper-middle-income countries.

The region also continues to rely heavily on institutional care models rather than community-based approaches. In Jordan, 49% of patients in mental hospitals stay for more than five years. Even in MENA countries where mental hospitals are primarily intended for short-term care, long-term institutionalization remains common. This hospital-centric approach persists despite global shifts toward integrating mental health services into primary care and community settings.

Still, there are promising signs of progress. Mental health is gaining greater government attention across the region, with recent efforts to strengthen mental health policy and workforce quality from many leaders. Qatar has made significant strides in integrating mental health into primary care, while Saudi Arabia has increased its mental health spending to 4% of its healthcare budget, which surpasses the global average for high-income countries.

It's safe to say, the pandemic accelerated some of these changes. In a 2022 Economist Impact report on mental health in the Middle East, Dr. Yasmin Altwaijri, Principal Scientist and Chairman of Epidemiology at King Faisal Specialist Hospital and Research Center in Saudi Arabia, noted that, during the pandemic, almost "everybody was suffering from anxiety, lack of sleep and depression, or all of those. So, the dialogue surrounding mental health and the stigma really improved." As part of the change, several countries established mental health helplines—and to clearly great effect. The mental health helpline in Qatar received 46,000 calls in its first two years. Due to sustained demand, most countries' helplines have remained in place.

While stigma remains a major barrier to care, particularly for severe mental illness, there has been a notable decline in stigma toward mild to moderate conditions like anxiety and depression, especially among younger generations. This shift is supported by increasing mental health awareness campaigns and initiatives across the region, including government-led mental health campaigns introduced in Egypt, Kuwait, Qatar and Saudi Arabia. Civil society organizations and community groups are also playing an increasingly active role in mental health outreach and education.

Organizations operating in the Middle East must understand these dynamics in order to navigate traditional cultural values while working to reduce stigma, expand access to care, and create culturally appropriate mental health resources for employees in these countries. Considering the central role of religion and family support in the cultural fabric of the region, figuring out how to integrate those aspects into the mental health initiatives and services provided through workplaces, will help increase the reach and impact organizational initiatives can have on the lives and mental wellbeing of these employees.

GLOBAL NEEDS, LOCALIZED APPROACHES

As this global tour illustrates, the mental health landscape around the world is as diverse as the cultures it encompasses. While universal challenges exist, effective solutions must be tailored to local contexts. "What works in one country may not work in another," said Yvonne Sonsino, Total Well-being and Longevity Lead at Mercer U.K., "so we need to develop strategies that are both flexible and inclusive." For multinational organizations, this means moving beyond one-size-fits-all approaches.

Sometimes, it may even require creative, highly customized solutions—something Amy Glynn realized at OpenText, the global enterprise information management software company where she serves as Senior Director of Benefits and Wellness. "We spend a lot of energy on making sure that anything we do for mental health is accessible to everybody in the company. It's an important goal and, truthfully, an obligation. With that, though, comes a big challenge because we have team members in 47 countries," she said. In the past two years, Glynn has spent a lot of time with OpenText's regional managers—who, she says, are closer to the employees within their region—to make sure that the company's mental health offerings in each region make sense culturally. How to serve its teams in India, where the company tripled its employee population in the past year alone, became the biggest question mark to solve. "We've started to look for a completely bespoke solution for mental health programming in the country, because we need to expand and change our mental health solutions to serve the growing employee base there."

Glynn and her colleagues have the right approach. By embracing cultural sensitivity, leveraging technology, and collaborating with local resources, companies can create mental health strategies that resonate across borders. Alorica landed on this approach as well, and to great success. After a global rollout of Journey's Proactive EAP—including customized engagement strategies for each country, diverse content and counselors, and digitally accessible options for 24/7 resources and care—Alorica saw 10 times the employee engagement levels they saw with their previous EAP, reaching 30% overall engagement within the first year.

As workforces like Alorica become increasingly global, organizations have a unique opportunity—and responsibility—to champion mental wellbeing on an international scale. In doing so, they not only support their employees but also contribute to the broader effort to prioritize mental health as a fundamental human right and democratize access to care worldwide.

EXERCISE
Global Mental Health Support Assessment

Use this exercise to evaluate your organization's mental health support across different regions and identify areas needing attention.

List all regions/countries where your organization has employees:

Rate current mental health support level by region, where
1 = minimal support and 5 = comprehensive support:

- North America _____
- Latin America _____
- Europe _____
- Asia _____
- Africa _____
- Middle East _____

Which regions currently have . . .

- Employee Assistance Program (EAP):

- Digital Mental Health Tools:

- In-Person Counseling Services:

- Other Mental Health Resources:

Identify regions where mental health resources are insufficient and why:

What cultural considerations need to be addressed in these regions?

For your top two priority regions, outline specific steps needed:

1. Region 1:
    a. Needed Resources:

b.   Cultural Considerations:

c.   Timeline & Implementation Plan:

2.   Region 2:
   a.   Needed Resources:

   b.   Cultural Considerations:

c. Timeline & Implementation Plan:

Every organization's mental health strategy should evolve to meet diverse needs. While universal challenges exist, success lies in understanding and respecting local contexts while working toward consistent, quality care for all employees, no matter where they are.

CHAPTER 7

CUSTOMIZING PROACTIVE MENTAL HEALTH FOR YOUR INDUSTRY

Leaving law school, Rohan faced a difficult choice: He had two attractive job offers from different firms—one from a small, boutique firm in Charlotte, North Carolina, where he'd interned throughout law school, and one from a major corporate law firm with a strong reputation in New York City. The offers promised very different things.

On the one hand, the boutique firm had highly respected attorneys, Rohan was comfortable there, and while there were stressful periods, the work culture was generally pretty balanced. There, the starting salary was $95,000. On the other hand, the big firm offered the prestige of its name, a new experience, and new connections, plus a rigorous environment where he could cut his teeth learning from some of the best. To top it off, that firm was offering him upwards of $200,000 for his first year, excluding bonuses—more than double what he'd make at the smaller firm.

However, he didn't have rose-colored glasses on; Rohan knew the big firm pushed people hard. He'd heard plenty of stories about people having no life outside of work, working between 70 and 100 hours a week for months on end, burning out, and even developing illness because of it.

The statistics are, in fact, more serious than Rohan realized. A 2023 study published in *Healthcare* surveying nearly 2,000 lawyers in California and Washington, D.C., found that 66% of the lawyers felt their profession worsened their mental health, and 46% contemplated quitting due to stress or burnout. The study also determined that the average lawyer in the U.S. is between two and three times more likely than professionals in other industries to have suicidal thoughts. To make matters even worse, another 2023 survey of partners, associates, and staff from six large U.S. law firms reported that one-third of respondents felt their firm wasn't committed to supporting employee mental health, and over half said they'd taken at least one day off for mental health reasons in the three months prior. Those mental health days add up for employees and businesses alike. Projections indicate that big firms lose roughly $22 million per firm per year due to the effects of poor mental health—in lost workdays, turnover, and decreased performance.

The legal sector, and Big Law in particular, is known to be stressful. Lawyers at those firms work for big clients with lots of money on the line, often with international teams accommodating multiple time zones and exceptionally high expectations. As the data bears out, these stressors lead to unique mental health concerns for the employees in the field. To help their employees cope and ensure they can perform their best, these firms would benefit from employing unique mental health strategies, customized for the requirements of the job.

Every industry has unique stressors, not just Big Law. Building a proactive mental health culture and supporting employees requires tailoring your approach in ways that will serve them best, based on the outlines of their jobs. When employees feel supported in their mental health, companies win, too. This chapter highlights several industries with particularly demanding environments, the ways we can tailor mental health approaches to fit those environments, and the benefits both companies and employees gain in doing so.

PROFESSIONAL SERVICES

Since we started with Big Law, let's stay there for a minute. Law fits more broadly into the realm of professional services, which encompasses a number of fields, including consulting, financial services, architecture, engineering, and IT, among others. Professional services industries present unique challenges that can profoundly affect employee mental health.

Workforce Challenges in Professional Services

By nature, all professionals in these fields work for their clients, who often want two things at odds with one another: high-quality work and work delivered as fast as possible. The success of these businesses relies on the satisfaction of their clients. Thus, the pressure in these dynamic environments tends to be perpetually high and the pace unrelentingly fast, which can cause chronic stress, anxiety, and feelings of inadequacy among employees. Complicating matters is "scope creep," an all-too-common situation where the parameters and deliverables of a project gradually expand beyond what was initially agreed-upon, often resulting in increased workloads and tighter deadlines without corresponding adjustments in fees or resources. Navigating these changes while maintaining high performance and client satisfaction can add another layer of mental strain for employees.

That's to say nothing of the strain of long working hours, especially common in law, finance, and consulting, where it's typical to work 12- to 14-hour days (or more) six to seven days a week over an extended period of time. Long workdays and weeks not only disrupt personal lives and worsen physical health to sometimes detrimental or even fatal degrees, but they can also lead to feelings of isolation, depression, and burnout.

A large part of the long workdays, too, is the constant stream of incoming information and communication. These professionals routinely manage an overwhelming volume of emails and meetings at all hours. The perpetual connectivity and need to be online impacts focus and productivity considerably, and blurs the lines between work and personal life, leaving little room for genuine downtime.

Effects on Mental Health

Collectively, these factors make maintaining good mental health a significant challenge, and employees feel the effects. A 2024 survey by *The American Lawyer* found that 36% of lawyers are currently experiencing depression (twice the national average), and 69% reported having anxiety. Those in IT and engineering are in a similar boat. A 2015 academic study of health problems and stress in IT and business process outsourcing employees in India found that 54% of IT workers had depression, anxiety, or insomnia. And in a 2020 survey by *Professional Engineering*, 53% of engineers said that workplace stress has negatively affected their mental health. Two-thirds also reported going to work despite feeling mentally or emotionally unwell, with 42% agreeing that having poor mental health negatively affected their work.

Speaking to Chris Kim, Global Head of Employee Experience, Benefits and Wellness at the investment firm KKR, he recognized the difficulty of working in professional services industries or any high-performing organizations because "the boundaries of one's mental, physical, and emotional wellbeing are often tested as employees perform at a high level of intensity over sustained periods of time." To help counter that, Kim established KKR's global wellness program and designed a multi-year healthcare strategy that included building a sustainable culture of wellbeing and implementing progressive family support and work-life programs.

Unfortunately, the traditional work culture in these environments doesn't often promote wellbeing, mental or otherwise. Less than 30% of employees in IT said they'd feel comfortable bringing up their mental health with a supervisor, and even though many human resources leaders in professional services want to improve mental health support at their organizations, nearly 60% have said the company culture, including leadership, prevents them from doing so. "Big Law firm culture is toxic," one attorney told *The American Lawyer* in 2024. "The economics drive a hierarchical structure that is and will always be opposed to any genuine culture of caring or wellbeing."

Yet, the argument for the reverse seems clear: With the need for exceptional communication, collaboration, and quality in professional services work, the mental wellbeing of employees transcends personal wellness. Embracing mental health isn't just an option for these companies; it's an absolute necessity.

Challenges for Mental Health Engagement in Professional Services

As evidenced by the data and sentiments noted above, one of the greatest engagement challenges in the professional services sector is the culture. The focus on billable hours and maintaining client satisfaction often comes at the expense of employee mental health, where employees are reluctant to step away from work to engage with mental health activities due to the stigma associated with seeking help. Simultaneously, companies and leaders can be reluctant to support employees stepping away for fear of not meeting clients' demands and looking uncompetitive in the industry—or simply because "that's not the way things have been done." One result of the cultural stigma and traditional lack of leadership support is a lack of employee awareness of or even access to companies' mental health benefits. Michelle Eckert noticed this at her global consulting firm with 125,000 employees in over 70 countries, where she serves as Director of Human Resources. "When we took a closer look at how employees were using our support programs, like the EAP, we found that there was a stigma attached to seeking help. So, we had to change the narrative around it, making mental health conversations normal and expected," Eckert said.

Sometimes, utilization rates lag because employees aren't fully aware of their benefits due to communication challenges across global, dispersed teams. They may also worry about privacy and fear that speaking openly about their mental health challenges could lead to professional consequences. Mercer U.K.'s Total Well-being and Longevity Lead Yvonne Sonsino brought up another valuable point: Some employees in these industries (and all industries) simply don't have the knowledge and awareness of mental health issues period. "Education around mental health is crucial," Soninso said. "Employees need to understand the signs of mental health struggles, both in themselves and others, so they can get the support they need early on." Regardless of employees' reasons for not engaging, it's up to the companies and leaders in these professional services to provide better resources *and* create communication strategies to ensure all employees know about and can access the resources provided, no matter where they are.

KKR's Chris Kim has, thankfully, noticed a recent shift. "I've been incredibly encouraged by the greater openness we've seen in our industry in the past few years to discuss mental health issues, with employers significantly increasing their investment in behavioral health resources and communications efforts around this topic," he told me. "I think we're seeing progress within our industry toward finding a place where performance continues to be paramount while acknowledging and supporting each individual as a human and all the challenges associated with that today."

How to Support Mental Health in Professional Services

There are no quick fixes or easy answers here. However, there are some meaningful steps that forward-thinking leaders can take to improve the wellbeing of their workforce:

1. **Restructure your working norms and normalize taking time off.** Whether your team is fully remote, in-office, or hybrid, all employees benefit from flexible working arrangements, collaborative spaces that foster community, and improved boundaries and expectations around email, response times, and working hours. Encourage employees to use their PTO and normalize taking both vacation and mental health days when they're needed, especially after intense work periods.

2. **Recognize achievements and encourage open communication about mental health.** Recognize and celebrate achievements, both big and small, and encourage

employees to discuss their mental health openly to foster a supportive environment and be able to provide better support.

3. **Offer robust mental health resources and broadcast them widely and often.** Provide access to counseling or workshops tailored to address the unique mental health challenges faced in professional services. If your existing EAP doesn't provide adequate mental health support, look for an enhanced EAP that provides proactive support and rapid access to counseling services. Make sure, in every way possible, that all employees know about these resources and have ready access to them at all times; and then build in consistent reminders and engagement campaigns to amplify employee awareness and increase utilization.

   To Geetika Bhojak, that piece—consistently communicating about the resources—is crucial. Bhojak is the Global Mental Health Lead at Accenture. She said, "Beyond just offering benefits or resources, we need to integrate mental health into daily routines. This means offering gentle reminders regularly, continually encouraging employees to take care of themselves, and making it easier for employees to access support before they feel overwhelmed."

4. **Promote stress management and mindfulness.** Use virtual tools for remote mindfulness sessions, including concepts like "no on-camera days" or "no meeting days." Offer workshops on stress-relief techniques like meditation and deep breathing.

5. **Provide specialized training.** Provide training on issues and practices that are unique to this field—or that are prevalent among employees in it. For instance, client communication is a big part of the job, and it can cause a lot of stress. Providing training on how to communicate with clients effectively can help employees navigate tricky client demands and

relationships, including conversations around scope creep, by offering workshops and best practices for communication.

At Goldman Sachs, they provide training on perfectionism—something that a lot of employees in high-intensity fields relate to. "It's different from striving for excellence," Noah Morgan, Vice President of Benefits and Wellness, explains. "It's crucial to help people understand that perfectionism can be harmful to their mental health." Their training tries to parse out those differences and help employees understand when perfectionistic thoughts or behaviors may be cropping up and getting in their way.

ADVERTISING

Advertising is undoubtedly a part of the professional services industry, and with its fast pace, tight deadlines, and high-stakes client relationships, the dynamics and challenges are similar to those listed above. However, the substantive differences are worth highlighting.

Workforce Challenges in Advertising

Advertising work revolves around crafting compelling, innovative campaigns within stringent time constraints. Agencies live and die by their ability to not just meet but exceed client expectations, which sets up a culture where creativity must flourish under intense pressure. This environment—coupled with scope creep, which comes up just as often as in other professional services, and sometimes more so—can breed chronic stress, spark anxiety, and foster self-doubt among even the most talented professionals.

The nature of agency work also tends to demand long and irregular hours, especially when preparing for pitches or during campaign launches where late nights and weekend work becomes the norm. Add to this the constant pinging of emails and client messages at all times of day, and the boundary between professional and personal life becomes increasingly fuzzy. The imbalance of employees' work hours and personal life can lead to physical and mental exhaustion.

"Burnout is common, with creative minds juggling multiple projects while striving to meet demanding client expectations," said Claude Silver, Chief Heart Officer at VaynerMedia, when I asked her how the industry's unique demands affect employee mental health. "Criticism and competition add further stress, but what stands out the most is the need to keep up with trends while maintaining creativity."

Effects on Mental Health

These industry pressures take a significant toll on mental health among advertising professionals. A 2023 survey of 19,000 advertising professionals in the U.K. revealed that 33% of marketing and advertising professionals have been affected by stress or anxiety, with 14% attributing it primarily to work-related factors. A *Guardian* report further revealed that 65% of advertising and media employees have experienced stress so severe they felt unable to cope. Underscoring Silver's remark above, the Association of National Advertisers also found that a staggering 83% of marketing and communications professionals report experiencing burnout, and over a quarter of marketers said they were likely to leave their jobs due to poor work-life balance.

Despite these distressing trends, there's a reluctance to address mental health openly in many ad agencies. The same *Guardian* report found that 69% of advertising professionals worry about telling senior staff they're feeling stressed, fearing it might be viewed as a sign of weakness and cause professional harm. This stigma creates a significant barrier to seeking help and addressing mental health issues proactively.

Challenges for Mental Health Engagement in Advertising

Engaging advertising professionals in mental health initiatives comes with its own set of hurdles. The fast-paced nature of the industry often leaves little time for employees to participate in wellbeing programs.

Plus, when professionals' enthusiasm for the creative side of the work gets in the mix, the cross between personal fulfillment and professional obligation stops some employees from disengaging with work when they should take a break.

Moreover, the diversity of roles and working styles in advertising agencies, from art directors to designers to account managers to data analysts, means that one-size-fits-all approaches to mental health support are often ineffective. Tailoring programs to meet the unique needs of each different group and role within an agency is essential but can be logistically challenging.

Finally, the advertising industry has a high turnover rate, which makes implementing consistent mental health initiatives challenging. Ensuring that programs are resilient to employee turnover and that new hires are quickly onboarded into these initiatives is crucial but often overlooked.

How to Support Mental Health in Ad Agencies

Tackling mental health in advertising agencies requires a comprehensive strategy:

1. **Foster a culture of creative wellness.** Encourage brief respites during intense work sessions and create quiet spaces for recharging or working without distractions. Nurture an environment where discussing mental health challenges is as normal and common as pitching ideas.

2. **Embrace flexible work models.** Offer remote work options and adaptable schedules to help employees better juggle their professional and personal lives, acknowledging the often unconventional hours demanded by advertising work.

3. **Invest in comprehensive mental health support.** Provide access to counseling and workshops tailored to the unique pressures of the advertising world, and upgrade your EAP to

one that offers proactive support that resonates with your creative team and is accessible at all times.

4. **Introduce innovative stress management practices.** Beyond traditional techniques, consider incorporating creative stress-relief methods that align with the more artistic nature of advertising and media, such as expressive art practices or mindfulness-based brainstorming sessions.

5. **Recognize achievements and foster growth.** To boost morale, celebrate successful campaigns and personal milestones. Offer diverse professional development opportunities, demonstrating a commitment to employee growth while providing refreshing breaks from daily routines.

HEALTHCARE

The healthcare industry, particularly hospitals and medical centers, stands as a critical pillar of support for society. However, the noble profession of caring for others often comes at a real cost to the mental health of those providing that care. In an environment characterized by life-and-death decisions, long shifts, and relentless patient-care responsibilities, healthcare professionals frequently find themselves at the forefront of challenges that extend far beyond their clinical duties.

Workforce Challenges in Healthcare

Healthcare professionals face the weighty responsibility of making complex clinical decisions that directly affect patient lives and outcomes every single day. This constant pressure to perform flawlessly can lead to chronic stress and anxiety. During illness outbreaks and unprecedented pandemics, as in the COVID-19 pandemic, such stress and anxiety accumulated to burnout and significant turnover for many healthcare professionals.

The demanding nature of healthcare is a constant feature of the industry—not one that just shows up during acute outbreaks. These professionals frequently work extended work hours—often 12-hour shifts or longer. Their grueling schedules can disrupt sleep patterns, personal relationships, and overall work-life harmony in substantial ways. Additionally, healthcare workers, especially those in emergency or intensive care settings, are regularly exposed to traumatic events and human suffering, leading to emotional exhaustion, compassion fatigue, and increased rates of anxiety and depression.

Finally, healthcare workers, especially those in the United States, face an increasing administrative burden. The need to navigate complex insurance systems, maintain detailed documentation, and adhere to ever-changing regulations can detract from patient care and add to the mental load these professionals carry day in and day out.

Effects on Mental Health

Add up the impact of all these challenges and we see profound mental health effects in the healthcare workforce. According to a survey conducted by Mental Health America on healthcare workers in 2020, 93% reported feeling stressed out and stretched too thin, and 82% shared feeling emotionally and physically exhausted or burnt out. The mental health toll extends to specific professions within healthcare, too, with 69% of physicians reporting experiencing depression.

This mental health crisis in the field has far-reaching consequences. The CDC reports that 32% of nurses considered leaving their positions within a year, citing insufficient staffing, intense workloads, and emotional toll as primary reasons. Moreover, a disconcerting 13% of physicians reported having thoughts of suicide, which points to the severe impact of workplace stress.

And yet, there's often a reluctance to address mental health openly. The culture of resilience and self-sacrifice that permeates the medical profession can make it difficult for healthcare workers to seek help or admit to struggling. Ironically or not, the healthcare industry is not set up to support the very health of the professionals who keep it running.

COVID may have changed some of this, according to Christine Pfeiffer, the Director of WorkLife and Well-being at Memorial Sloan Kettering Cancer Center. "In the wake of COVID, we realized that the way people approach mental health has shifted dramatically, and we need to be flexible and responsive to these changes," she said.

Challenges for Mental Health Engagement in Healthcare

Engaging healthcare professionals in mental health initiatives is a singular task. The round-the-clock nature of hospital work, with its varying shifts and unpredictable emergencies, makes it challenging to implement consistent mental health programs that all staff can access. The intense focus on patient care can also lead healthcare workers to deprioritize their own wellbeing; there's often a sense that taking time for oneself detracts from patient care, creating guilt around engaging in mental health activities.

Additionally, as in professional services fields and many industries and organizations, healthcare settings employ incredible numbers of people in a wide range of roles—from surgeons to nurses to administrative staff—that all have different schedules and mental health needs. This customization, while essential, can be complex to implement across large hospital systems. Pfeiffer acknowledged this, too. "We try to focus on equipping people with the tools they need when they're ready. With 22,000 employees, we can't push resources all the time," she said. "But when they come to us, we're prepared." One thing that's helped, she noted, is integrating mental health strategies into the everyday work life of MSKCC's employees. "We provide resources that employees can access whenever they need, helping them take ownership of their mental health."

How to Support Mental Health in Healthcare

Healthcare necessitates a multi-pronged approach to build in increased support for mental health:

1. **Prioritize mental health at the leadership level.** Encourage your leadership team (both clinical and administrative) to openly discuss mental health in the workplace and exhibit their commitment to prioritizing it for themselves. Have leadership provide and participate in mental health education programming to help healthcare workers recognize concerns in themselves and their colleagues.

2. **Create a culture of support, including relaxation spaces and breaks.** Encourage open dialogue about mental health challenges and implement peer support programs. Normalize taking breaks and seeking help when needed—especially when employees have been working longer and more emotionally and physically taxing shifts. Designate quiet areas in hospitals or clinics where employees can decompress during shifts.

3. **Offer accessible, confidential, and tailored mental health resources.** Provide easy access to counseling services, support groups, and crisis intervention tailored to the unique needs and experiences of healthcare professionals.

4. **Address systemic issues.** As much as possible, work on improving staffing ratios, reducing administrative burdens, and creating more flexible scheduling options to alleviate some of the structural stressors in healthcare work.

5. **Implement regular check-ins and screenings.** Conduct routine mental health check-ins and offer voluntary screenings to identify and address issues early and often.

6. **Proactively help reduce stigma in healthcare.** Start by employing messaging campaigns, integrating mental health awareness into new employee onboarding, providing mental health awareness training to all staff, engaging in activities

during Mental Health Awareness Month, and establishing a wellness committee focused on employee wellbeing.

HIGHER EDUCATION

The realm of higher education, a bastion of knowledge and growth, harbors its own issues affecting the mental health of faculty and staff. Despite their mission to nurture minds, universities and colleges sometimes struggle to provide adequate support for the mental wellbeing of those responsible for shaping the next generation of thinkers and leaders.

Workforce Challenges in Higher Education

Educators in higher education grapple with a demanding trifecta of responsibilities: teaching, research, and administrative duties. This complex balancing act often necessitates extended and unpredictable work hours, such that many faculty members find themselves in a perpetual work mode, unable to maintain any semblance of work-life harmony during the school year. This constant juggling of tasks and inability to fully step away from work frequently leads to chronic stress and a pervasive sense that there is always work they should be doing.

Associate Professor Hilal A. Lashuel is a neuroscientist and chemist who teaches at the École Polytechnique Fédérale de Lausanne (EPFL) in Switzerland and directs its Laboratory of Molecular and Chemical Biology of Neurodegeneration. He spoke to the distinct pressure of managing all these responsibilities in an essay he published in 2020 after experiencing two heart attacks in three years. "The life of a professor is a constant balancing act where we try to juggle personal and professional responsibilities under the pervasive stress of managing expectations in an often hypercompetitive culture," Lashuel wrote. "There is always a fear that we may drop the ball, a sense that if that were to happen, we would be alone and the only one to blame."

With technology constantly changing, professors and administrators must also continually adapt, retrain, and change their pedagogical approaches—all of which can be mentally taxing, particularly for faculty members who must stay current in their field while also mastering new teaching tools.

Add to the technical labor the emotional labor involved in addressing students' diverse academic and personal needs. Educators often find themselves investing considerable emotional energy in supporting students. Corey Griffin directs the Employee Counseling and Consultation Office at University of Massachusetts Amherst. In early 2024, he shared with *NEA Today*, a publication by the National Education Association in the United States, that "we are hearing more faculty who describe feeling overloaded by student need. A lot is expected of faculty." Providing that support can certainly be rewarding for some faculty, but it can lead to compassion fatigue and burnout if not properly managed.

Last, but by no means least, financial pressures add another layer of stress. Education is a notoriously underpaid field, and while certain professors and administrators at colleges and universities are compensated better than others, many—perhaps most—are not paid nearly enough to reflect their workload. This is especially true for those in entry-level and mid-management positions, as well as adjunct faculty and lecturers. This can lead to feelings of undervaluation and financial anxiety, which in turn affect overall mental wellbeing.

Effects on Mental Health

The mental health impact of these challenges on higher education professionals is profound and well-documented. As Lashuel wrote in his essay, "Pressure, stress, and anxiety frequently translate into sleep deprivation, irritability, and isolation. Chronic stress is also a major risk factor for developing many psychiatric and cardiovascular disorders," as evidenced, he remarked, by his two heart attacks in quick succession.

Lashuel speaks for many. A 2023 survey published in *Inside Higher Ed* found that 33% of higher education faculty are "often" or "always" physically exhausted, and 38% are "often" or "always" emotionally exhausted. Over 50% said they felt this way every day. Furthermore, a full 45% of educators in American colleges and universities have reported suffering from mental health distress, including 6% who have a serious mental illness, and 81% of educator respondents in a 2022 study reported experiencing work-related stress.

This trend extends to administrative staff. Another 2023 report from NASPA, the National Association of Student Personnel Administrators in higher education, found that 72% of student affairs staff said the mental health of employees had gotten worse in the previous year.

Disappointingly, the environment in higher education dissuades many employees from speaking up. One survey found that 60% of staff would not feel confident disclosing mental health problems or unmanageable stress to their employer, pointing to a persistent stigma surrounding mental health in academic settings. "In a culture of perfectionism and nearly constant peer pressure, the lines between disappointment and failure become very blurry. Most of us quickly learn that we must project an image of always being in control and unshaken by all the storms of academia," Lashuel wrote in his essay. "As faculty, many believe that admitting we are stressed or going through a mental health crisis would be a mistake; that if we do, [. . .] it may compromise our relationship with our students, our colleagues, and our superiors." It amounts to a near-impossible mental-health tightrope.

Challenges for Mental Health Engagement in Higher Education

Engaging higher education professionals in mental health initiatives presents real hurdles. As Lashuel elucidated, the culture and hierarchical structure of many institutions and often precarious nature of certain roles and positions may discourage open communication about mental health concerns, particularly for those on the tenure track who may fear that admitting to struggles could impact their career progression.

Additionally, the academic calendar, with its peaks of intense activity around exams and start-of-term periods, can make consistent participation in wellbeing programs difficult to attain. The diversity of roles within higher education—from lecturers to researchers to administrative staff—also necessitates a varied approach to mental health support, as what works for a tenured professor may not be suitable for an adjunct lecturer or an admissions counselor as the demands and stresses of their roles differ.

Moreover, the increasing prevalence of remote and hybrid work models in higher education has created new challenges in fostering a sense of community and providing accessible mental health support to all staff members, regardless of their physical location.

How to Support Mental Health in Higher Education

Addressing mental health in higher education requires a comprehensive and nuanced approach:

1. **Encourage openness on mental health.** Promote dialogue about mental health at all levels of the institution. Invest in mental health initiatives, share them widely and involve academic leaders in their promotion to set an example and reduce stigma. A network of universities recently created the Okanagan Charter, committing to promote health—including mental health—in a big way for faculty and staff as well as students on campus.

2. **Empower department leaders and supervisors through mental health training.** Involve leadership in promoting mental health initiatives and train staff to recognize signs of mental health concerns in their colleagues. This creates a more compassionate work environment and underscores your institution's commitment to employee wellbeing.

3. **Balance professional growth opportunities with a commitment to employees' personal wellbeing.** Offer professional development opportunities to demonstrate an investment in educators' professional growth. Additionally,

encourage work-life harmony by offering flexible scheduling and opportunities for self-care activities.

4. **Create supportive communities and solicit feedback and ideas.** Organize events and establish peer groups among faculty and staff that foster a sense of belonging, understanding, and mutual support. You may also benefit from using these support groups to occasionally solicit ideas about ways to provide more consistency to wellbeing programming throughout the ebbs and flows of the academic year.

5. **Provide comprehensive mental health resources.** Offer a range of mental health support options, from counseling services to workshops focused on stress management and work-life harmony, and ensure these resources are easily accessible to both on-campus and remote staff. Go a step further and provide training or discussion opportunities specifically focused on the areas that cause the most stress, such as emotional fatigue, setting necessary boundaries with students, learning the latest technologies affecting faculty's work, etc.

6. **Rebalance faculty workloads and provide fair pay.** "When you think about what makes people happy at work, it's things like having a voice in decisions. It's being respected. It's feeling well-compensated," said UMass Amherst's Corey Griffin. If people are consistently overworked, managing too much without their concerns being heard or addressed, and aren't making enough money to live without significant financial stress—and in the case of higher education, that's most people—they have more anxiety and a greater likelihood of developing both mental and physical health conditions. Institutions can change mental health outcomes for their employees in significant ways simply by reducing their workloads and providing fairer wages.

MANUFACTURING

With the manufacturing industry's focus on production and physical output, employees in the field experience different pressures from knowledge workers and many industries today.

Workforce Challenges in Manufacturing

Manufacturing jobs often involve standing for long periods, lifting heavy objects, and making repetitive motions, thereby fatiguing and stressing the same muscles over and over, which can cause unique physical stress and exhaustion. The repetition and monotony of those tasks can lead to mental fatigue, boredom, and a lack of engagement among workers while the physical stress can translate to mental stress and anxiety about the toll the work takes on one's body. And not just the cumulative toll—safety concerns are very real. Working with heavy machinery and handling potentially dangerous equipment is highly risky, prompting fears about accidents or injuries. Even when no incidents occur, the constant vigilance required can be mentally draining.

Many manufacturing operations call for shift work, including night shifts and rotating schedules. These irregular hours can disrupt natural sleep patterns and, thus, overall wellbeing. Also prone to seasonal fluctuations and economic challenges, work in this industry can lead to job instability and financial stress for many workers.

Effects on Mental Health

The mental health concerns in manufacturing are serious. A 2015 study on mental health across 55 industries found that manufacturing employees had 36% higher rates of mental health conditions compared to the national average. The situation is particularly dire in construction. Recent studies show substance abuse rates among construction workers at two times the national average, coupled with alarmingly high suicide rates—twice as high for men in construction and four times as high for women compared to the general U.S. population.

The 2021 Manufacturer's Alliance Cost of Mental Health Report reveals that among the manufacturing companies surveyed, 89% feel that productivity is adversely affected by employee mental health issues. Jae Kullar, the Global Head of Benefits, Health Services, and Wellbeing at a large agricultural machinery manufacturer, understands this implicitly. "Mental health is closely tied to how well people manage work-life balance. If companies don't provide the right conditions for balance," she said, "employees suffer, leading to burnout and disengagement." So, not only are mental health concerns in the industry widespread, so too are the negative business outcomes.

Challenges for Mental Health Engagement in Manufacturing

When it comes to tackling the problem, one of the primary challenges is a lack of awareness. Due to the nature of shift work and limited HR communication channels, many manufacturing employees do not fully understand the scope of their benefits, and with the industry's emphasis on speed and productivity, they may have little time to ask questions. Many employees have limited access to computers or smartphones during their workday, making it difficult to implement digital mental health platforms or communication strategies. High diversity among the workforce means that many employees speak other languages. Resulting language barriers can pose challenges, complicating efforts to communicate benefit information effectively.

Stigma presents another major barrier in this industry. Manufacturing is heavily male-dominated. Numerous studies have shown that men generally speak about their mental health and seek treatment far less often than women, a situation that's compounded when in groups of other men. Couple that with the focus on keeping production lines moving, and the result is a culture that heavily weighs physical safety over mental health. These priorities may discourage employees from slowing down and asking for help or seeking out support for their mental health when they need it.

How to Support Mental Health in Manufacturing

Addressing mental health in manufacturing requires tailored strategies that account for the unique aspects of the industry:

1. **Encourage regular breaks.** In addition to mandatory breaks, encourage your employees to take time for a mental and physical reset every few hours. Offer healthy snacks in the breakroom and encourage employees to step outside for some fresh air when possible.

2. **Integrate mental health into safety protocols.** Combine safety training with mindfulness practices, emphasizing the importance of mental clarity in ensuring physical safety. This approach can help bridge the gap between physical and mental health concerns.

3. **Create accessible mental health resources.** Implement breakroom apps or digital platforms that are easily accessible during breaks for quick mental health exercises. Use traditional marketing materials like posters and ID card attachments to share mental health tips and resources.

4. **Implement shift-specific support.** Offer tailored mental health sessions for workers transitioning between shifts, ensuring inclusivity for all employees regardless of their work schedule.

5. **Allow schedule flexibility and offer mental health days.** Provide some flexibility to accommodate appointments, personal concerns, and family needs. Also, be specific and let your employees know they can take time away from work when they need to tend to their mental health.

    As Kullar notes, supporting employees' mental health is "not just about offering programs; it's about creating a workplace where employees feel mentally supported. This includes flexibility in how they work and encouragement to prioritize self-care."

6. **Foster community and connection.** Encourage peer support networks where employees can connect with colleagues who share similar experiences and challenges. This can be particularly effective in an industry where team cohesion is often already strong due to shared work experiences.

7. **Address substance abuse proactively.** Given the higher rates of substance abuse in related industries, implement robust substance use disorder programs and promote them actively through various channels.

RETAIL

Retail workers interface directly with customers constantly and commonly have unpredictable work environments, which create their own stressors.

Workforce Challenges in Retail

Retail employees often contend with long and irregular hours, including evenings, weekends, and holidays. Schedule unpredictability can disrupt personal routines, making work-life harmony hard to maintain and leading to increased stress and fatigue. The physical demands of the job, such as prolonged standing and constant movement, exacerbate these symptoms.

Customer interactions, while potentially rewarding, can also be a significant source of stress. Retail workers frequently face challenging customers. In fact, a 2022 survey of retail workers found that 64% experienced an increase in verbally abusive customers since March 2020. Worse, in a 2024 survey, 80% of retail workers reported being scared to go to work every day, and 72% had experienced threatening incidents that went unaddressed because of understaffing issues. These incidents can be traumatizing and clearly cause lasting stress and anxiety.

The industry also grapples with job insecurity, low wages, and high turnover as a result. Many retail positions only offer minimum wage or slightly above, which creates substantial financial pressure for many workers. In fact, many full-time retail workers have reported having additional income sources—a sign of their strain to make ends meet on retail wages alone.

Effects on Mental Health

The impact of these challenges on retail workers' mental health is intense. A 2017 study published by Mental Health America found that 84% of retail workers reported declining mental health in recent years, while another survey found that 9 in 10 retail managers noticed an increase in mental health issues among staff in recent years.

The holiday season, a critical period for retailers, intensifies these mental health challenges, with 73% of retail workers reporting work-related stress around the holidays. This seasonal pressure adds to the already considerable stress of day-to-day retail work.

Challenges for Mental Health Engagement in Retail

So how do forward-thinking retail employers tackle employee mental health in their industry? Start with an assessment of the engagement challenges at play.

The retail workforce is diverse, with employees of a wide range of ages, cultures, languages, and backgrounds. Outreach and communication strategies will need to reflect that. The mix of full-time, part-time, and seasonal employees—plus ongoing turnover and team changes—can make it difficult to implement consistent mental health programs and long term engagement strategies. Part-time and seasonal workers are often ineligible for comprehensive benefits as well, which poses a challenge when trying to promote mental health programs only available through benefits providers.

Furthermore, limited access to devices during work hours, short break times, and the fast pace of the job—especially during peak shopping seasons—can make it difficult to ensure that everyone can receive timely information or participate in mental health activities.

How to Support Mental Health in Retail

Here are some proactive mental health strategies specifically designed to combat the challenges that employees in retail face:

1. **Schedule additional breaks—and enforce break time.** Encourage and enforce regular breaks during shifts, especially during peak hours or busy seasons. Further these efforts by instituting additional break periods during the holiday season to help reduce physical and mental fatigue and boost overall morale.

   Sandy Pilon is the Chief People and Values Officer at RH, a global luxury home furnishings company. She makes a concerted effort to promote breaks—"getting some fresh air and some steps in"—among her employees. "It's important to remind people that taking time for their wellbeing, even amidst work craziness, can make all the difference," she told me.

2. **Create comfortable break rooms.** Design inviting and comfortable break rooms where employees can relax and disconnect from customer interactions, enhancing overall wellbeing and job satisfaction. Use this space to post and share information about upcoming engagement events and/or employer-sponsored mental health initiatives.

3. **Rotate tasks and provide additional training.** Allow employees to switch between tasks like cashier, stocker, or customer service to keep the job interesting and reduce

burnout. To help employees develop new skills so that they feel better equipped to shift roles, offer opportunities to attend training sessions or workshops.

4. **Offer targeted mental health resources and encourage communication about mental health.** Provide access to counseling services or workshops that address the specific mental health challenges faced by retail employees, such as dealing with difficult customer interactions or managing holiday stress. Encourage employees to voice their mental health concerns and their concerns about the environment, and share ideas for building trust.

5. **Promote team building and recognition.** Organize team activities and implement recognition programs to boost morale and foster a sense of community among employees. As Christopher Dysinger, Vice President of Global Benefits at Walgreens, explained, "Friends and colleagues want to be there for each other. Creating systems that foster peer support within the workplace can make a big difference."

6. **Recognize efforts.** Show your employees that they're valued by rewarding outstanding performance and letting them know that their feedback matters. "Inspiring and celebrating employees doesn't just impact productivity," RH's Pilon said. "It also boosts their mental health and creates a sense of belonging."

THE BENEFITS OF CUSTOMIZED MENTAL HEALTH APPROACHES

While each industry faces its own unique set of challenges, the impact of these industry-specific stressors on employee mental health is clear. By tailoring mental health approaches to address these distinct needs, organizations can reap significant benefits that extend far beyond individual wellbeing.

Increased Employee Engagement

When mental health initiatives resonate with employees' daily experiences, they're more likely to participate actively in those initiatives. For instance, in manufacturing, integrating mental health check-ins into safety protocols can help link the two measures, placing mental health on par with physical safety in importance for these workers. This alignment can help workers view mental health support and resources as essential tools rather than optional add-ons—or worse, "fluffy" programs—further encouraging them to engage more deeply and consistently with the mental health resources provided.

As another example, in the retail sector, where customer interactions can be a significant source of stress, targeted workshops on handling difficult customer situations can draw high participation. Employees recognize the immediate applicability of such support, increasing their likelihood of engaging with broader mental health initiatives and utilizing other support structures in place.

Improved Employee Performance and Effectiveness

Addressing industry-specific mental health challenges head-on can lead to marked improvements in job performance. In professional services, where long hours and high-pressure client demands are the norm, strategies to manage stress and maintain work-life harmony can enhance employees' focus and decision-making abilities. This targeted support allows employees to navigate their demanding roles more effectively, ultimately delivering higher-quality work. For healthcare workers, who face unique emotional burdens, tailored support for managing compassion fatigue, for instance, can significantly impact patient care quality. By providing tools specifically designed to address the emotional toll of their work, healthcare organizations enable their staff to maintain empathy and attentiveness—crucial components for delivering effective care.

Additionally, when employees feel their unique challenges are understood and addressed, job satisfaction tends to soar. In higher education, where balancing teaching, research, and administrative duties can be overwhelming, targeted support for time management and work prioritization can alleviate stress and increase overall job satisfaction. For retail workers, acknowledging the physical and emotional demands of the job through initiatives like comfortable break spaces and peer support networks can foster a sense of being valued by their employer. This recognition of their specific needs contributes to a more positive work experience and greater overall satisfaction.

Greater Retention

Perhaps one of the most tangible benefits of tailored mental health approaches is improved employee retention. In industries like advertising, known for high turnover rates, addressing the specific pressures of creative work and tight deadlines can make employees feel supported and understood, increasing their likelihood of staying with the company. Manufacturing companies that proactively address safety concerns and the mental strain of repetitive work may find their skilled workers more inclined to remain in their roles long-term. This retention of experienced staff is invaluable in an industry where expertise and familiarity with specific processes are crucial.

By crafting mental health strategies that speak directly to the unique challenges of each industry, organizations demonstrate a deep understanding of their employees' needs. This tailored approach not only addresses immediate mental health concerns but also fosters a culture of care and support. The result is a workforce that feels valued, understood, and equipped to handle the specific demands of their roles.

Ultimately, investing in industry-specific mental health initiatives pays dividends in the form of a more engaged, effective, satisfied, and stable workforce. As organizations continue to recognize the importance of employee mental health, those that take the time to understand and address the unique needs of their industry will find that they are better able to attract, retain, and nurture top talent, giving them a significant advantage among competitors in their fields.

EXERCISE

Assess the Unique Mental Health Needs of Your Organization and Industry

Having read about the mental health needs of a variety of industries, take a few minutes to reflect on the impact your specific industry has on your own mental health and that of your colleagues.

What are some of the distinct mental health and wellbeing concerns of your industry?

How have the stressors of your industry directly affected you and your wellbeing?

What does your organization and its leaders already do to help support employees with these concerns?

How could they do more to support employees' mental wellbeing? In what ways could support and programming be improved?

CHAPTER 8

MEASURING SUCCESS IN PROACTIVE MENTAL HEALTH

More and more companies today recognize the value of supporting their employees' mental wellbeing. But before investing significant resources to expand mental health programming or amplify their support efforts, leaders want to know: *How do we measure the success of these efforts?* It's a fair and important question. As the old adage goes, what gets measured gets managed, and we want to ensure that the initiatives and programs put in place produce the outcomes they're meant to—in this case, improve employees' mental health, thereby improving the organization's ability to drive positive business outcomes.

Measuring the outcomes of proactive mental health initiatives isn't just a perfunctory exercise in data collection; it's a fundamental necessity to understand their effectiveness, demonstrate their value, and continuously improve them over time. Yet, in an area as nuanced and personal as mental health, traditional metrics often fall short. We're not simply counting widgets produced or sales made; we're attempting to gauge improvements in human wellbeing, resilience, and overall quality of life and how those things affect our businesses. This means we need many different kinds of data to give us a full picture of what's happening.

This chapter delves into the comprehensive approach required to get that full picture. We'll explore why tracking these outcomes is so crucial, examine four categories of key metrics to track and use to gauge success, and discuss both the important role of data analysis and challenges presented by it.

WHY IT'S IMPORTANT TO TRACK OUTCOMES FOR PROACTIVE MENTAL HEALTH

Measuring the impact of proactive mental health programs is essential for several reasons. First and foremost, in a business world often driven by ROI, or return on investment, concrete data on the effectiveness of mental health initiatives can tip the scales between a program thriving or getting cut. Leaders want their programs to help employees, but they also want to make sure those programs materially aid their businesses. Yet, as Lauren Goldstein, Senior Director of HR at the management consulting firm Gartner, acknowledged, tracking ROI is not always a direct line. "With mental health initiatives, it's not always about immediate ROI. Sometimes, success looks like a more engaged workforce or lower absenteeism rates."

So, has overall engagement increased? Has absenteeism decreased? Have health insurance claims decreased? These are some of the questions and answers that show leaders how their mental health programs affect the bottom line. If absenteeism and health insurance claims both decrease, that means the company's saving money. Demonstrating appreciable benefits like this through evidence can justify continued investment and even expansion of these critical programs. But if you don't measure the outcomes and have data from your own organization's efforts to show the positive effects, it's often hard to get and keep executives on board.

Second, measuring the impact allows organizations to determine if their efforts are making a real difference in employees' lives and enabling them to show up their best at work. Are they experiencing reduced levels of stress and anxiety? Are they sick less frequently? Has their sleep improved? Do they have more energy? If, over time, a proactive mental health program doesn't help improve things for your employees, you'll need to change your efforts.

In this way tracking outcomes additionally paves the way for continuous improvement. By gaining a clear understanding of what's working and what's not, your organization can refine its approach, allocate resources more effectively, and ultimately create more impactful programs. Guided entirely by feedback and data, this iterative process ensures that mental health initiatives evolve to meet the changing needs of employees and the organization as a whole.

KEY METRICS OF SUCCESS

To measure the efficacy and success of proactive mental health initiatives, there are four categories of metrics to look at: activity metrics, mental health progress metrics, business metrics, and cultural metrics.

Activity Metrics

Activity metrics show how much employees know about and use the mental health program and tools provided—in other words, their awareness and engagement. Engagement takes two forms: preventive and clinical. But let's look at awareness first.

Awareness

Awareness is a measure of how many people know about the mental health benefits and support services available at the organization. If employees aren't aware of the services, they certainly can't engage with them. Unfortunately, on average, less than 20% of employees are aware of the mental health benefits their company offers. This comes down to communication. How frequently, clearly, and effectively do employees hear about the benefits they provide? Companies with low employee awareness should amp up their communication efforts so employees become familiar with the programs and start using them—and redouble efforts when implementing a new program, since uptake on new programs takes more time. Consistently connecting with employees about mental health specifically helps keep their wellbeing top of mind, helps break down stigma, and ensures that they know how to get support through the company's benefits and services when needed.

Thankfully, awareness is fairly easy to measure. Simple employee surveys, conducted regularly and at important junctures, such as after onboarding or during busy seasons, can tell you what percentage of employees know about the mental health support available. Ask questions as broad as, "Did you know that our company's health benefits include mental health?" and as specific as, "Did you know our company has a robust EAP with an app providing classes on a range of mental health–related topics like mindfulness, stress management, and navigating grief?" Including questions with varying levels of specificity helps give organizations more detailed information about the degrees of employee awareness about their mental health benefits generally and about each specific service provided so that you can adjust your strategies accordingly.

Preventive Engagement

Preventive engagement describes the actions employees take to maintain and support their mental wellbeing using the company's proactive mental health programs. These include things like completing a daily mental health check-in, doing a morning meditation, taking an on-demand class on mental wellness for new parents, or participating in an ongoing peer support group for women in the workplace, for example.

With these actions, you want to look at two different measures: overall usage and consistency. It takes time for employees to adopt and regularly engage with the program, so when you first implement proactive mental health initiatives, your primary goal should be to see overall usage grow. Eventually, though, consistency becomes more important. Maintaining consistency with self-care practices—in other words, building healthy habits—statistically reduces stress and promotes better mental health outcomes, so one-time use isn't as valuable as consistent use. You want employees to utilize preventive care as regularly and as much as is helpful for them to maintain positive wellbeing.

Sometimes, changes in the levels of preventive engagement, as well as the types of content employees engage with, can tell you valuable information about the general state of your employees' mental wellbeing. For example, if you see precipitous increases or decreases in employee engagement with content or programming around stress and anxiety, it may be worth having some bigger discussions or check-ins to learn whether or not these changes are caused by issues at work and could, therefore, be addressed by the organization.

Clinical Engagement

Clinical engagement is the measure of employees utilizing the clinical benefits of their EAP or healthcare package—for example, seeing a therapist, requiring medication for a mental health disorder, participating in a substance use or other mental health–related treatment program, or needing an intervention for acute mental health concerns.

Here, too, you want to look at two different metrics: overall usage and usage by demographic. We know that most traditional EAPs see an average of 3% employee engagement. This number should be significantly higher, because the vast majority of workforces have more than 3% of people who would use or benefit from their EAP if they were aware of it and it served them well. After all, studies have proven that clinical care keeps employees healthy and engaged, as timely clinical interventions help avert larger potential issues, promote employee wellbeing, and cultivate a resilient workforce.

However, driving as much clinical care as possible is not the goal. Ideally, proactive mental health programs help people develop consistency, as mentioned above, so that they need to use clinical care less frequently.

Breaking down clinical engagement by demographic serves another purpose: It can reveal patterns that may not be immediately obvious, such as whether certain departments or demographic groups are struggling more or certain initiatives are having a greater impact. For instance, if your sales team consistently uses more clinical benefits than other teams, that may warrant further investigation into the working environment and dynamics of that team. Similarly, if you notice that your male employees in Eastern Europe utilize clinical services significantly less than other groups, it may be worth amplifying engagement strategies speaking to them in particular, or surveying them to learn how the services could serve them better. Noah Morgan, Vice President of Benefits and Wellness at Goldman Sachs, said, "We work with vendors to review employee mental health trends to provide a comprehensive view that helps us fine-tune our programs."

Breaking anything down by demographic or department comes with the disclaimer that this can and should only be done when that data represents a sizable group of employees. While all usage data is anonymized in reporting, if the representative group you're looking at is small—for instance, if one department has only six people, or only two employees live and work in Latin America—don't break the data down further.

Mental Health Progress Metrics

Next to activity metrics, you want to look at the actual mental health progress of your teams. This is where you find out how they're doing, and if their mental health is changing—and, hopefully, improving—as they utilize the services provided. There are three different progress metrics to keep track of: results of daily check-ins, changes to monthly assessments, and overall clinical outcomes, including scores of clinical assessments.

Daily Check-Ins

Daily check-ins are just a quick, non-clinical pulse-check, taking mere seconds, for people to share how they're doing. In the Journey platform, for example, we prompt people with emojis when they log in. People can select from four different emoji faces that correspond with four responses for how they're feeling that day: great, good, okay, or bad. If you're using a proactive or digital EAP with check-ins like this, the platform will allow you to track responses over time. Individual employees can track their own patterns, and companies can track anonymized responses in aggregate and watch for trends.

If you start to see upward trends in employees' reported daily well-being—more and more people reporting that they feel "good" or "great" instead of "okay" or "bad," for instance—that's a good indication that your proactive programs are having a positive effect on your employees. Likewise, if you see those responses start to migrate downward, or stay consistent at just "okay" or "bad" for too long, that tells you there's work to be done to help employees' mental health.

Monthly Assessments

More detailed assessments, conducted monthly, or at regular intervals, can gather data on employees' sense of their mental health, stress levels, and satisfaction with your organization's available mental health resources. While daily check-ins are a quick pulse-check, monthly assessments should ask a few clinically validated questions in an approachable way, and take one to two minutes to fill out. The idea is to provide a bit more insight on the overall state of the employees' wellbeing after which point they can receive a personalized plan for proactive mental healthcare that month. Organizations can track data from monthly assessments to get a fuller picture of employees' wellbeing as the year progresses.

Clinical Outcomes

Clinical assessments, such as the Outcomes Ratings Scale (ORS), the Generalized Anxiety Disorder-7 (GAD-7), and the Patient Health Questionnaire-9 (PHQ-9), come into the picture when people call for clinical support. These assessments help screen, diagnose, measure, and monitor progress for people's mental health conditions. The GAD-7 assesses anxiety, the PHQ-9 assesses depression, and the ORS assesses therapy patients' wellbeing covering four areas: individual wellbeing, interpersonal relationships, social roles, and overall sense of wellbeing. These three are among the most commonly used clinical assessments, but there are several others. I've included a fuller list in Appendix C in the back of the book.

Monitoring the results of these assessments, coupled with usage data for clinical care, can bring to light how mental health initiatives are impacting people at the clinical level. As Joel Axler, National Behavioral Health Leader at Brown & Brown, put it, "If you put a robust proactive mental health program in place with an employer, you want to see an improvement in their depression and anxiety rating scales. You want to see an improvement in all their clinical assessments."

Business Metrics

Beyond progress and engagement with the mental health programs themselves, companies can also look to key business metrics to assess the success of their proactive mental health approach. These metrics include healthcare costs, absenteeism rates, turnover rates, productivity, and overall return on investment.

Healthcare Costs

Healthcare costs are crucial to measure, in both aggregated and individual metrics, as a successful proactive mental health approach should lead to reduced mental health–related medical claims, prescription drug costs, and even overall health claims. A 2022 study conducted by inZights Consulting showed that employers using Journey saved, on average, $580 per engaged employee per year in healthcare costs.

Absenteeism

Absenteeism is the amount of sick days or mental health–related absences employees have over time. Remember, the average employee misses 10 to 12 days of work per year due to mental health, which costs businesses as much as $10 billion per year. Effective mental health initiatives bring these numbers down. In 2022, Humana, a leading U.S. health insurance company conducted a clinical study on the impact of Journey within organizations and found a 51% reduction in absenteeism. Seeing reduced absenteeism may, therefore, indicate improvement in overall employee mental health as a result of a proactive mental health approach, and it undoubtedly indicates increased savings for employers.

Turnover Rates

Employee turnover often increases in unsupportive work environments where employees aren't able to sustain positive mental health. When organizations invest in employee mental health and employees feel more supported on the whole, however, engagement and job satisfaction tend to improve, resulting in decreased turnover rates. Seeing lower turnover could indicate a successful mental health initiative.

Productivity Metrics

Productivity metrics, such as improvements in output, quality of work, and efficiency, can also demonstrate the impact of better mental health on business outcomes, as employees with better mental health tend to be more focused, efficient, and creative. In fact, a recent study by Mind Share Partners revealed that 60% of employees reported that their productivity had improved when their mental health was supported at work. The inZights Consulting study on Journey also found that employers saved $216 per employee per year in productivity and absenteeism loss savings. Pair that with a $580 savings in healthcare costs and a $232 savings in employee turnover, and you get a total savings of over $1,000 per engaged employee per year.

Return on Investment (ROI)

ROI compares the financial benefits of mental health programs to their costs, and it tends to be the most compelling metric to many stakeholders. According to the research, you're more than likely to see great cost reductions and significant ROI when you invest in mental health programs. A study by Deloitte found the ROI to be $1.62 for every dollar spent on mental health. Meanwhile, multiple studies put out by the World Health Organization, the World Economic Forum, and the National Safety Council and NORC at the University of Chicago found that the median return on investment for workplace mental health initiatives is an impressive 4 to 1, meaning that for every dollar spent on mental health programs, companies see $4 in return.

Cultural metrics

The final category to measure is cultural metrics, which help gauge how mental health initiatives are impacting your workplace environment and overall organizational culture. Cultural metrics typically come from quarterly pulse surveys and annual measurements of employee satisfaction.

Quarterly Pulse Surveys

Pulse surveys are meant to, exactly as their name suggests, get a pulse on employees' experiences with and perceptions of mental health in the workplace. These brief, focused questionnaires can track changes in stigma levels, assess the effectiveness of mental health communications, and measure employees' comfort discussing mental health with colleagues and managers. Conducting these surveys quarterly provides organizations with regular snapshots that can readily show changes happening over shorter periods of time.

Annual Employee Satisfaction

Tracking different employee satisfaction measurements annually offers deeper insights into the long-term cultural impact of mental health initiatives. Between surveys and analyzing certain utilization data points from healthcare plans and proactive platforms, look at the following categories of information:

- **Workplace Climate:** Has stigma decreased? Have mental health conversations become more commonplace? Do employees feel psychologically safe discussing mental health concerns? Asking these questions on employee surveys and in 1-on-1s can give you key insights into how much your employees feel that the work environment supports improved mental health and wellbeing, as well as whether support has changed as a result of the mental health programming.

- **Managerial Support:** Including survey questions that evaluate how well-equipped employees feel their managers are to handle mental health conversations, and how well they support their teams, can provide useful information as to whether or not your mental health programs and training have translated into better help on the day-to-day. Looking at mental health training completion rates of managers can also indicate whether or not your managers are well-equipped in this area.

- **Reactive vs. Proactive Care:** Reviewing metrics like the ratio of preventive to reactive service usage and healthcare claims, you can track the balance between reactive and proactive care, showing whether the organization is successfully shifting from crisis response. The goal is to see movement toward more proactive care with less reactive care in the balance.

- **Employee Advocacy:** You can also track how many employees recommend mental health programs to colleagues. While gathering this data is slightly more challenging, it's a strong indicator of both program effectiveness and cultural acceptance. Crafting survey questions where employees indicate their own level of advocacy, as well as asking whether they started using the proactive mental health services because another employee recommended them, can provide data for you to gauge advocacy efforts among your team.

Together, these cultural metrics provide crucial context for the other categories of measurement, helping organizations understand not just what employees are doing with mental health resources, but how the workplace environment supports or hinders their mental wellbeing.

HOW DATA ANALYSIS HELPS ORGANIZATIONS CONTINUOUSLY IMPROVE

Collecting data is only part of the equation in measuring success. Analyzing and interpreting that data is how you drive meaningful improvements in mental health initiatives. Thorough analysis allows organizations to benchmark their performance against their own historical data or industry standards, if that data is available, both of which give essential context for their progress.

By measuring their own data against others in the industry, Walgreens improved their mental health programming to reach award-winning levels. Elizabeth Burger, Executive Vice President and Chief Human Resources Officer of Walgreens Boots Alliance, described the company's methods. In addition to evaluating various measurements—including engagement, utilization, absenteeism, productivity, healthcare costs, and changes to clinical assessments, among others, "We've also compared our practices, programs and policies with those of other employers," she said. "In 2023, we were awarded Mental Health America's Bell Seal for Workplace Mental Health at the Gold Level, and in 2024, we achieved the Platinum Level. The Bell Seal for Workplace Mental Health national certification program acknowledges employers dedicated to creating mentally healthy workplaces. The program evaluates employer practices based on Mental Health America's extensive research and advocacy, taking into account the entire employee experience."

Aside from setting and surpassing industry standards, strong data collection and analysis enable organizations to clearly communicate the benefits of their mental health programs to stakeholders, establishing transparency that boosts buy-in and engagement at all levels of the organization, from the C-suite down.

For example, Bell Canada's Bell Let's Talk initiative, which focuses on improving mental health awareness, reducing stigma, and expanding access to care by funding mental health initiatives in over 1,500 organizations across the country. Bell has tracked the impact of Bell Let's Talk since the start of the initiative, which has supported nearly seven million Canadians with access to its services. Among the many data points they've collected, they've found that short-term disability claims related to mental health—which usually account for one-third of disability claims in Canada—have fallen by over 30%, and relapse and recurrence has dropped by more than 50%. They also found increased productivity and engagement among employees at organizations with mental health support. With this data, they've been able to point to Bell Let's Talk's wide-ranging benefits, allowing them to not just continue but also expand funding for the initiative in recent years.

Importantly, not all data does the same job. This chapter has listed measurements of both quantitative and qualitative data, and we learn different things from each one. Quantitative data helps indicate *what* is happening as a result of mental health initiatives, or the lack thereof—for example, how many more or fewer people participated in programming? How much did EAP utilization change? Or how many more or fewer mental health–related claims went to insurance? But quantitative data doesn't tell you *why* those things happened, or *how* people experienced something and how experiences could be improved. Those answers lie in the qualitative survey data and feedback from employees.

Regular feedback, as collected in some of the surveys listed in previous sections, helps organizations identify blind spots that may not be apparent from the numbers alone. It can guide how you refine existing initiatives as well as help you generate new ideas for mental health support strategies. The very act of soliciting and acting on feedback can even improve employee engagement and trust, which helps create a more positive work culture.

To get the most feedback from your employees, give them multiple channels for input—anonymous surveys, manager and leadership reviews, open forums, and even suggestion boxes. Again, emphasize the option for anonymity, and close the feedback loop by communicating specifically how input is being used to improve programs and employee support, further demonstrating the organization's commitment to hearing employee voices and continuing to make things better.

The multinational professional services firm EY exemplifies this approach with their "r u ok?" campaign, an EAP extension launched in 2016 that's aimed at addressing mental illness and addiction for EY employees. According to the first campaign lead, Dr. Sandra Turner, they incorporated employee feedback from the get-go. "When we began designing the program, we had everyone at the table—human resources, diversity and inclusion, the communications team and more," Turner told *Forbes*. This allowed them to build a campaign based on input from real employees actively managing teams and navigating the workplace culture surrounding mental health. Over the years, they've continued to collect consistent feedback on the campaign, conducting regular pulse surveys and tracking EAP usage. This feedback helps them keep refining "r u ok?" and ensure the program remains relevant and effective.

Ensuring Anonymity, Confidentiality, and Data Privacy

When collecting and analyzing mental health data of any form, protecting employee privacy and confidentiality is absolutely essential. All data must be anonymized, and organizations need to ensure that data collection methods comply with privacy laws and regulations. These measures must also be communicated clearly with employees at all times so they (1) know that their private medical information will remain private, and (2) understand how the data will be used within the organization. Communicating this information well helps encourage participation with mental health initiatives as well as honest responses to the surveys and assessments provided.

This point can't be overstated. People don't trust companies, or large entities in general—especially when it comes to their mental health. It can take a lot of reassurance for employees to trust that their responses to check-ins, surveys, or assessments, and their activity on company-provided digital apps, will truly be anonymous and kept that way. It can also take a lot of reassurance for them to believe that the organization won't use data on their mental health against them. So, for proactive mental health initiatives to work and provide benefits for anyone—employee or organization—it is paramount that employees trust the organization to handle their data with utmost integrity.

CHALLENGES TO ANALYZING MENTAL HEALTH–RELATED DATA

There is a caveat associated with all data analysis for proactive mental health programs: Due to the anonymous nature of data related to mental health, as well as the number of variables that affect people's mental health in and outside of work, it's difficult to make hard-and-fast connections between fluctuations in any of these metrics and the proactive mental health programming. Utilization of the proactive services can change because people's levels of stress go up or down, for example, or because it takes time for mental health conversations to become commonplace within an organization and for people to get comfortable using the services.

Further, you can't know if the people using the services are those who'd be inclined to use them anyway, or those experiencing more acute issues and in need of support. Never mind the effects that changes in people's personal lives and world events have on people's mental health. If one person on a team experiences a death in the family at the same time that another person is going through a divorce, and another has a close friend dealing with depression, they may all start consuming more proactive content, which could look like there's an issue on this team when in reality, these utilization instigators have nothing to do with those employees' experiences at work. Again, there are innumerable variables that can affect people's mental health at any given time, and organizations can't conduct non-anonymized clinical studies that would provide all the context they'd need to understand the exact impact of their proactive mental health program.

When interpreting and analyzing data, all organizations have to face this reality. This is where surveys and qualitative feedback on employees' experiences in the workplace can help provide the context lacking in the numerical data and utilization statistics. Rest assured, however, every study conducted on mental health benefits in organizations has shown that investments in mental health do reduce absenteeism, improve productivity, and cut costs for organizations.

LEVERAGING METRICS TO MOVE FORWARD

Measuring the success of mental health initiatives is not just about lowering costs or ticking leadership boxes. It's about understanding the real impact these programs have on people's lives and on the organization as a whole and using the data to create better work environments. Every step taken towards better measurement and understanding of mental health initiatives is a step towards a healthier, more productive workforce and healthier, more successful companies.

EXERCISE
Evaluate Your Organization's Measurement Efforts

Use the following checklist to understand which mental health metrics your organization currently tracks and identify potential gaps in measurement.

Check all that apply and note areas where you may need increased measurement.

Activity Metrics:
- ☐ Awareness of mental health benefits and resources
- ☐ Preventive engagement
- ☐ Clinical engagement

Mental Health Progress Metrics:
- ☐ Daily check-in results
- ☐ Monthly assessment scores
- ☐ Clinical assessment scores

Business Metrics:
- ☐ Overall healthcare costs
- ☐ Absenteeism rates
- ☐ Turnover rates
- ☐ Productivity
- ☐ ROI

Cultural Metrics:
- ☐ Quarterly pulse survey responses
- ☐ Employee satisfaction
- ☐ Manager mental health training completion rates

☐   Preventive vs. proactive care usage
☐   Employee advocacy

Looking at your responses, think through the following questions:

- Which categories have the most checks? The fewest?
- Where are the biggest gaps in your measurement approach?
- Which additional metrics would be most valuable to start tracking?
- What barriers exist to implementing new measurements?
- What resources or support would you need to start tracking everything you'd like to?

I recommend bringing these thoughts and ideas forward to discuss with the rest of your team and/or share with leadership. Taking steps to close measurement gaps for mental health initiatives helps organizations build more effective, data-driven programs, which improves outcomes for employees and the organization on the whole.

CHAPTER 9

THE ROLE OF TECHNOLOGY IN PROACTIVE MENTAL HEALTH

Technology, as we all know, is everywhere, and its role in our lives seems to increase with every passing day. In general, that has its positives and its negatives for our mental health. On the one hand, certain kinds of technology, and ways of using them, can contribute to worsening mental health and wellbeing for some individuals. On the other hand, though, advances in technology have ushered in unprecedented opportunities to support people's mental health proactively, playing an absolutely integral role in broadening access to care. From apps to virtual reality, these technologies provide personalized support, on demand and at scale, and can help step in before issues escalate. In reality, technology makes many prongs of a proactive mental health approach possible.

This chapter explores the distinct role technology plays in proactive mental health and organizations' mental health programming generally, examining various digital tools and resources available, the benefits and challenges of these tools, and how organizations can effectively integrate them into their proactive mental health programs and daily practices.

DIGITAL TOOLS AND RESOURCES AVAILABLE FOR PROACTIVE MENTAL HEALTH

In the digital mental health landscape today, we have a wide array of tools, apps, and resources designed specifically to support different aspects of mental wellbeing. Understanding what's out there helps organizations determine which tools will be most effective for their workforces.

Mental Health and Mindfulness Apps

Numerous apps available today aid proactive mental health, focusing on a range of things from meditation and mindfulness to mental health maintenance more broadly. Meditation and mindfulness apps such as Headspace and Calm offer resources like guided meditation sessions, sleep aids, and stress management techniques. Other apps like MindDoc, Clarity, and Moodfit help individuals track their mood daily, keep a mental health journal, learn coping skills, and access both self-assessments and external support. All of these apps can be particularly useful for individuals who aren't comfortable with traditional mental health services, or who want to dive into specific topics on their own.

Digital Mental Health Platforms

Comprehensive digital mental health platforms integrate various tools and resources, offering a centralized hub for mental health support. These platforms can include features such as mental health assessments, personalized support plans, access to counseling services, and educational resources, such as guided and on-demand classes on various mental health topics. These all-in-one solutions provide a seamless experience for employees, allowing them to access different levels of support as needed and engage as frequently as they want. For instance, an employee might start with self-guided exercises, move on to coaching for specific issues, and then transition to therapy if needed—all within the same platform.

Integrating a digital mental health platform is a vital component of a proactive mental health approach. These platforms provide the resources, privacy, data, and personalization organizations need to support employees no matter where they are. Further, they allow for, and even help facilitate, the consistency of practice and engagement with mental health that people need to be truly proactive about their wellbeing.

Virtual Support Groups

Digital platforms can also facilitate virtual support groups, where individuals can connect with others who share similar experiences. These virtual support groups can be particularly beneficial for employees dealing with specific issues, such as work-related stress, parenting challenges, or managing chronic illnesses. They can also provide valuable social support in the circumstance where there isn't a designated peer support group for an individual's particular area of interest, identity, or concern already at their organization. Platforms like Slack, Microsoft Teams, or dedicated mental health forums can be used to facilitate these groups.

Wearable Technology

Wearable devices like smartwatches and fitness trackers that track physical health indicators can also provide insights into an individual's mental health. By tracking physical indicators of stress, such as elevated heart rate or disrupted sleep patterns, they can provide real-time—one could even call it *proactive*—feedback to users and prompt them to do certain activities to ease their stress. For example, the Apple Watch has a Breathe app that reminds users to take deep breaths throughout the day, while Fitbit devices offer guided relaxation sessions.

Some companies are now exploring how to use aggregated, anonymized data from these devices to identify trends in employee stress levels and tailor their wellness programs accordingly. While certain companies may not want or be able to use such data or provide wearable technology to their employees, you can share information about the proactive uses of these devices for those employees who have them to better inform their own mental health practices.

Online Counseling Services

While not exactly a proactive measure, I'd be remiss not to mention telehealth and online counseling services. The rise of telehealth use during the COVID-19 pandemic made mental healthcare vastly more accessible. Platforms like BetterHelp and Talkspace connect users with licensed therapists through video calls, messaging, and phone calls, providing flexible and convenient access to professional support. Allowing individuals to receive counseling and therapy from the comfort of their homes, or whatever location is available and comfortable for them, as opposed to having to travel to participate in person, broadened the scope of who can receive therapy tremendously. Beyond allowing for location flexibility, telehealth has also expanded scheduling options, making it possible for employees to schedule sessions outside of traditional 9-to-5 work hours, including early mornings, evenings, and weekends, even further lowering barriers to seeking help.

"In COVID, we saw how quickly employees adapted to virtual mental healthcare and telemedicine," said Eddie Gammill, Senior Director at WTW. "The convenience and accessibility of those offerings have made it easier for a wider range of people to prioritize their mental wellbeing, and I hope we continue to embrace innovations like this in the mental health space."

THE BENEFITS PROVIDED BY TECHNOLOGY IN PROACTIVE MENTAL HEALTH

The integration of technology into proactive mental healthcare offers numerous advantages, particularly in the context of workplace wellness programs. As Gammill noted, digital mental health tools offer unprecedented convenience, providing support 24/7. This on-demand nature means that help is always just a few taps away. An employee experiencing a panic attack at 2 AM can immediately access guided breathing exercises or connect with a crisis counselor, rather than having to wait until business hours. Similarly, an executive feeling overwhelmed before a big presentation can use a mindfulness app for a quick mental wellness session to center themselves.

Hand in hand with convenience is perhaps the most significant advantage of digital mental health tools: their ability to democratize access to mental health resources. As long as an individual has a smartphone or a device with an internet connection, they can access a wealth of mental health support. This is particularly valuable for employees in remote locations or areas with limited mental health services. For instance, a multinational corporation can ensure that an employee in a small branch office in rural India has access to the same quality of mental health support as their colleagues in New York or London. Population Health Leader at WTW, Jeff Levin-Scherz underscored this point. "Working globally, you need to find ways to support wellbeing regardless of where your team is located—no matter how many different time zones they're stretched across," he said.

In addition to accessibility, the privacy afforded by digital tools can help people overcome, or at least circumvent, the stigma that often prevents people from seeking help. This can be particularly beneficial in workplace settings where employees might worry about the professional implications of seeking mental health support. For instance, an employee, or even high-level executive, who might feel uncomfortable being seen entering a therapist's or company counselor's office might be more willing to use a discreet app on their phone. This anonymity is also extremely helpful in countries, cultures, and industries where mental health issues are still taboo.

Another very tangible benefit is cost savings. Many digital proactive mental health solutions are more affordable than traditional in-person therapy and counseling programs, allowing organizations to provide comprehensive mental health support to a larger portion of their workforce. While the initial investment in digital platforms may be substantial, the scalability of these solutions often results in a lower per-employee cost over time, which can be particularly beneficial for small and medium-sized enterprises that might not have the resources for extensive in-house mental health programs. Furthermore, with digital solutions, you don't need to set up physical infrastructure in every single office for employees to use the tools. Instead, once set up in an organization, a proactive mental health platform can serve thousands of employees simultaneously, ensuring consistent quality of mental health support across the organization.

More than that, the personalization capabilities of many digital tools allow for highly individualized support as machine-learning algorithms can analyze user data to provide tailored recommendations and interventions. For example, a digital platform or app might learn that a particular employee responds better to guided imagery exercises for stress relief than breathwork sessions and thereafter prioritize imagery exercises in its recommendations for that employee. This kind of personalization is more challenging to achieve in traditional, one-size-fits-all workplace wellness programs.

Tools using predictive analytics can further facilitate early intervention as well. For instance, many of the mental health platforms available enable people to track their mood and emotional state every day. Tools with predictive analytics also often have the ability to conduct sentiment analysis, which uses machine learning and natural language processing to identify and categorize whether the sentiment of certain text is positive, negative, or neutral. In other words, it can analyze the language employees use, or the moods they select, in their check-ins and track whether someone's emotional state is declining. It can then suggest specific resources or potential interventions to help prevent minor issues from escalating into more serious mental health problems.

Lastly, as discussed in Chapter 8, digital mental health tools can collect and analyze vast amounts of data, which provide valuable insights for leaders into the mental health trends of their organization. When properly anonymized and aggregated, this data can help companies identify potential stressors in their work environment, measure the effectiveness of their mental health initiatives, and make data-driven decisions about resource allocation. For instance, if data shows that employees in a particular department are experiencing higher levels of stress, the company can investigate the root causes and implement targeted interventions.

TECHNOLOGY'S CHALLENGES AND LIMITATIONS IN PROACTIVE MENTAL HEALTH

While technology offers many benefits for mental health support, it's important to acknowledge its limitations and potential drawbacks. The same devices used to access proactive mental health resources can also be sources of stress and distraction. Many of us spend much of our days on our phones and at our computers. We're spending hours upon hours on various apps, interfacing with technology that, in almost all cases, is designed to suck us in and keep us coming back for more. It's the attention economy—and technology is winning.

Even apps designed with good intentions may prioritize engagement metrics over actual mental health outcomes. Success metrics for companies that create apps—even mindfulness and meditation apps—often include measurements like monthly active users and time spent on the platform. Some mindfulness apps are even using gamification techniques to engage users in activities designed to boost mood and build resilience. We should be wary of gamifying anything related to mental health. It's valuable to get people engaged in proactive activities that will benefit them, but gamification is a slippery slope toward keeping people on an app or device longer than is beneficial to anyone but the technology company behind it all.

As organizations implement proactive mental health and integrate digital tools to support their efforts, they must also carefully evaluate the tools they offer, ensure they align with genuine mental health goals, verify their credibility, and consider how to encourage healthy technology use alongside their digital mental health initiatives.

Another significant challenge within mental health and tech is ensuring the privacy and security of sensitive personal data. Mental health information is among the most private data an individual can share, and any breach of confidentiality could have serious consequences. Organizations must ensure that any digital mental health tools they implement adhere to the highest standards of data protection and comply with relevant regulations such as GDPR in the European Union or HIPAA in the United States, or equivalent health regulations in other countries and regions. Moreover, employees need to feel completely confident that their mental health data won't be used against them in workplace decisions.

While digital tools can increase accessibility, they also risk exacerbating existing inequalities. Not all employees may have equal access to or comfort with digital technologies. Older employees, those in lower income brackets, and those in regions with poor internet connectivity might be at a disadvantage.

Furthermore, there's a risk that some organizations might view digital tools as a complete solution to proactive mental health support, neglecting other crucial elements like creating a supportive work environment or addressing systemic issues that contribute to poor mental health. Offering benefits and digital tools are just the start; technology should complement, not replace, human-centered care, organizational change, cultural shifts, and community-based support. Erin Young agrees. Young is Director for Health, Equity, and Wellbeing at WTW. "The stressors and impacts people feel at work are so unique; assuming one set of benefits will meet everyone's needs just doesn't work," she said. "We need adaptable options and multiple pathways for support." Proactive offerings in organizations should all incorporate in-person options to facilitate greater community and a shared experience. These forms of support should be available and advertised to everyone in the organization just as readily and as often as the digital tools.

Finally, the use of AI and predictive analytics in mental health raises ethical questions. As of early 2025, these technologies are still in the initial stages of their development. They do not have enough source data to serve whole populations adequately in regards to mental health. AI tools also hallucinate, making up information and answers regularly. Additionally, these tools are biased by their source data, which can make them both less accurate and less sensitive to the needs of minority groups. They may reinforce biases or inaccuracies if the training data used is not diverse or representative, leading to flawed predictions and potentially harmful outcomes for some users. Predictive models can also produce false positives or false negatives when analyzing mental health data, resulting in unnecessary alarm or missed warnings for those who need intervention, and potentially impacting users' trust in the tool. Ultimately, these tools cannot by any stretch replace human interaction and intuition in mental healthcare, and they should not be solely relied upon with.

HOW TO INTEGRATE PROACTIVE MENTAL HEALTH TOOLS

To successfully integrate technology into organizational mental health programs, start by considering the unique needs of your workforce and their specific mental health needs. Then, look at the technological options available to you, how the tools would serve your workforce, and the overall goals of your mental health initiative. You may want to conduct surveys, focus groups, or analysis of existing health data to aid your assessment. Understanding prevalent issues, preferences, and potential barriers to adoption will help you select the most appropriate digital tools to help your teams.

Choose Tools With Offerings That Align With Your Company's Values

The chosen digital solutions, and how they're configured, should align with your organization's culture and values. For instance, a company that values work-life harmony might prioritize tools and resources that help employees manage stress and set boundaries, while a high-performance culture might focus on resilience-building resources.

Ensure the Tools Meet Your Employees Where They Are

Whatever tools you choose, ensure all employees can access them and that the tools meet them where they are, so to speak. This means considering factors like language, disability accommodations, and technological literacy. It also means integrating the tools into the day-to-day experience of your employees and the platforms they already use regularly, such as the company HR software and communications tools like Slack, Microsoft Teams, or Zoom. This makes employees more likely to use them, thereby making the tools more effective.

Chief Heart Officer Claude Silver noticed a huge difference in VaynerMedia's culture around mental health when the organization implemented Journey Proactive EAP, which we intentionally created to integrate easily into the day-to-day activities of modern workforces. "Through company-wide awareness campaigns, Slack and calendar integrations, and Daily Journey emails, our employees now have the tools necessary to proactively tackle mental health challenges like never before," Silver said.

These software integrations are particularly helpful for employees, like knowledge workers, who spend most of their days on their computers. For employees in other fields that spend more time on their feet, on the service floor, or managing customers—industries like hospitality, construction, retail, entertainment, etc.—you may need to provide more site-specific tools, such as standalone tablets, digital kiosks, or posters with QR codes directing employees to apps or specific resources. By providing tools that meet employees where they are, both literally and metaphorically, organizations can reduce barriers to engagement and make mental health support a natural part of the workday.

Broadcast the Tools' Availability and Benefits Consistently

Just having these tools set up will only get you so far, however; you must also communicate clearly and consistently about the availability of these tools and the benefits they provide to remind employees to use them. Create strategic communications campaigns to put the resources in front of employees regularly—and when they most need them. Tailoring your engagement strategies helps tremendously, and not just tailoring these strategies to your industry, but also to the needs of employees specific departments, roles, geographic locations, cultures, and seasons of the working year. For example, during tax season, an accounting firm might promote resources for managing work-related anxiety or getting a good night's sleep. A global manufacturing company with offices in Mexico, where mental health stigma is high, might implement a months-long messaging campaign aimed at normalizing mental health support and reducing stigma. These kinds of targeted approaches ensure that employees are aware of relevant support when they need it most.

Train Employees on How to Use The Tools

To make sure they also know *how* to use the tools, provide training to teach employees how to use them effectively and where to find what they need when they need it. Some digital mental health platforms and apps use AI to recommend relevant resources based on employees' usage patterns. These recommendations can be beneficial to employees, helping them find the mental health content that's most useful to them.

However, using those tools also requires high levels of transparency with employees around their data privacy and usage. Implement robust data protection measures, and as you train employees and communicate about the programs, make sure to clarify how employee data is collected, used, and protected.

Get Leaders to Promote the Tools

Encourage leaders to openly support and use the digital mental health tools as well, as this can reduce stigma and encourage wider adoption among all employees. "Leaders need to take an active role in promoting mental health within their organizations," said Elisha Engelen, Partner, Human Capital Solutions Client Leader at Aon. "Employees look to leadership for guidance, and when leaders prioritize mental health, it sets the tone for the entire company." That means promoting and prioritizing *every* part of the organization's mental health approach, digital tools included.

Evaluate the Tools' Impact Regularly

Identify what your organization's key metrics for success with its proactive mental health program are, and then regularly evaluate the impact of digital mental health initiatives against those metrics. Are employees using them? Are they moving the needle? Do you need more offerings, or different ones? As part of that evaluation, regularly solicit feedback from employees about their experience with these tools and use this feedback, along with usage data, to continuously improve and refine the proactive offerings you provide.

Maintain In-Person Support Always

Finally, to reiterate an important point, while digital tools can be powerful, they shouldn't completely replace human interaction. Ensure that employees also have access to in-person support, at work and outside of it, whenever they need it.

THE FUTURE OF DIGITAL PROACTIVE MENTAL HEALTH TOOLS

The field of digital mental health is continually evolving, and recent advancements have the potential to transform proactive mental healthcare moving forward.

While still emerging as tools in the mental health field, virtual reality (VR) and augmented reality (AR) technologies are being developed and tested for their potential to help treat—or even prevent—conditions like anxiety disorders and PTSD. Both VR and AR technologies enhance or replace a user's real physical surroundings with a simulated environment. VR involves wearing a headset designed to "transport" you visually to another fully immersive, virtual space, whereas AR is typically partially immersive and can be accessed through a smartphone.

In the realm of proactive mental health specifically, the tech and scientific communities are exploring the use of these technologies as a form of exposure therapy to help people overcome fears and work through context-specific anxiety. For example, a VR or AR program might allow an employee with a fear of public speaking to enter a virtual auditorium or conference room and practice giving presentations, allowing them to get more comfortable in those settings and gradually build their confidence. Some companies are also exploring the use of AR for mindfulness exercises, creating immersive, calming environments that employees can enter to relieve stress. Using the simulation capabilities of both of these technologies may also help in training leaders, HR professionals, and managers how to navigate certain mental health–related situations and concerns involving employees.

AI and machine learning have also burst on the scene, and they may play an increasingly significant role in mental health support in the coming years. AI-powered chatbots are already being used to provide limited support 24/7. These tools use natural language processing to engage in conversations with users, offer coping strategies, and even help with cognitive behavioral therapy techniques. While limited in use now, as the technology improves, these chatbots will use machine-learning algorithms to improve their responses over time, potentially enabling more sophisticated, accurate, and personalized recommendations and interventions to users as well as more accurate prediction of mental health issues. As human connection underlies mental wellbeing in every way, chatbots are in no way a replacement for human therapists; however, these AI assistants can provide immediate support when needed and serve as a first line of intervention.

Additional technologies to watch include wearable technology and biosensors, which can provide more detailed and accurate data on physical and mental health indicators, such as heart rate variability and cortisol levels, to provide insights into stress and anxiety and recommend things like relaxation exercises or resources for professional support—all of which takes the current wearable tech tools to the next level. Similar technologies are being developed to detect differences in external factors, like vocal intonation, typing speed, or social media usage, that could also indicate changes in mental or emotional wellbeing. In the coming years, we're likely to see more holistic health platforms that integrate mental and physical health data, providing a more comprehensive view of an individual's overall wellbeing.

Though still in early stages, advances in genetics and neuroscience, combined with big data analytics, could lead to highly personalized mental health interventions based on an individual's unique biological and psychological profile using brain-computer interfaces. Brain-computer interfaces, or BCIs, are technologies that translate neural signals or brainwave activity into data or commands for an external technological device. There are both non-invasive and, more recently, invasive BCIs. Non-invasive BCIs use external sensors to detect brain activity, whereas invasive BCIs involve implanting electrodes directly into the brain. Neuralink, the leading BCI technology company, made headlines in early 2024 for having the first successful human brain implantation of a neuromodulation device. Up to this point, BCIs have largely been used to aid those with severe physical disabilities and communication impairments, including perhaps most famously Steven Hawking in the technology's early days. Now, with continued advancements in the field, scientists anticipate using BCIs for neurofeedback therapy to treat symptoms of ADHD, anxiety, and depression.

Yet, while many of these technological innovations are exciting, we cannot overlook the ethical concerns involved in all of these technological advances—not the least of which pertain to the brain-computer interfaces and AI-powered therapy chatbots. Mental health is not a field to play lightly in, and people's safety, privacy, and wellbeing must be paramount. Any advanced technologies in this field should be treated skeptically until they are thoroughly tested, vetted, and regulated, and we can ensure that the data connected to such devices is absolutely secure.

EMBRACING TECHNOLOGICAL ADVANCEMENTS, MAINTAINING CONNECTION

The integration of technology into proactive mental health strategies presents both exciting opportunities and significant challenges for organizations. As we've explored in this chapter, digital tools offer unprecedented accessibility, convenience, and scalability of mental health support as well as the option of increasingly personalized interventions and early detection of mental health issues. The goal is not to replace human-centered care, but to augment and extend it, creating a more accessible, personalized, and effective approach to mental health support for all employees.

However, these benefits must be balanced against concerns about data privacy, the digital divide, and the risk of over-reliance on technology at the expense of human connection. Technology is not a panacea, but rather a powerful tool that, when wielded thoughtfully and ethically, can significantly enhance our ability to support mental health in the workplace. As we move forward in this digital age, the organizations that will thrive will be those that can harness the power of technology while still prioritizing the human element in mental healthcare.

EXERCISE

Assess Your Organization's Use of Digital Tools for Mental Health

Take a moment to evaluate your organization's current use of digital mental health tools and consider opportunities for expanding or improving their integration into your workplace.

Which digital tools have you already incorporated in your organization's approach to mental health?

- Mindfulness apps
- Comprehensive digital mental health platform
- Virtual support groups
- Virtual counseling and telehealth options

For the tools that you haven't incorporated, what are the barriers your organization faces to being able to provide those tools? Or what steps need to be taken to set them up?

On a scale of 1 to 10, rate your organization's efforts to integrate the tools into the day-to-day work environment. _____

Based on the rating you chose, what else do you think your organization could and should do to integrate the technology and encourage employees to use them?

As you think through strategies to improve tech integration into your proactive mental health approach, remember that you don't need to implement every available digital tool. Instead, thoughtfully select and integrate technologies that align with your organization's culture and your employees' needs while maintaining a balance with human-centered support.

CHAPTER 10

PROACTIVE MENTAL HEALTH TRAINING FOR MANAGERS

Six months ago, Zuri started working on the sales team at a recently public software company. She reports to the Regional Sales Manager of the Southeastern U.S., which happens to be you. You've helped orient Zuri to the procedures at work, and in fact, the two of you have become friendly, chatting regularly about what's going on in your lives. In the past month or so, she's told you about a few interactions with personnel from key accounts that really impacted her.

Just last week, for example, one senior account contact from a national consumer goods brand was extremely upset when Zuri couldn't accommodate a last-minute request to include a huge, customized data set in their quarterly analytics report, which she was supposed to deliver that afternoon. The data set to be included in this report had been determined months before, and the new, customized portion the client wanted would have taken Zuri several days to prepare. There was no way she could accommodate their request and deliver the report on time.

The account contact called back three times, insisting that Zuri fulfill her request. In their last exchange, despite Zuri offering to provide an additional report on the new data within a few days—for which she would have had to work overtime—the contact said, "No one else at this organization has ever given me this much trouble. Apparently, you're new here, so hear me: This is completely unacceptable. We'll see if we keep working with you!" Zuri was rattled. It's the end of the fiscal year—an important time for the sales teams to secure contract renewals with existing accounts—which means it's an important time to keep those accounts happy. However, it's also a time for high stress and high expectations. This particular account contact was just one of a handful who'd passed their stress onto Zuri in recent weeks.

Being new to the organization, Zuri has doubted herself after these interactions, and as her manager, you've noticed that she's been on edge because of them. You've been able to make space for Zuri to process the conversations and assure her she didn't do anything wrong. Still, recently, instead of showing up early to your weekly check-ins and swapping stories, as she had previously, Zuri's seemed distracted, worried, and uncharacteristically serious. This morning, when another prominent account contact called with a question she didn't know the answer to, she froze and quickly asked them to email another colleague for the right answer.

You're concerned for Zuri and would like to talk about how she's feeling, however, you wonder if there's something serious outside of work impacting her as well. You also know that your own stress level has ticked up. Considering how things have gone with Zuri lately, you don't know if or how to approach such a conversation. You want to provide actual help without making Zuri uncomfortable, accidentally bringing your stress into the mix, or stepping into territory you're not equipped to handle.

You're not alone in this situation. Managers everywhere have to navigate sensitive circumstances and conversations with their direct reports all the time, and when an employee's mental health is a consideration, not to mention the manager's as well, knowing what to say or do is especially challenging. Elizabeth Burger is the Chief Human Resources Officer at Walgreens Boots Alliance, the global pharmacy and health retail company. She recognizes the difficulties managers face when having these conversations. "Leaders and managers have a responsibility to ensure their teams know about the resources available to them, and also be able to spot when someone might be struggling," Burger said. "It's a fine line to walk—not wanting to pry into someone's personal life, but also ensuring they know they are cared for and supported especially if it's clear they need it." These interactions require managers to tap into many different skills.

The reality is, however, a lot of managers simply aren't taught these skills. Yet, since managers are culture carriers, organizations trying to build proactive mental health cultures have an obligation to everyone—leaders, managers, and direct reports alike—to explicitly train managers on how to approach mental health with their teams. Better still, train them on how to be proactive about their own mental health so they can help their direct reports do the same.

In this chapter, we look at the role managers have in building and maintaining a proactive mental health culture and why training is important. We'll also walk through some of the key elements and messages to include in this training.

THE ROLE OF MANAGERS IN BUILDING A PROACTIVE MENTAL HEALTH CULTURE

Managers play pivotal roles in every organization. They're the team leaders. They're both teachers and executors, facilitators and supporters—all rolled into one. They have the most frequent touchpoints with individual team members, and they often see the seeds of potential issues before they grow. Moreover, because managers have all of these important functions, they have an outsized impact on a company's culture. The environment they create and the dynamic they foster for their teams really determines their team members' experience and wellbeing at work. As the saying goes, people don't quit companies, they quit managers. But the reverse is also true: People stay when they have managers that support them. Whatever culture a company wants to create will have to be nurtured, sustained, and reinforced through its managers.

To create a proactive mental health culture, this means having every manager foster an affirming, open team environment where people feel supported in discussing mental health, privately and as a team, and asking for help. It means having every manager check in with individual team members daily or weekly to keep a pulse on how each of them are doing. It means having every manager encourage participation in the company's proactive mental health programs and help direct people to additional resources when needed. It also means having every manager flag potential concerns when they arise so people can get the support they need before issues become acute.

For managers to be able to do any of that, though, their own mental health is paramount. Typically, managers are people on the go. They're high-achievers who tend to put the needs of their team before their own. They may not always realize, however, the impact that has. If a manager is struggling, that will affect their team and, by extension, the rest of the organization. By that measure, one of the most fundamental pieces to building a proactive mental health culture is prioritizing the mental health of managers and ensuring they have the education, resources, and tools they need to feel supported, competent, and healthy themselves, as well as to be able to support their teams appropriately.

It's also important to note that organizations may face some resistance from managers at first. "One of our most rewarding opportunities has been helping managers recognize that supporting mental health is a core leadership responsibility. By actively engaging with their teams on well-being—both proactively and during challenges—they can create a healthier, more supportive workplace culture." said Erika Loperbey, HR Manager of Employee Well-being and Talent Management an American multinational IT services company with over 100,000 employees. Loperbey realized that to deliver impactful training, the organization embraced the opportunity to prepare managers for meaningful conversations, addressing potential uncertainties or discomfort with discussing mental health with their teams. "By integrating this preparation into the training, we empowered managers to feel confident and capable in fostering open, supportive dialogues."

It's crucial to emphasize, too, that in no way do you (or should you) expect, require, or endeavor to turn your managers into mental health professionals. "Managers are not there to rescue people in mental health crises," said Wagner Denuzzo, former Vice President of Leadership and Management Development at IBM and the author of *Leading to Succeed:*

Essential Skills for the New Workplace. "Team members don't need their managers to rescue them or provide solutions. They need support and understanding. So, we need to train managers to maintain empathy while also setting healthy boundaries." Ideally, Denuzzo said, organizations train managers to help their team members navigate challenges—what he calls "moments of impact" where they can make the most difference by providing support—and to celebrate them, which has a tremendous positive impact.

Regardless of the levels of expertise or comfort managers get to with facilitating conversations about mental health with their direct reports, they need training to know what to do and where to point people.

HOW TO TRAIN MANAGERS ON PROACTIVE MENTAL HEALTH

To incorporate all of these points and provide realistic, holistic guidance, proactive mental health training for managers focuses on four primary outcomes:

1. Managers have the knowledge and tools to be **able to prioritize their own mental health** and take care of themselves first.
2. Managers **know what to look for and can recognize signs** that someone may be struggling with their mental wellbeing.
3. Managers **have the skills to approach struggling team members thoughtfully** and without judgment.
4. Managers **know the available resources**, within the workplace and beyond, to which they can direct people.

It bears repeating that nowhere in this outcome list do you see anything about requiring managers to find solutions or become workplace therapists. The goal with manager training is not at all to place the burden of care on managers. The goal of training is to equip managers with the knowledge and tools to be able to provide the level of support that makes sense for them, give their team members a good place to turn to, and then direct team members to the right resources for further care as needed.

Educating Managers on Mental Health

The first step in proactive mental health training is to educate managers on the basics of mental health. Define it—*a state of mental wellbeing that enables people to cope with the stresses of life, realize their abilities, learn and work well, and contribute to their community*—and discuss the varying factors that affect our mental health. Have mental health professionals walk through some of the most common mental health conditions affecting people around the world, and explain the signs that managers should be aware of and look out for in their team members that may indicate they're struggling or need help.

Further explain the cultural contexts surrounding mental health that impact the employees at the organization, depending on the organization's size and location, and if possible, specifically highlight the contexts and attitudes the managers' team members may have or encounter. This includes discussing how the culture of the organization and its industry impacts the mental health of employees and what stressors play the biggest roles in the organization's day-to-day environment.

Finally, focus on proactive steps vs. reactive care for mental health. Help them understand what steps they can take preventatively for themselves as well as where and how they can direct their team members. Make sure they are trained on any and all digital tools and technologies involved in the proactive mental health approach for the organization. And provide them with all the information for internal and external resources they may need for themselves or their team members.

Creating Conversations with CARE

Demonstrating genuine care is a choice that every manager can make, but it becomes essential when an employee seeks help. Managers should strive to approach these conversations with empathy, respect, and understanding, ensuring that every individual feels heard and supported. The "CARE" framework offers a helpful structure for how to approach conversations about mental health with team members:

- **Connecting with safety:** Managers need to be able to make themselves available to those who may be struggling and offer social support.

- **Attending with empathy:** Managers can recognize signs and listen without judgment.

- **Responding with compassion:** Managers respond in ways that show kindness and affirm others.

- **Empowering with resources:** Managers share support strategies and foster a team dynamic that prioritizes mental health.

Connecting with Safety

Connection matters for mental health. Research has proven time and again that social support and connection reduces the effects of depression, anxiety, and stress, so it's important for team members to feel a sense of safe connection with their managers.

To have a container for connection with a team member requires first establishing psychological safety. KKR's Global Head of Employee Experience, Benefits and Wellness, Chris Kim, acknowledged the importance of this when we spoke. "We know that managers play a critical role in the overall psychological safety that employees experience within their teams," Kim said. "To further bolster an environment of optimal mental wellbeing, we have to help managers learn how to communicate this effectively and empathetically."

This starts by making sure the conversation is welcome and asking if it's okay to step into that territory. Deepen that sense of safety by letting the team member determine how they want to structure the conversation—give them the autonomy. Since disclosing a mental health issue can feel like a significant social and professional risk, assure them that the conversation is private where possible. Then, reaffirm that you're there in support of their interests and wellbeing rather than out of concern for their performance.

Attending with Empathy

Kim also alluded to empathy, which is the ability to understand another person's emotional experience and imagine their situation from their point of view without judgment. Since fear of being judged or treated differently is the top reason people are reluctant to open up about their mental health, especially at work, managers' ability to listen with empathy, to be fully present with no agenda, is a critical link in creating a culture of care.

To do this, offer team members your undivided attention, set aside any distractions, and keep comfortable personal space and eye contact. Aim to simply listen without evaluating. The goal is to connect with that person's emotional experience. When you notice your own judgments arising, refocus on your team member and what they are sharing with you. Keep your focus there, on the experience, not the outcome. You don't need to identify a problem or find a solution.

When Empathy isn't Enough:
Transforming Empathy into Compassion

Some people struggle to access their empathy. Others experience empathetic distress, which is having an aversive reaction to the suffering of others, leading to a desire to withdraw and protect oneself from another's negative feelings. As Wagner Denuzzo, former VP, Leadership and Management Development at IBM and the author of *Leading to Succeed,* has witnessed working with various teams, "It's very easy for a person who is empathic to become immersed in the emotions of the individual they're talking to and start taking on that person's mental health symptoms as their own."

When this is the case, tapping into compassion can help keep the conversation safe for both parties and transform the manager's experience from feeling *with* another person in need to feeling *motivated to help* them.

Think of the journey from empathy to compassion in three stages:

1. **Fostering empathy = Stepping in.** You offer your attention, and expand your circle of care by tuning into the feelings they express.
2. **Creating space = Stepping back.** When you notice empathic distress, distinguish between their experience and yours, and understand that showing care and concern doesn't mean we have to take on their emotions.
3. **Offering support = Stepping up.** Consider what you can confidently and appropriately offer, share the resources you can give, and remember that simply being present is of value.

If you start with empathy, or stepping in, by offering your attention and tuning into the feelings your team member is expressing, but then notice your own feelings or empathic distress cropping up, you can step back (metaphorically speaking). This gives you the brain space to remind yourself that their experience isn't yours. With that space, you can then step up to offer your support in the form of listening and sharing resources.

Responding with Compassion

Responding compassionately when someone shares a mental health struggle breaks the cycle of stigma and silence and makes it more likely they will seek support. Christopher Dysinger, Walgreens Vice President of Global Benefits, agrees. "Caring and compassion are at the core of mental health support. When employees feel supported in their mental health journey, they're more engaged and productive," he said.

To respond compassionately, express your care and compassion for their situation in your own words. Use mirroring language to reflect back what they shared with you, using the same words and phrases they used. Paraphrase what you understand from their situation. And finally, clarify with them to make sure that what you heard is correct, highlighting the key points and double-checking with them.

This facet of manager training is valuable for organizations on many levels, and particularly for big corporations, because you need multiple ways to translate care from the top levels of the organization down when you're dealing with large teams. Lee Lewis, Chief Strategy Officer and General Manager of Medical Solutions for the healthcare cooperative Health Transformation Alliance, said, "It's tough to be compassionate at scale. Executives are eager to help people in their organizations, but it's hard to disseminate care through enormous organizations with teams across time zones and continents, even when the benefits teams do a great job of communicating mental health programs' value." Managers who can respond with compassion become the linchpin to close any gaps in messaging, employee understanding, and care.

Empowering with Resources

After responding with compassion, we reach the final stage in the CARE framework: Empower with resources.

Keep these data points in mind: Despite the fact that 15% of global workers live with a mental health condition, and workplace stress has hit a record high, according to a 2022 Gallup report, only 2–3% of employees utilize the mental health services available to them at work. The more managers can encourage their team members to seek help when needed and be a source for them to find resources, the greater likelihood we have of improving these numbers and the lives of our team members all over.

So, first, express gratitude for the team member's willingness to be vulnerable, share their experience, and place trust in you. Check in by reaffirming your intent to support them and asking if they're open to you sharing resources that may help. Ask how you can support them further. Then, offer to keep checking in with them and keep communication open if they'd appreciate that.

Note that *none* of these steps or responses include diagnosing any-one, prying or probing for details, offering advice, suggesting treatments, minimizing or criticizing someone, or violating someone's privacy by sharing the information with HR or anyone else, unless necessary for someone's safety. These are inappropriate responses when someone is struggling and can have the opposite of the desired effect, making them close down or fearful of speaking up about their mental health again in the future.

Note, too, that the conversation must shift if a team member's situation escalates. If there are concerns for a team member's life or safety, managers should contact HR and emergency services immediately. (I've included a list of helpful resources and hotlines in the back of this book.)

Self-Regulating and Prioritizing Self-Care

When you're in the position of providing support to others often, which managers are, it's incredibly important to give yourself breaks and prac-tice self-compassion. The mental load of caring for others can take a real toll. Lesli Marasco has experienced this firsthand. The Vice President of Global Benefits and Well-Being at AbbVie, a pharmaceutical research and development company, Marasco said, "I've dealt with some difficult situations in HR, and it taught me how important it is for team managers and HR leaders to manage their own mental health. You can't help others if you're not taking care of yourself first."

RAIN is another easy framework to help you practice self-compas-sion when you realize these conversations are affecting you, and you're unable to show up for your colleagues as you'd like to:

1. **Recognize** what's happening, and name the emotions coming up for you.
2. **Allow** some space for things to be just as they are for a moment.
3. **Investigate** what the emotion is trying to tell you.
4. **Nurture** yourself with kindness and affirm your ability.

All of these point to self-regulation, or the skill of staying aware of yourself and your emotions. Beyond awareness, regulating involves the ability to manage your thoughts, feelings, and behaviors so that you show up with the energy and presence that the moment needs from you and what you need in the moment.

As hundreds of studies have affirmed, mindfulness practices can significantly strengthen our self-regulatory skills, which further reduces biases we may have and boosts our empathy toward others. Mental wellness and mindfulness classes offered by proactive mental health platforms and apps can be helpful partners in learning how to self-regulate. When you are well-regulated, not only do you feel better, but you also create a space where others can self-regulate more easily, too.

ADDITIONAL TRAINING AND CONSIDERATIONS

When you look at the stages in the CARE framework, you can see two throughlines underscoring every aspect of care: understanding and a lack of judgment. It's often easy to have understanding for people going through things we've been through ourselves. It's also easy to hold our judgment of someone else when they are similar to us as individuals. But managers cannot be understanding only of those with whom they feel the most kinship; they have to embody understanding for anyone who might come to them for help. While the CARE framework and similar empathy and active listening training help with this, anti-bias and diversity and inclusion trainings are others that organizations should provide so that managers better understand where their biases might show up, what to do when they notice them, and how to maintain an open and supportive environment for all team members no matter what.

Additionally, fostering an open environment where people feel supported in discussing their mental health can bring up challenging topics. Living in a time of increasingly divided politics, culture clashes, rapidly advancing technology, life-altering pandemics, global conflict, economic uncertainty, and extreme climate change—to name just a few concerns—prompts tricky conversations in the workplace that managers find themselves having to navigate, or even mediate, with their teams. By no means do managers need to be arbiters of team members' thoughts, opinions, or experiences, but ideally, we want them to be able to acknowledge the dynamics at play, hear where people are at, and help guide conversations to be safe for everyone involved. This is no small feat, and it makes training all the more important.

Each of these kinds of training are, ultimately, in service to your employees—which, according to Ali Hasan, the Commercial Director at AXA Health, makes them strategic imperatives for mental health programs. "When I think about people who understand the provision of mental health services in the workplace, the best leaders go far beyond the possession of technical knowledge and structural design experience," he said. "They implement effective strategies that truly—and measurably— support better outcomes for employees." Ensuring your managers and leaders at all levels receive training on all of these elements that affect employees' lives and experiences at work helps you truly support them.

EMPATHY BETWEEN EQUALS

There's a quote from Brené Brown that I love that helps remind me what my role is when people come to me for support:

> *Compassion is not a relationship between the healer and the wounded. It's a relationship between equals. Only when we know our own darkness well can we be present with the darkness of others. Compassion becomes real when we recognize our shared humanity.*

As Brown says, showing empathy and compassion for people is not about finding solutions or fixing the situation. It's also not about taking on people's pain as our own. It's about simply being with them and helping them feel that someone cares about what they're going through. When managers can do that, they help employees feel supported. They help promote wellbeing in their organizations. They help create a caring, proactive mental health culture.

EXERCISE
Manager Mental Health
Training & Support Assessment

This assessment will help you evaluate both your organization's current mental health training for managers and your personal readiness to support team members' mental wellbeing. Use these insights to identify areas for improvement in your organization's training programs and your own skill development.

Part 1: Organizational Assessment

Rate your organization's current mental health training and support for managers on a scale of 1 (strongly disagree) to 5 (strongly agree):

Our organization provides managers with:

- Basic mental health education and awareness training
  _____

- Training on recognizing signs of mental health struggles
  _____

- Guidance on having supportive conversations about mental health _____
- Clear protocols for crisis situations _____
- Regular updates about available mental health resources
  _____

- Training on maintaining boundaries while providing support _____
- Education on cultural factors affecting mental health
  _____

- Anti-bias and diversity training related to mental health
  _____

Total Score: _____ / 40

Scoring Key:
32–40: Comprehensive training program
24–31: Good foundation but room for improvement
16–23: Basic program needing significant enhancement
Below 16: Limited training requiring immediate attention

Part 2: Personal Readiness Assessment

Reflect on your own comfort and capability supporting team members' mental health.

How comfortable do you feel discussing mental health with your team members?
- Very comfortable
- Somewhat comfortable
- Neutral
- Somewhat uncomfortable
- Very uncomfortable

What aspects of mental health conversations are most challenging for you? List your top concerns:

What additional training or resources would help you feel more equipped to support your team's mental health?

On a scale of 1 to 5, where 1 = not at all confident and 5 = very confident, rate your confidence in:

- Recognizing signs of mental health struggles _____
- Creating psychological safety in conversations _____
- Listening without trying to "fix" _____
- Setting appropriate boundaries _____
- Directing people to mental health resources _____

What is one specific step you can take in the next month to improve your ability to support your team's mental health?

Consider reviewing this assessment periodically to track improvements in both organizational training and personal capabilities.

CHAPTER 11
THE ROLE OF POLICY AND ADVOCACY

Throughout this book, you've read multiple sections highlighting pivotal policies and procedures that support proactive mental health and bolster employee wellbeing in the workplace. At the organizational level, we've covered everything from foundational measures like ensuring that health insurance plans cover mental healthcare, counseling services, and substance abuse treatment to providing employees with regular assessments, to instituting organizational policies like ample paid time off, mental health days, and reasonable workloads. We've talked about guaranteeing the availability of digital proactive mental health tools no matter what physical space employees work in. And we've walked through other day-to-day practices like consistent mental health check-ins with employees, forward-thinking email practices, and messaging campaigns and digital reminders to utilize the proactive mental health tools available—among many other things.

These policies and practices aren't just nice-to-haves; they're the building blocks that make a real difference in the lives of employees and their loved ones. They raise awareness, reduce stigma, and turn mental health from an abstract concept into a tangible, manageable thing for every person. These measures transform team dynamics and company cultures, allowing for people to get the support they need, support others better in turn, and as a result, bring their best, healthiest, most creative selves to the table.

They also, incidentally, serve as advocacy measures for proactive mental health more broadly. By instituting mental health policies and raising awareness internally, organizations can drive meaningful change within their communities, advance socio-cultural systemic change surrounding mental health norms, and help improve mental health outcomes for all. That said, we must also have policies promoting mental health *outside* the workplace to drive even greater change. This chapter explores the importance of proactive mental health policy and advocacy in and out of the workplace as well as key areas for greater policy development, strategies for effective advocacy, and some of the dedicated organizations doing great advocacy work already.

THE BROADER SIGNIFICANCE OF PROACTIVE MENTAL HEALTH IN THE WORKPLACE

At the base level, instituting organizational proactive mental health policies ensures that employees and their loved ones have access to the mental health services they need. However, as even the WHO wrote in its latest World Mental Health Report, when workplaces put proactive mental health policies in place, it turns out, they don't just serve the people in those workplaces; they also pave the way for more proactive mental health policies elsewhere. As more and more organizations get on board, it creates a ripple effect, promoting awareness and access to care beyond individual organizations and into communities on a larger scale. This only encourages wider discussions about mental health, which can facilitate greater support for action in the public sector, leading to, for example, increased funding for mental health programs, both proactive and reactive, as well as more mental health education in schools, and mental health training programs for professionals in healthcare, human resources, leadership, management, education, and more. Proactive mental health policies in organizations—especially those addressing discrimination and protecting privacy—also help protect the rights of individuals with mental health conditions, ensuring that they receive fair and equitable treatment.

Michelle Blair-Medeiros, the Employee Engagement Program Manager for the California Department of Human Resources (CalHR), sees this as a crucial point. "We often think of mental health as something personal, but in reality, it's shaped by broader social conditions," Blair-Medeiros told me. "The work we do to promote mental health among employees is about bringing those two together to create better outcomes for everyone."

The cumulative effect of increased proactive mental health in organizations helps spur systemic change by increasing attention on the issues at the root of mental health conditions, including important social determinants of health like housing, education, and employment. When expansive mental healthcare isn't already codified in government legislation, as is the case in many countries and communities, organizations with robust proactive mental health policies can serve as the model for governments and public agencies in creating policies on a macro level, improving access to care, protecting the rights of individuals with mental health conditions, and promoting mental health awareness more broadly.

KEY AREAS FOR INCREASED POLICY DEVELOPMENT

Even with robust proactive mental health policies in organizations, we need more policy development in several key areas at the public level that can improve mental healthcare broadly and support proactive mental health strategies.

Mental Health Parity

Mental health parity policies ensure that mental health services are covered by insurance plans on par with physical health services, which helps improve access to care and reduces financial barriers for individuals seeking mental health services. For example, the Mental Health Parity and Addiction Equity Act in the United States requires insurance plans to provide equal coverage for mental health and substance use disorder services—but that's just the beginning. As discussed in Chapter 6, Employing a Global Perspective, many countries throughout the EU have passed legislation covering a wider array of services. In regions with reduced social stigma surrounding mental health, legislative parity is easier to come by. Many other regions, however, have yet to create such laws, and even in the United States, despite having legislation for mental health–physical health parity, coverage for mental healthcare is still limited in certain areas and finding quality, affordable coverage isn't always easy.

That's to say nothing of the remaining stigma or limiting cultural perspectives, which Noah Morgan, the Vice President of Benefits and Wellness at Goldman Sachs, brought up when I spoke with him. "Getting people to see mental health as equally as important as physical health remains one of the biggest challenges," he said. That goes for individual employees, full organizations, regional cultures, and governments alike.

Integrating Mental Health into Primary Care

Integrating mental healthcare into primary care improves access to care and reduces stigma. What does that look like? To start, having policies that support the integration of mental health screening, assessment, and treatment into primary care settings. For instance, policies that provide funding for training primary care providers in mental healthcare can enhance the integration of mental and physical health services.

It can help shift the approach of some medical providers where necessary, too. The VP of Total Rewards for the furniture and design company MillerKnoll, Bill Tompkins, shared a story with me about a medical doctor he'd previously worked with at a major global beverage company. This physician had realized that traditional medical training doesn't prepare doctors to help people thrive; it focuses mostly on fixing what's broken. "But," Tompkins said, "we need to focus on keeping people healthy and helping them thrive. That's where mental health plays a critical role in wellbeing strategies." The doctor ended up spending as much time out of the clinic working on mental wellbeing in corporate settings as he did working with patients because he felt so strongly about the difference that mental healthcare creates in people's lives and overall health. Integrating mental health more thoroughly into primary care could allow more doctors like Tompkins' former colleague to help patients thrive and more patients to get the well-rounded care they deserve.

Youth Mental Health

Youth mental health has become an increasingly alarming concern around the world in recent years. Just look at the statistics: According to the WHO, depression, anxiety, and behavioral disorders are among the leading causes of illness and disability among adolescents, and suicide is the fourth-leading cause of death among young people aged 15 to 29. In fact, 13% of the global burden of disease among 10- to 19-year-olds can be attributed to mental disorders, which affect 1 in 7 teens worldwide. Just last year, U.S. Surgeon General Dr. Vivek Murthy issued an advisory warning about the effects of social media on the mental health of children and teens, noting the growing prevalence of mental health disorders among youth alongside the growth of social media's presence in their and our daily lives.

Policies can play a major role here. Instituting policies that support youth mental health promotes early intervention and preventive care. This includes policies that provide funding for mental health programs in schools, support mental health education, and promote access to counseling services. As Dr. Murthy recommends, it could also include governmental regulations and health warnings on social media platforms, which disproportionately affect teens and the effects of which are as of yet under-studied and under-regulated.

Community-Based Mental Health

Finally, we have community-based mental health, an approach that views mental health disorders as layered issues that both affect and are affected by communities surrounding individuals instead of as issues relegated to individuals alone. This approach focuses on the human rights and recovery of the individuals struggling with mental health, aiming to deliver collective aid and solutions.

Dr. Randy Martin, the clinical director of the CopeNYP EAP at Weill Cornell Medicine, learned the importance of community-based mental health early in his career. "I worked in a community mental health center, and it really showed me how much impact we could have by meeting people where they are—offering therapy and support right in the heart of the community," Martin told me. "It wasn't about waiting for people to come to us when they were in crisis. It was about being proactive, offering resources, and creating a network of care that supported people before things got worse."

As such, community-based mental health policies can improve access to care and provide culturally sensitive support. This can include policies that support training for community health workers, funding for community-based programs, and the development of community mental health centers that Dr. Martin spoke of. For example, Brazil's community-based approach, mentioned in Chapter 6, included setting up community mental health centers known as the Centro de Atenção Psicossocial (or CAPS III). These centers, funded by the federal and municipal governments, provide 24/7 mental health services and crisis support to adults and children in settings designed to mimic homes. They also host community events open to the public.

ENGAGING IN EFFECTIVE ADVOCACY

Purposeful advocacy can make a big difference in the realm of mental health. Beyond the passive accumulation of awareness through greater numbers of organizations implementing mental health programs, organizations and leaders can advocate for mental health proactively as well.

Building coalitions and partnerships with other organizations, healthcare providers, and community groups can amplify advocacy efforts for mental health policy initiatives and create a stronger voice for change.

Running public awareness campaigns, social media outreach, and community events centered on mental health can engage the public and build support for more policy initiatives. Engaging policymakers and advocating for mental health policies at the local, state, and national levels can make a great difference. This can include meeting with policymakers, providing testimony at hearings, and submitting policy recommendations. Additionally, empowering individuals within your organization with the education and resources to advocate for the mental health of their communities, whether through organizing public meetings or writing to policymakers, for example, can help create a grassroots movement for change.

TOP U.S. MENTAL HEALTH ADVOCACY ORGANIZATIONS TODAY

Thankfully, outside of the private sector, there are several organizations and initiatives successfully advocating for mental health policies already. This list only covers select organizations within the U.S., but you can find organizations across every country and region doing incredible work to promote mental health within their communities.

Mental Health America (MHA) is a leading community-based advocacy organization that works to promote mental health policies and raise awareness about mental health issues in the United States. MHA advocates for policies that improve access to care, protect the rights of individuals with mental health conditions, and promote mental health awareness. The organization also provides resources and tools for individuals and organizations to advocate for mental health policies, including policy recommendations, advocacy toolkits, and opportunities for public engagement.

The **National Alliance on Mental Illness (NAMI)** is a grassroots organization that advocates for mental health policies at the local, state, and national levels, focusing on policies that improve access to care, promote early intervention, and protect the rights of individuals with mental health conditions. The organization also provides education, support, and advocacy for individuals with mental health conditions and their families as well as resources and training for individuals to advocate for mental health policies within their own communities.

The **World Health Organization (WHO)** works to promote health around the world, address global health challenges, and advocate for universal health coverage, including for mental health. The WHO's Mental Health Action Plan specifically provides a framework for developing and implementing mental health policies, with a focus on promoting mental health, preventing mental health conditions, and expanding access to care. The organization collaborates with governments, organizations, and stakeholders to advocate for mental health policies and raise awareness about mental health issues.

AFFECTING GREATER CHANGE FOR THE FUTURE

The path to better mental health clearly isn't just about what happens behind closed doors in therapy sessions or one-on-one, doctor-patient assessments. It's also about the policies we create, the conversations we have, and the way we advocate for change in our workplaces and communities. Whether you're an employee, a manager, or a CEO, you have the power to make a difference. The journey to get there won't be a sprint but a marathon. Like any long race, it will require persistence, adaptability, and teamwork. As we move forward, we have to remember that every small step counts. From normalizing mental health discussions in your team meetings to lobbying for better mental health coverage in your local government, it all furthers the cause. Together, we can build a future where proactive mental health isn't a progressive move for companies at the forefront of a movement, but rather a fundamental part of how we live and work.

EXERCISE
Mental Health Advocacy Assessment

Now, evaluate your organization's current mental health advocacy efforts and identify opportunities to create greater impact, both within your organization and beyond.

Rate your organization's current mental health advocacy efforts on a scale of 1 (not at all) to 5 (extensively):

Internal Advocacy:

- Has comprehensive mental health policies that exceed legal requirements_____
- Openly communicates about mental health initiatives and resources_____
- Provides mental health education and awareness programming_____
- Ensures mental health benefits are on par with physical health coverage_____
- Creates structural support for mental wellbeing (break spaces, etc.) _____

External Advocacy:

- Partners with mental health organizations or initiatives _____
- Participates in community mental health events or programs_____
- Engages with policymakers on mental health issues _____
- Shares mental health resources with the broader community_____

- Supports employees' mental health advocacy efforts

  _____

Total Score: _____/ 50

Scoring Key:

40–50: Excellent—Your organization has a strong, supportive mental health culture.

30–39: Good—Your organization is on the right track but has room for improvement.

20–29: Fair—Your organization needs significant improvements in its mental health culture

10-19: Poor—Your organization urgently needs to prioritize mental health initiatives.

What areas present the greatest opportunities for expanding your organization's advocacy efforts?

Which mental health policy areas are you most passionate about? (Check all that apply)

- ☐ Mental health parity in insurance coverage
- ☐ Integration of mental health into primary care
- ☐ Youth mental health initiatives
- ☐ Community-based mental health programs
- ☐ Workplace mental health policies

☐   Other: _____

What specific changes would you like to see in . . .
- Your workplace:

- Your local community:

- Your state/country:

3. What resources or support would help you become a more effective mental health advocate?

4. What is one concrete action you can take in the next month to advance mental health advocacy in your sphere of influence?

Every step toward better mental health policies and awareness, no matter how small, contributes to meaningful change.

CHAPTER 12

PRACTICAL MENTAL HEALTH STRATEGIES FOR INDIVIDUALS

This whole book has focused on the importance of implementing proactive mental health in organizations, as well as the strategies for how to do so. But a big part of being proactive about our mental health is our commitment to consistent, preventive practices as individuals. In other words, what we do daily, weekly, and in particularly sensitive or uncertain moments to support our own mental health.

While not exhaustive in the slightest, this chapter aims to give an overview of some of the personal mental health practices people can do on their own to help take care of their mental wellbeing every day.

PROACTIVE SELF-CARE PRACTICES

There are several ways to approach self-care and proactive mental health on a personal level.

Mindfulness and Meditation

Mindfulness and meditation practices vary widely, each offering unique benefits. While many forms emphasize awareness of the present moment—observing thoughts, emotions, and sensations as they arise—

others focus on visualization, mantras (words, phrases, or sounds repeated during the practice), or cultivating a sense of compassion or gratitude. Rather than seeking to eliminate thoughts or feelings, these practices typically encourage building a more conscious, non-judgmental relationship with them. Over time, those who regularly engage in mindfulness or meditation may experience benefits like improved self-regulation, a sense of balance, and greater self-awareness.

More than that, in fact: According to the American Psychological Association, over 200 studies with over 12,000 participants have found mindfulness practices to be incredibly effective at managing and reducing stress, anxiety, and depression among healthy adults. Mindfulness and meditation have also been proven to help treat chronic pain and substance misuse. In our early days, Journey conducted a clinical study on meditation with neuroscientist Dr. Wendy Suzuki at New York University, which showed that participants demonstrated significant reductions in stress, increases in focus, and improvements in mood.

Thankfully, finding resources for mindfulness and meditation practices is very easy today. Dozens of apps offer guided meditation sessions that can help individuals incorporate mindfulness into their daily routines. For example, setting aside just five minutes a day for meditation can significantly reduce stress and improve overall wellbeing. Additionally, many cities have meditation centers where people can participate in group mindfulness and meditation classes, which also provide the built-in community and accountability that are helpful for creating new mental health habits. As I shared early in the book, meditation sessions were among my first forays into proactive mental health practices—before I even knew what that meant—and they changed my mental wellbeing, and my entire life, in hugely beneficial ways.

Mental health practitioners may also recommend more specific mindfulness-based therapeutic interventions, including mindfulness-based stress reduction (MBSR) and mindfulness-based cognitive therapy (MBCT), which may be more effective for certain people. MBSR involves weekly group mindfulness sessions and daily individual exercises, as well as yoga and meditation, completed over a multi-week period. MBCT combines elements of MBSR and cognitive behavioral therapy

(CBT)—a talk-therapy practice focused on identifying and changing harmful or persistent thought patterns that affect our behavior—to treat people with depression. If you're curious about MBSR or MBCT, please consult a mental health professional.

Physical Activity

While obviously crucial for physical health, regular physical activity and exercise are essential for mental health, too. Exercise releases endorphins, our bodies' natural mood boosters. Commonly called the "feel good" chemicals, endorphins reduce perceptions of pain and increase pleasure and positive emotions in our bodies. Exercise also releases other positive chemicals—neurotransmitters like serotonin, dopamine, and norepinephrine, which help boost our mood, motivation, focus, and arousal. Multiple studies have shown that increasing all of these neurochemicals through exercise can help reduce and prevent symptoms of anxiety and depression. At the same time, exercise also reduces our bodies' levels of stress hormones, like cortisol and adrenaline, and generates new neurons in our brains, which improves overall brain function—both critical factors in maintaining our mental health.

Beyond the chemicals released in our brains, regular physical activity improves our sleep, and when we sleep better, our mental health improves. Exercise can also improve our self-esteem and help us feel physically stronger and more capable, all of which helps improve and maintain positive mental health.

Incorporating physical activity into your daily life doesn't mean that you need to start running marathons or get on a training plan. It simply means moving your body in ways that feel good and are accessible to you. Even taking a walk to get away from your desk in the middle of the day is one great way to proactively take care of your mental wellbeing through physical activity.

Healthy Eating

In the same way that our physical health and physical activity intersect with our mental health, so does our nutrition. More specifically, recent research has highlighted the connection between our digestive system and our mental health. Research shared by the American Psychological Association shows that the microorganisms in our intestines play a crucial role in producing some of the same neurochemicals essential for regulating both our physical and psychological functions mentioned above. It's estimated that a remarkable majority—around 95%—of the body's serotonin is actually produced by bacteria in the gut. Additionally, studies suggest that stress may have a negative effect on the beneficial bacteria in our digestive system, potentially creating a cyclical relationship between gut health and mental state.

Being proactive about our mental health, then, includes eating healthily and making sure our diet includes a balanced variety of fruits, vegetables, whole grains, fats, and proteins that will support brain function and emotional wellbeing. Staying hydrated and limiting the intake of caffeine and sugar can also help stabilize mood and energy levels.

Getting Adequate Sleep

Sleep is our bodies' time to rest, regroup, process memories and emotions, incorporate things we've learned, and create new neural pathways. Needless to say, it's important. As such, when we don't sleep well, studies have shown it can affect our mental health in numerous ways. Poor sleep can exacerbate symptoms of anxiety, depression, and PTSD, among other mood disorders. Meanwhile, getting quality sleep can improve mood, cognitive function, and overall wellbeing. The links are clear.

To promote better sleep, and by extension your mental health, work to improve your sleep conditions. Establish a regular sleep routine, create a restful sleep environment, and avoid screens before bedtime. Developing a calming bedtime routine, such as reading, drinking herbal tea, or listening to soothing music, and aiming to get seven to nine hours of sleep each night—or however many hours your body naturally needs—can all help improve sleep quality and aid your mental health, too.

Engaging with Your Hobbies and Interests

Research has shown that engaging in hobbies that bring joy and fulfillment can have significant positive effects on mental health and overall wellbeing. A comprehensive study published in *Nature Medicine* in 2023 explored this connection, analyzing data from over 93,000 adults aged 65 and older across 16 countries. Over a period of four to eight years, researchers found that those who regularly engaged in hobbies they enjoyed reported better health outcomes, increased happiness, fewer depressive symptoms, and greater life satisfaction compared to those without hobbies.

While not causal, the results showed that activities such as arts and crafts, gaming, gardening, volunteering, or participating in clubs, for example, offer benefits like creativity, sensory engagement, self-expression, relaxation, and cognitive stimulation—all of which improve mental health. Additionally, the social connections formed through group hobbies may help combat loneliness and isolation, further contributing to improved overall wellbeing.

Whether you prefer painting, playing a musical instrument, or cooking, setting aside time each week to engage in a hobby or pastime outside of work is a great way to proactively and positively impact your mental health.

Journaling

Making time to write down our thoughts and feelings might seem simple, but it's actually one of the most evidence-backed ways to support our mental health. A 2022 analysis of several scientific studies found that expressive writing—the practice of writing deeply about emotional experiences—can reduce symptoms of anxiety and depression, help process stress and trauma, and improve overall psychological wellbeing.

Additional research from 2018 has demonstrated that regular journaling can help reduce mental distress and increase resilience. This is well-documented across various populations and people of all backgrounds, professions, and socioeconomic categories, too. One 2013 study found that people who engaged in expressive writing for just 20 minutes over three consecutive days showed significant decreases in depressive symptoms, with improvements lasting at least four weeks.

The best part of all of this is, you don't need a doctor or therapist to facilitate journaling for you, nor do you need special training or equipment to begin. All you need is something to write on and with—whether a paper and pen, or your phone or laptop. While some people prefer structured prompts or gratitude journaling, others prefer something more free-form, writing whatever comes to mind and following their thoughts as they go. What's most important is finding an approach that feels comfortable and sustainable for you.

To gain the most benefit from journaling, mental health professionals often recommend setting aside 15-20 minutes a few times per week to write about your thoughts, feelings, or experiences without judgment or concern for grammar or structure—but even just a few minutes a day can help.

Taking Occasional Breaks

Speaking of areas where even a few minutes can help us, taking regular breaks from work, even short ones, is another vital practice for maintaining our mental health. Research has shown that our brains are designed to respond to short bursts of stress rather than prolonged periods of intense focus. When we work for extended periods without breaks, our mental resources become depleted, leading to decreased productivity and increased risk of burnout. So, while it may seem counterintuitive at first, stepping away from tasks actually helps us perform better.

Plenty of studies back this up. A 2017 study by a group of psychologists found that five-minute breaks improved attention and performance on cognitive tasks compared to working straight through. Other research has shown that breaks are most effective when taken in the morning, before our mental resources are most depleted. One pair of researchers who surveyed administrative workers in 2016 on their workday break habits found that those who took breaks to do something enjoyable reported fewer physical health symptoms like headaches and eye strain, as well as higher job satisfaction and lower burnout rates—and those benefits increased when they took breaks in the morning rather than at midday or in the afternoon.

To maximize the benefits of breaks, experts recommend choosing activities that are different from your work tasks. Go for a walk, get some light exercise, or read a novel for a few minutes. Simply gazing out a window can actually help restore mental energy. The key is making breaks a regular priority rather than pushing through until exhaustion sets in.

Spending Time in Nature

You might even want to think about taking your hobby outside to reap the countless mental health benefits of spending time in nature. Numerous scientific studies over many years have shown that exposure to natural environments can reduce stress, anxiety, and depression in addition to improving overall mood and cognitive function. It doesn't take much, either. Spending as little as five minutes in nature can help regulate our nervous system and alleviate stress.

There are a few possible reasons for this. For one, time outdoors, even in urban settings, often involves physical activity, which releases mood-boosting endorphins and improves our overall wellbeing. Second, natural settings provide a respite from the constant stimulation many of us experience in cities and urban environments, which allows our minds to rest and recover. This aligns with attention restoration theory, which posits that nature offers a restorative sensory environment that alleviates the cognitive fatigue we get from periods of focused thinking—likely a common experience at work. Moreover, exposure to green spaces has been linked to improved sleep quality, increased happiness, and enhanced creativity.

For city-dwellers with limited access to the outdoors, even small doses of nature can be beneficial. Urban parks, gardens, and indoor plants can provide some of the mental health benefits of larger natural environments. One study found that merely having a *view* of a park or green space can, essentially, trick our brain into believing our surroundings are less noisy, and therefore more calming, than they are.

By making a conscious effort to incorporate nature into our routines—whether through lunchtime walks in a nearby park, weekend hikes, or tending to houseplants—we can harness the restorative power of the natural world for our mental wellbeing.

Spending Time with Friends and Loved Ones

People often think of self-care as things we do alone, and clearly, as evidenced by many of the listed items above, many self-care practices can be done by ourselves. However, it's also a form of self-care to spend time with our friends and loved ones—and a powerful one at that. Research has consistently shown that stable, healthy friendships are crucial for our wellbeing and longevity. A 2020 review of 38 different studies on adult friendships found that people with close social connections report greater life satisfaction and wellbeing and are less likely to experience anxiety and depression. This backs up earlier studies showing that they also have a lower risk of premature death from various causes, including heart problems and chronic diseases.

This seems to make sense implicitly, but there's science to explain why. As it turns out, being with friends changes our stress responses. For instance, studies have found that having a supportive friend nearby during challenging tasks can lower heart rate reactivity and blood pressure. In some cases, we may even view the task as less difficult than it objectively is. Interestingly, even casual interactions with acquaintances can boost our mental wellbeing: A study in 2014 found people tend to be happier on days when they have more interactions with "weak ties"—a.k.a. individuals we know but aren't close to, such as the barista we buy coffee from every morning, the UPS delivery worker on our route, or the corner crossing guard we say "hi" to when dropping off and picking up our kids from school.

Psychology professor Catherine Bagwell, who teaches at Davidson College in the United States and has studied the mental health implications of social interaction in her own work, validated the reports in an interview for the American Psychological Association's monthly magazine. "In the face of life's challenges, having a close friend to turn to seems to be a buffer or protective factor against some of the negative outcomes we might otherwise see," she said. By prioritizing time with friends, nurturing close friendships, and cultivating social connections—even brief encounters with acquaintances—we can harness these mental health benefits.

Strategies for Building Resilience

Resilience is the ability to bounce back from adversity and cope with challenges. Having strong resilience can help people move through difficult moments and challenges better, and therefore maintain their mental wellbeing throughout.

Certain industries—particularly fast-paced, high-growth sectors like tech, law, and finance—place a strong emphasis on resilience-building as a mental health tool. While this focus can be valuable, it's important to ensure that resilience-building programs align with a broader culture of support and well-being, rather than inadvertently reinforcing high-pressure environments. For resilience-building efforts to be truly effective, they should complement other initiatives that foster sustainable workloads, psychological safety, and a positive workplace culture.

However, building resilience is also genuinely necessary. High-intensity work in stressful or volatile environments does require people to have real endurance and fortitude in order to maintain strong performance amid challenges. The reality is, too, that challenges will come up no matter what industry you're in, so having skills around resilience is helpful whatever your role. To Rich Krutsch, President of the U.S. Employers division at Abett, a large healthcare analytics software company, this is critical in a workforce. "We need to teach employees how to build mental health resilience. It's not just about offering counseling services;

it's also about helping people develop the skills they need to handle stress and adversity," he said.

Plain and simple, resilience is important for mental health, and many individuals reap innumerable benefits from resilience-building practices. Simply Human's Jill Santercier, a member of Harvard University's Global Flourishing At Work Network, swears by them. "Being rooted in resilience has been my guiding principle, both personally and at work," she told me. "Furthermore, creating environments that foster resilience can have a profound impact on mental health."

Whether it's something a company encourages and provides support for, or something individuals do entirely on their own, there are practices and skills that can help people become more resilient over time. Here are a few:

1. **Cultivating a positive mindset** involves focusing on strengths, practicing gratitude, and reframing negative thoughts. Practicing mindfulness or keeping a gratitude journal can help people shift their focus to positive elements of their lives.

2. **Setting realistic and achievable goals** can provide direction and motivation. Breaking larger goals into smaller, manageable steps can make them feel more attainable and reduce feelings of overwhelm.

3. **Building strong relationships**—with family, friends, colleagues, neighbors, etc.—helps give us the social support and sense of belonging we can rely on when we're struggling. Making time for regular social activities and reaching out for support when needed can strengthen these connections. For example, scheduling weekly coffee dates with friends or participating in community groups can enhance social support and wellbeing.

4. **Practicing self-compassion**, and being kind to yourself, especially during difficult times, is an important aspect of resilience. Beating oneself up for mistakes or emotional distress and muscling through will not help you regain your footing. Instead, recognizing that everyone makes mistakes and that setbacks are a natural part of life helps us learn that we can get up again after a tough time and encourages us to keep going. Practicing self-compassion involves affirming our self-worth and treating ourselves with the same kindness and understanding that we would extend to a friend.

5. **Reflecting on past challenges** allows us to identify lessons learned and gain valuable insights to help us cope in future challenges. Viewing challenges as opportunities for growth in this way can strengthen our resilience as we move forward.

Seeking Further Support

No matter how diligent we are with our mindset, personal proactive mental health practices, and resilience-building efforts, sometimes we may need additional help. That is a normal part of mental health management, and there are many services individuals can take advantage of.

Professional counseling and therapy can provide evidence-based interventions to help manage symptoms of mental health conditions and develop coping strategies, or even simply help you learn more about your psychology and improve your relationship with yourself and your thoughts. Your health insurance company should have a list of in-network therapists in your area. Your organization's EAP should also provide short-term confidential counseling and support services for employees and their families. These counselors can provide referrals to other mental health professionals as needed as well as additional resources for managing stress and individual mental health.

Support groups offer another option to help maintain strong individual mental health. Whether ERGs or peer support groups at work or elsewhere, groups like these can provide a sense of understanding, a safe space to share experiences, and the support of individuals facing similar challenges.

If, however, you find yourself in serious distress or in need of immediate support, there are several hotlines and crisis support services available to help you. I have provided a list of crisis support hotlines at the end of the book.

EXERCISE
Mental Health Self-Assessment

Understanding your current mental health status as an individual is an important step in your proactive mental health journey, regardless of your organization's mental health initiatives.

This brief self-assessment will help you gauge your current mental wellbeing. While it's not a diagnostic tool, it can provide insights into areas that may need attention. Remember, if you have concerns about your mental health, it's always best to consult with a mental health professional.

Rate each statement on a scale of 1 to 5, where
1 = "strongly disagree" and 5 = "strongly agree".

1. I often feel overwhelmed by daily tasks. _____
2. I have trouble sleeping or experience changes in my sleep patterns. _____
3. I find it difficult to concentrate on work or other activities. _____
4. I frequently feel anxious or worried. _____
5. I have lost interest in activities I used to enjoy. _____
6. I often feel irritable or easily frustrated. _____
7. I experience physical symptoms like headaches or stomach issues when stressed. _____
8. I have difficulty maintaining relationships with friends or family. _____
9. I often feel lonely or isolated. _____
10. I struggle to maintain a work-life balance. _____

Add up your total score: _____

Your total score indicates the level of risk that you may have, or may develop, a mental health condition or concern. Here's how the scores break down:

10-20: Low risk
21-30: Moderate risk
31-40: High risk
41-50: Very high risk

If your score is in the "high risk" or "very high risk" range, please consider seeking professional support. A list of resources can be found in the back of this book.

BONUS EXERCISE
Develop a Personal Mental Health Plan

If you don't already have a consistent proactive mental health practice—or if you want to approach yours more intentionally—it's a great idea to develop a personal mental health plan.

Start by reflecting on your current personal mental health practices to learn how effectively you are managing your wellbeing today and where there may be opportunities for improvement:

1. What proactive mental health practices do you currently use?
2. What aspects of these practices do you appreciate the most?
3. How effective are these practices in managing your stress and wellbeing?

Now, identify what other actions or next steps would make the most sense for you:

1. **Identify your stressors.** List the primary sources of stress in your life:

2. **Set targets for change.** Define certain changes and improvements you'd like to see in your mental health over the next few months (e.g. better sleep, reduced work stress, reduced overall stress, less anxiety around finances, etc.)

3. **Choose strategies.** Select up to three new or different proactive mental health strategies to add to your personal practice to achieve the targets you set above (e.g. set a sleep schedule, meditate daily, journal, etc.)

4. **Create a schedule.** Plan when and how often you'd like to practice these activities and techniques.

5. **Check in.** Is there anything else you need to facilitate your proactive mental health practice?

Consider keeping a journal of your experience and/or tracking your progress so you can keep in touch with what works best for you.

Remember, your plan can change. If you find the techniques or schedule you set now don't work for you or don't fit into your daily life, try something else and make as many adjustments as needed. It might be helpful to return to this reflection periodically to track how your personal proactive mental health practice evolves over time and learn what you find most useful.

CLOSING THOUGHTS

As we reflect on the trajectory of mental health support in organizations, it's clear we've come a long way. From the days when mental health was shrouded in overwhelming misunderstanding and stigma, we've progressed to an era where mental health is increasingly recognized as essential for individual and organizational wellbeing—and not just reactive mental health, but proactive mental health, too. This shift didn't happen overnight; it's the result of decades of research, advocacy, and changing cultural attitudes.

Today, we're witnessing a surge in proactive mental health initiatives within organizations. Companies are realizing that supporting employee mental health isn't just the right thing to do, it's also a strategic imperative. Employees, too, are raising their expectations. They're looking for workplaces that prioritize mental wellbeing and work-life harmony, offer comprehensive support, and create cultures where it's safe to be their full selves and discuss mental health openly.

This evolving landscape is paving the way for exciting trends in proactive mental health everywhere. We're moving toward more personalized approaches within organizations as well as our healthcare systems, leveraging scientific advances and data analytics to tailor interventions to individual needs. The artificial intelligence boom is accelerating this trend, with AI-powered tools offering personalized recommendations and support based on vast amounts of data.

Simultaneously, we're seeing a growing recognition of the intricate connection between physical and mental health. The future of healthcare is likely to be more integrated, treating the mind and body as inter-connected systems rather than separate entities. This holistic approach extends to the increasingly wider acceptance and adoption of integrative therapies like mindfulness, yoga, and nutrition counseling as comple-mentary tools for mental wellbeing.

Preventive mental health practices are also becoming more wide-spread, with regular mental health check-ins being integrated into pri-mary care settings, including annual physical exams. This shift towards prevention is a game-changer, promising to help reduce the incidence and severity of mental health issues before they escalate.

Technology, of course, is playing a pivotal role in transforming men-tal healthcare. As we explored in earlier chapters, digital platforms and apps are making mental health support more accessible—and widely accepted—than ever. Looking ahead, we can expect even more inno-vative applications of technology; the possibilities within virtual and augmented reality alone show great promise in treating anxiety disor-ders and PTSD through immersive exposure therapy. However, as we embrace these technological advancements, we cannot lose sight of the definitive issues they raise. Issues of data privacy, technological misuse, and wrongful intervention, the potential for algorithmic bias, and the importance of maintaining human connection in mental healthcare will need ongoing attention and careful navigation.

The future of proactive mental health isn't just about new tech-nologies, either; it's also about fostering supportive communities and environments. I'm hopeful that we will see more community-based ap-proaches to mental health and more investment in community-building generally, recognizing that wellbeing isn't solely an individual respon-sibility but a collective one and that our social support systems are, in fact, the lifeblood of a mentally healthy society. I also hope to see en-hanced global collaboration on proactive mental healthcare. As mental health challenges transcend borders, so too must our solutions and our commitment to combating the stigma that persists surrounding mental health in so many corners of the world. International knowledge-sharing and collaborative research efforts can accelerate progress and ensure that effective strategies are disseminated widely.

Policy and advocacy will play a vital role in shaping this future. We need robust policies that mandate mental health coverage in insurance plans, integrate mental healthcare into primary care settings, protect the rights of individuals with mental health conditions, and further institutionalize proactive, preventive care in workplaces and communities of all kinds. Advocacy efforts from organizations will be essential in pushing for these changes, as will education and training. We need to equip not just mental health professionals, but also leaders, managers, educators, and the general public with the knowledge and skills to support mental wellbeing proactively. Mental health literacy should be as fundamental as physical health education in our schools and workplaces.

I envision a world where mental health is treated with the same seriousness and urgency as physical health. A world where proactive mental health practices are woven into the fabric of our daily lives, our workplaces, and our communities. A world where seeking support for mental health is as natural and understood as going to the doctor for a physical ailment. This future isn't just a pipedream; it's a possibility we can actively work towards. By implementing the strategies discussed in this book, by advocating for better policies, and by fostering supportive cultures in our workplaces and communities, organizations everywhere can help realize this vision and bring about better outcomes and better lives for everyone.

ACKNOWLEDGMENTS

Writing this book has been an extraordinary journey, and I could not have completed it without the support, inspiration, and contributions of so many remarkable people.

To my wife, Ita; my mother, Sheryl; my brother, David; and my son, Sam:

I am nothing without you. You mean the world to me, and I am eternally grateful for your never-ending love and support. I love you more than words can say.

To my grandmother, Miriam:

Your wisdom, love, and guidance continue to shape who I am, and you are with me every single day. The lessons you taught me are a part of everything I do, and your spirit lives on in my heart and actions.

To my entire family:

Thank you for teaching me so many lessons about what life is all about. From you, I have learned the values of hard work, perseverance, and strength. I am forever grateful for all you have done to shape me into the person I am today.

To Marjie Shrimpton, my fearless collaborator:

Thank you for your unwavering dedication, creativity, and insight. Your partnership brought clarity and heart to this book, and I am endlessly grateful for your belief in this vision and your incredible contributions.

To my teachers, coaches, and mentors—David Nichtern, Sharon Salzberg, Ben Seaman, Bryan Franklin, and so many more:

Thank you for your patience, guidance, and wisdom. You gently showed me the way when I couldn't see it myself, and your lessons continue to shape my path.

To the communities I've been lucky enough to be part of—Reality, Summit, AJC, Breakout, Junto, Evryman, Medi Club, Vipassana, Vistage, Venwise, YPO, and countless others:

These communities have been spaces of profound growth, connection, and learning. Thank you for helping me connect deeply with others and discover more about myself.

To all the team members at Journey, past and present:

Your tireless efforts, passion, and commitment to making the world a better place inspire me every day. I am deeply grateful for each of you and the incredible work you do to bring our mission to life.

To all the Journey investors, advisors, consultants, and contributors, past and present:

Thank you for your invaluable contributions of time, money, energy, and support—whether one or all of the above. Your belief in this mission has been instrumental in shaping what Journey is today, and for that, I am profoundly grateful.

To Claude, Kristen, Charles & Chris:

Thank you for believing in us and me, and for your unwavering support. Your trust, insights, and encouragement have been instrumental in bringing our vision to life.

To Peter, Erika, Michelle, Elizabeth, Eddie, Geetika, Barbara, Marco, Randy, Desiree, Lisa, David, Christine, Chris, Elisha, Ali, Lee, Yvell, Danielle, Shawnte, Jeff, Joel, Lauren, Marcela, Amy, Noah, Jae, Sandy, Wagner, Lesli, Ali, Michelle, Bill, Jill, Rich, Bayard, Wolfgang, Yvonne, Erin, Joe:

I am deeply grateful for your willingness to share your time, insights, and expertise. Your contributions have brought this book to life. Thank you for your generosity and support.

To all the HR leaders who have shared their insights with me over the years:

Thank you. Your dedication and passion for helping your people is inspiring. I'm grateful to have learned from you and count many of you as teachers, mentors, and friends.

To Aidi, Bearce, Bruce, Joao, Hoosh, Horse, Magic, Mango, Paz & Wiz:

You are my chosen family, and I am forever grateful for you. If I were to have just one close friend like you, I would be lucky—to count all of you as brothers is beyond words. You have taught me so much—and put up with me for so long! You have been with me through thick and thin (literally), ups and downs (also, literally), and every part of my story. Thank you.

To Bard & Andy:

So much to say and yet some things are better left unsaid. Seriously, I'm profoundly grateful for both of you and the laughter (and tears), and discussions (and debates) we've shared over the many long years we've spent together.

To Joshua:

From your support with Journey to getting Ita and I back into the country, your willingness to help knows no bounds. I feel truly grateful to call you both a friend and family.

To Tash & San:

You took me in when you barely knew me and made me feel like family. From best friends in Australia and New York to this lifetime, realm, and beyond, our bond is something I will treasure forever.

To AA:

What I thought was a favor to my brother turned out to be one of the greatest gifts. I'm so grateful for our friendship and look forward to many more years of laughter and deep connection. (I wonder if by the time you read this, I'll still owe you a sushi dinner!)

To Chris & Molly:

Thank you for making the dark days of COVID so much brighter, and for bringing joy into my life every day since. Chris, I deeply appreciate your guidance on this project—I truly would not be here if it wasn't for you.

To Eddie:

From Australia to New York, Altrum to Journey, Unique World to Skor, and Bondi Pizza to Buddhakan, your friendship, guidance, wisdom, and optimism have been constants in my life. Thank you for being you and for always understanding my dietary needs!

To Brian Miller:

Thank you for being my ride-or-die, day-to-day partner on one hell of a ride. Thank you for your unwavering support, loyalty, belief, humor, and friendship. It was an honor.

To Sharon:

Thank you for loving me, Ita, Sam, David, and, most importantly, my mom, so deeply. You are truly a blessing, and I am endlessly grateful for your presence in our lives.

Finally, to you, the reader:

Thank you for being part of this vital conversation about mental health. Your interest, curiosity, and commitment to fostering a better, healthier world make this work worthwhile.

This book is the result of collective effort and shared belief in the importance of mental health. To everyone who played a role, thank you from the bottom of my heart.

MENTAL HEALTH RESOURCES & CRISIS HOTLINES

The following is a list of crisis support hotlines and other mental health organizations and online resources to provide additional and/or immediate support for those interested or in need.

Please note that the inclusion of these resources does not constitute an endorsement of any particular service or organization.

HOTLINES AND CRISIS SUPPORT

988 Suicide & Crisis Lifeline

The 988 Suicide & Crisis Lifeline is a network of local crisis centers in the United States that provides free and confidential emotional support to people in suicidal crisis or emotional distress 24 hours a day, 7 days a week.

They also provide prevention and crisis resources for loved ones as well as best practices for mental health professionals in the United States.

Dial 988 for immediate support.

Crisis Text Hotline

The Crisis Text hotline is free and available 24 hours a day, 7 days a week, throughout the U.S.

The Crisis Text Line serves anyone, in any type of crisis, connecting them with a crisis counselor who can provide support and information.

Text "HELLO" to 741741.

You can text the hotline, message via WhatsApp, or use the chat feature on their website at www.crisistexthotline.org.

National Domestic Violence Hotline

The National Domestic Violence Hotline provides essential tools and support 24 hours a day, 7 days a week, to help survivors of domestic violence so they can live their lives free of abuse.

Contacts can expect highly-trained, expert advocates to offer free, confidential, and compassionate support, crisis intervention information, education, and referral services in over 200 languages.

Call 1-800-799-SAFE (7233) for help.

Or text START to 88788.

RAINN—National Sexual Assault Hotline

RAINN is the Rape, Abuse & Incest National Network, the largest non-profit anti-sexual assault organization in the United States, committed to supporting survivors of sexual violence and cultivating communities of anti-sexual violence activism.

The organization partners with over 1,000 local sexual assault service providers to provide free, confidential support from trained specialists 24/7.

Call 800-656-HOPE (4673) for help.

Or visit online.rainn.org to chat one-on-one with a specialist.

Visit hotline.rainn.org/es to chat in Spanish.

Veterans Crisis Line

The Veterans Crisis Line is a free, confidential resource that connects veterans 24 hours a day, seven days a week with a trained responder. The service is available to all veterans, even if they are not registered with the VA or enrolled in VA healthcare.

Call 1-800-273-TALK (8255) and press 1, or text 838255.

People who are deaf, hard of hearing, or have hearing loss can call 1-800-799-4889.

SAMHSA—The Substance Abuse and Mental Health Services Administration

The disaster distress helpline provides immediate crisis counseling for people who are experiencing emotional distress related to any natural or human-caused disaster. The helpline is free, multilingual, confidential, and available 24 hours a day, seven days a week.

Call or text 1-800-985-5990.

The Trevor Project

The Trevor Project provides 24/7 crisis support services to LGBTQ+ young people.

Text, chat, or call 1-866-488-7386 anytime to reach a trained counselor.

Trans Lifeline

Trans Lifeline is the only peer-support hotline in the United States offering direct emotional and financial support to trans people in crisis. Trans Lifeline is run by and for trans people.

Call 1-877-565-8860 in the U.S. and 1-877-330-6366 in Canada.

MENTAL HEALTH ORGANIZATIONS AND ONLINE RESOURCES

Alcoholics Anonymous (AA)—www.aa.org

A fellowship of individuals who share their experiences and support each other in recovering from alcoholism.

Anxiety and Depression Association of America (ADAA)—www.adaa.org

Provides resources, support groups, and information on anxiety and depression.

Beyond Blue (Australia)—www.beyondblue.org.au

Offers information, resources, and support for anxiety, depression, and suicide prevention.

Mental Health America (MHA)—www.mhanational.org

Offers resources, screening tools, and information on mental health conditions.

Mind (U.K.)—www.mind.org.uk

Provides advice and support to empower anyone experiencing a mental health problem.

National Alliance on Mental Illness (NAMI)—www.nami.org

Provides education, support, and advocacy for individuals affected by mental illness.

SMART Recovery—www.smartrecovery.org

Provides support groups and resources for addiction recovery using a self-empowering approach.

Veterans Affairs Mental Health Support— mentalhealth.va.gov

If you're serving on active duty in the United States uniformed services, including active National Guard and Reserve with federal pay as well as traditional or technical members, you can get connected with mental healthcare—no matter your discharge status, service history, eligibility, or enrollment status for VA healthcare.

To access free VA mental health services right away:
- Call or walk in to any VA medical center—anytime, day or night.
- Call or walk in to any Vet Center during clinic hours.
- Call the VA at 877-222-8387, open Monday through Friday, 8:00 a.m. to 8:00 p.m. ET.
  - › If you have hearing loss, call TTY: 800-877-8339

APPS AND DIGITAL TOOLS

BetterHelp—www.betterhelp.com

Offers online counseling and therapy sessions with licensed therapists through video, phone, or messaging.

Calm—www.calm.com

Provides meditation, sleep stories, and relaxation exercises to help reduce stress and anxiety.

Headspace—www.headspace.com

A meditation and mindfulness app offering guided sessions, sleep sounds, and mindfulness exercises.

MindDoc—www.minddoc.com

A mental health app that offers mood tracking, assessments, and resources to support mental wellbeing.

Talkspace—www.talkspace.com

Provides online therapy with licensed therapists via text, audio, and video messaging.

COMMON MENTAL HEALTH CONDITIONS

The information provided in this appendix is for informational purposes only and does not constitute medical advice or an endorsement of any particular diagnosis, treatment, or provider. For personalized support, please consult a qualified healthcare professional.

Anxiety Disorders

Anxiety disorders are incredibly common, and there are numerous forms: generalized anxiety disorder, social anxiety disorder, panic disorder, and separation anxiety disorder, among others. These disorders can cause overwhelming fear and concern, with symptoms including excessive worry, restlessness, and physical manifestations like increased heart rate and sweating. In particularly acute states, people can experience significant distress and/or impaired functioning.

Attention-Deficit/Hyperactivity Disorder (ADHD)

ADHD is characterized by patterns of inattention, hyperactivity, and impulsivity that interfere with daily functioning. Symptoms include difficulty focusing, following instructions, completing tasks, or remaining still. It can affect children and adults alike, and untreated ADHD can impact work performance, relationships, and mental wellbeing.

Bipolar Disorder

Characterized by extreme mood swings, bipolar disorder includes manic episodes in which people experience high energy, reduced need for sleep, and hyperactivity, followed by episodes of depression, low energy, and an inability to complete daily activities. When untreated, bipolar disorder can greatly impact daily life, relationships, and work performance, though there are effective treatments.

Borderline Personality Disorder (BPD)

BPD involves intense emotional instability, impulsive behavior, and difficulty in maintaining relationships. People with BPD may experience mood swings, fear of abandonment, distorted self-image, and self-destructive behaviors. Treatment can significantly improve functioning and reduce distress.

Burnout

Burnout is a state of emotional, physical, and mental exhaustion caused by prolonged stress, often due to work and common in high-stress and high-stakes professions and industries, such as law, finance, medicine, and public education, to name a few. Symptoms include energy depletion, the inability to make decisions, emotional distance and compartmentalization, and reduced professional efficacy. Burnout is particularly pertinent, of course, to mental health in the workplace as it's directly impacted by an organization's culture, the expectations placed on employees, and the mental health resources provided (or lack thereof).

Depression

Depression is characterized by persistent feelings of sadness, hopelessness, self-doubt or self-loathing, a lack of interest or pleasure in activities, and/or in severe cases, suicidal ideation. It can also manifest physically, with symptoms such as changes in appetite, increased sleep disturbances, and fatigue.

Dissociative Disorders

These disorders involve a disconnection between thoughts, identity, consciousness, and memory, often as a result of trauma. Dissociative disorders include dissociative identity disorder (formerly known as multiple personality disorder) and depersonalization-derealization disorder.

Eating Disorders

People with eating disorders experience body dysmorphia and the preoccupation with food, weight, and body shape. Eating disorders can take the form of anorexia nervosa, bulimia nervosa, binge-eating disorder, and avoidant/restrictive food intake disorder, among others. People of all ages, genders, ethnicities, and body weights can experience eating disorders, and even people who appear to be healthy on the outside can have eating disorders and be incredibly sick.

Obsessive-Compulsive Disorder (OCD)

OCD is characterized by recurrent, uncontrollable thoughts and repetitive behaviors—in other words, obsessions and compulsions. These behaviors tend to be performed to alleviate the anxiety caused by the obsessions but can interfere with daily functioning.

Phobias

Phobias are intense, irrational fears of specific objects, situations, or activities, which can cause avoidance behaviors that interfere with daily life. Common phobias include fear of heights (acrophobia), flying (aviophobia), or social situations (social phobia).

Post-Traumatic Stress Disorder (PTSD)

PTSD develops after exposure to a traumatic event and is characterized by flashbacks, severe anxiety, and uncontrollable thoughts about the event. It is prevalent among the veteran population, however, traumatic events of widely varying natures can lead to PTSD for anyone.

Schizophrenia

Schizophrenia is a serious mental illness that affects how a person thinks, feels, and behaves. It can involve hallucinations, delusions, disorganized thinking, and an impaired ability to function. Early treatment is crucial for managing the symptoms and improving long-term outcomes.

Substance Use Disorders

Sometimes called addictions, substance use disorders involve the excessive use of substances such as alcohol or drugs. They can lead to significant impairment, distress, anxiety, paranoia, physical illness, and personality and behavior change, and often impact people's work and relationships to a great degree.

MENTAL HEALTH ASSESSMENTS

Mental health assessment tools can help individuals understand their mental health status and identify areas that may need attention. They are great tools for organizations to help support individual employees' mental health as well as learn more about the state of mental health of their workforce. This appendix provides a list of commonly used mental health assessments and resources.

Patient Health Questionnaire-9 (PHQ-9)

A self-administered tool for assessing depression severity. It includes nine questions that align with the diagnostic criteria for major depressive disorder.

Generalized Anxiety Disorder-7 (GAD-7)

A self-administered tool for assessing anxiety severity. It includes seven questions that measure the symptoms of generalized anxiety disorder.

Perceived Stress Scale (PSS)

A tool for measuring the perception of stress. It includes questions about feelings and thoughts during the past month.

Depression, Anxiety, and Stress Scale-21 (DASS-21)

A set of three self-report scales designed to measure the emotional states of depression, anxiety, and stress.

Mood Disorder Questionnaire (MDQ)

A screening tool for bipolar disorder. It includes questions about mood swings, behavior, and family history.

Beck Depression Inventory (BDI)

A 21-item self-report inventory measuring the severity of depression.

Hamilton Anxiety Rating Scale (HAM-A)

A clinician-administered scale that assesses the severity of anxiety symptoms.

Mini International Neuropsychiatric Interview (MINI)

A structured diagnostic interview for identifying psychiatric disorders.

Montgomery-Åsberg Depression Rating Scale (MADRS)

A clinician-administered scale that assesses the severity of depressive episodes.

Clinical Global Impressions (CGI)

A tool used by clinicians to assess treatment response in patients with mental disorders.

FURTHER READING

For those interested in exploring mental health topics in greater depth, here is a list of books I recommend.

The Body Keeps the Score: Brain, Mind, and Body in the Healing of Trauma **by Bessel van der Kolk, MD**

Explores the impact of trauma on the body and mind and offers insights into healing and recovery.

Mindfulness for Beginners **by Jon Kabat-Zinn**

An introduction to mindfulness practices and their benefits for mental health and wellbeing.

Feeling Good: The New Mood Therapy **by David D. Burns, MD**

A guide to cognitive-behavioral techniques for managing depression and improving mood.

Lost Connections: Uncovering the Real Causes of Depression—and the Unexpected Solutions **by Johann Hari**

Examines the root causes of depression and offers alternative approaches to treatment.

Man's Search for Meaning by **Viktor E. Frankl**

A powerful memoir and exploration of finding purpose and meaning in life, even in the most difficult circumstances.

How to Win Friends and Influence People by **Dale Carnegie**

A classic guide to building strong relationships and improving interpersonal skills, with implications for mental wellbeing.

The 7 Habits of Highly Effective People by **Stephen R. Covey**

Covey's influential work on personal development and creating balance in life, with a focus on habit-building for wellbeing.

The Power of Now: A Guide to Spiritual Enlightenment by **Eckhart Tolle**

Tolle's teachings on living in the present moment and freeing oneself from stress and anxiety.

Daring Greatly: How the Courage to Be Vulnerable Transforms the Way We Live, Love, Parent, and Lead by **Brené Brown**

Explores the importance of vulnerability in building resilience and connection in both personal and professional life.

Happier: Learn the Secrets to Daily Joy and Lasting Fulfillment by **Tal Ben-Shahar**

A guide to positive psychology principles and practical ways to cultivate happiness and meaning in life.

The Happiness Advantage: How a Positive Brain Fuels Success in Work and Life by **Shawn Achor**

Achor's research-based book on how happiness and a positive mindset can lead to better performance and overall wellbeing.

A Path with Heart: A Guide Through the Perils and Promises of Spiritual Life by **Jack Kornfield**

A practical guide to meditation and mindfulness, offering tools for inner growth and healing.

Real Happiness at Work: Meditations for Accomplishment, Achievement, and Peace by **Sharon Salzberg**

Salzberg explores the practice of meditation and its impact on mental health, compassion, and wellbeing in the workplace.

Radical Acceptance: Embracing Your Life with the Heart of a Buddha by **Tara Brach**

A guide to breaking free from self-judgment and embracing mindfulness and compassion to heal emotional wounds.

The Untethered Soul: The Journey Beyond Yourself by **Michael A. Singer**

This book explores mindfulness and spiritual awareness, offering insights into how we can free ourselves from mental and emotional limitations.

The Four Agreements: A Practical Guide to Personal Freedom by **Don Miguel Ruiz**

A spiritual guide based on ancient Toltec wisdom, focusing on principles that lead to personal freedom and happiness.

Self-Compassion: The Proven Power of Being Kind to Yourself by **Kristin Neff**

Neff's book on how practicing self-compassion can improve emotional wellbeing, reduce anxiety, and enhance personal resilience.

Buddhism for Busy People: Finding Happiness in an Uncertain World by **David Michie**

Michie offers an accessible introduction to Buddhist principles and mindfulness, tailored to those looking for balance and happiness.

REFERENCES

Abbas, Fatima. "Mental Health: An Urgent Priority for Africa." Omnia Health Insights. October 28, 2021. https://insights.omnia-health.com /show-news/mental-health-urgent-priority-africa.

Abrams, Zara. "The Science of Friendship." *Monitor on Psychology* 54, no. 4 (June 2023).

Adepoju, Paul. "Africa Turns to Telemedicine to Close Mental Health Gap." *The Lancet Digital Health* 2, no. 11 (2020): e571–e572. https://doi.org/10.1016/S2589-7500(20)30252-1.

Aderinto, Nicholas, Joshua Opanike, and Elizabeth Oladipo. "Accessing Mental Health Services in Africa: Current State, Efforts, Challenges, and Recommendation." *Annals of Medicine & Surgery* 81 (September 2022): 104421. https://doi.org/10.1016/j.amsu.2022.104421.

Africa CDC. "Mental Health: A Universal Human Right for Africans." October 10, 2023. https://africacdc.org/news-item/mental-health-a -universal-human-right-for-africans/.

Aladjem, Ruthi, and JoJo Platt. "2024 Is the Year for Brain-Computer Interfaces." *Technology Networks*. July 11, 2024. https://www .technologynetworks.com/neuroscience/blog/2024-is-the-year-for -brain-computer-interfaces-388563.

Amazon. "About Amazon: Leadership Principles." Accessed November 3, 2024. https://www.aboutamazon.com/about-us/leadership-principles.

American Psychiatric Association. "Mental Health Facts." Accessed November 3, 2024. https://www.psychiatry.org/psychiatrists/diversity/education/mental-health-facts.

American Psychological Association. "Mindfulness Meditation: A Research-Proven Way to Reduce Stress." October 30, 2019. https://www.apa.org/topics/mindfulness/meditation.

American Psychological Association. "Train Managers to Foster Healthy Workplaces." May 16, 2024. https://www.apa.org/topics/healthy-workplaces/mental-health/train-managers.

American Psychological Association. "Workforce Demographics." 2017. https://www.apa.org/workforce/data-tools/demographics.

André, Aurore S. "Mental Healthcare in Europe: Review 2023 and Outlook 2024." *LinkedIn.* January 23, 2024. https://www.linkedin.com/pulse/mental-healthcare-europe-review-2023-outlook-2024-aurore-s-andre-6dref/.

Atieh, Nada. "Barriers to Mental Health: The Middle Eastern Experience." *National Alliance on Mental Illness.* July 29, 2022. https://www.nami.org/education/barriers-to-mental-health-the-middle-eastern-experience/.

Bell Let's Talk. "Our Impact." Accessed November 3, 2024. https://letstalk.bell.ca/our-impact/.

Better Health Channel. "Exercise and Mental Health." Victoria State Government, Department of Health. Accessed November 3, 2024. https://www.betterhealth.vic.gov.au/health/healthyliving/exercise-and-mental-health.

Bisma, Anwar. "Journaling for Mental Health." Clinically reviewed by Kate Robsenblatt. Talkspace. Updated March 21, 2023. https://www.talkspace.com/blog/journaling-for-mental-health/.

BlackRock. "Together as One." Fact sheet. Accessed November 3, 2024. https://www.blackrock.com/corporate/literature/fact-sheet/together -as-one.pdf.

Brassey, Jacqueline, Anna Güntner, Karina Isaak, and Tobias Silberzahn. "Using Digital Tech to Support Employees' Mental Health and Resilience."McKinsey & Company. July 8, 2021. https://www.mckinsey .com/industries/life-sciences/our-insights/using-digital-tech-to-support -employees-mental-health-and-resilience#/.

Bright Network. "How This BlackRock Trader Is Destigmatizing Mental Health at Work." Accessed November 3, 2024. https://www.brightnetwork.co.uk/employer-advice/blackrock/how -this-blackrock-trader-is-destigmatizing-mental-health-at-work/.

Bush, Donna M., and Rachel N. Lipari. "Substance Use and Substance Use Disorder by Industry." Substance Abuse and Mental Health Services Administration. April 16, 2015. https://www.samhsa.gov/data /sites/default/files/report_1959/ShortReport-1959.html.

Business Wire. "80% of Retail Workers Feel Unsafe." May 21, 2024. https://finance.yahoo.com/news/80-retail-workers-feel-unsafe -131700285.html.

Centers for Disease Control and Prevention. "Mental Health for All." Accessed November 3, 2024. https://www.cdc.gov/ncbddd /disabilityandhealth/features/mental-health-for-all.html.

Centers for Disease Control and Prevention. "Mental Health and Healthcare Workers." Accessed November 3, 2024. https://www.cdc .gov/niosh/newsroom/feature/health-worker-mental-health.html.

Chen, Q., S. Huang, H. Xu, et al. "The Burden of Mental Disorders in Asian Countries, 1990–2019: An Analysis for the Global Burden of Disease Study 2019." *Translational Psychiatry* 14 (2024): 167. https://doi.org/10.1038/s41398-024-02864-5.

Clay, R. A. "A New Look at Racial and Ethnic Disparities in Mental Health Care." *Monitor on Psychology* 47, no. 1 (January 2016). https://www.apa.org/monitor/2016/01/publication-disparities.

Clarence, Anthony E. "A Shifting Landscape: Mental Health in the Workplace." National League of Cities. July 24, 2024. https://www.nlc.org/article/2024/07/24/a-shifting-landscape-mental-health-in-the-workplace/.

Cree, Robyn A., Catherine A. Okoro, Matthew M. Zack, and Eric Carbone. "Frequent Mental Distress Among Adults, by Disability Status, Disability Type, and Selected Characteristics — United States, 2018." *MMWR Morbidity and Mortality Weekly Report* 69 (2020): 1238–43. https://doi.org/10.15585/mmwr.mm6936a2.

"Current State of College & Student Mental Health Survey." NASPA Student Affairs Administrators in Higher Education, Uwill Student Mental Health & Wellness. Accessed November 3, 2024. https://uwill.com/NASPA-college-mental-health-survey/.

Deloitte. "Blueprint for Workplace Mental Health." 2019. https://www2.deloitte.com/content/dam/Deloitte/ca/Documents/about-deloitte/ca-en-about-blueprint-for-workplace-mental-health-final-aoda.pdf.

Douglas, Kate, and Joe Douglas. "Green Spaces Aren't Just for Nature; They Boost Our Mental Health Too." *New Scientist*. March 24, 2021. https://www.newscientist.com/article/mg24933270-800-green-spaces-arent-just-for-nature-they-boost-our-mental-health-too/.

Drobny, Kimberley. "2024 Retail Worker Safety Survey." *Theatro*. May 20, 2024. https://www.theatro.com/resources/2024-retail-worker-safety-survey/.

DuRose, Rachel. "How BlackRock's HR Executive Managed the Investment Firm Through the Pandemic." *Business Insider*. March 30, 2022. https://www.businessinsider.com/blackrock-hr-executive-managed-investment-firm-through-pandemic-2022-3.

Eaton, Nicholas R., et al. "An Invariant Dimensional Liability Model of Gender Differences in Mental Disorder Prevalence: Evidence from a National Sample." *Journal of Abnormal Psychology* 121, no. 1 (2012): 282–88. https://doi.org/10.1037/a0024780.

Economist Impact. "Mental health in the Middle East—Measuring progress towards integrated, accessible and equitable mental health." May 15, 2023. https://impact.economist.com/perspectives/sites/default/files/janssen-measuring_mental_health_integration_in_the_middle_east-report-a4-v4.pdf.

Edmondson, Amy. "What Is Psychological Safety?" *Harvard Business Review*, February 2023. https://hbr.org/2023/02/what-is-psychological-safety.

European Commission. "EU comprehensive approach to mental health." Accessed November 3, 2024. https://health.ec.europa.eu/non-communicable-diseases/mental-health_en.

Fioritti, Angelo, et al. "Mental Health and Work: A European Perspective." *Epidemiology and Psychiatric Sciences* 33 (April 5, 2024): e20. https://doi.org/10.1017/S2045796024000246.

Flannery, Mary Ellen. "The Mental Health Crisis Among Faculty and College Staff." National Education Association. March 7, 2024. https://www.nea.org/nea-today/all-news-articles/mental-health-crisis-among-faculty-and-college-staff.

Funer, F. "Admitting the Heterogeneity of Social Inequalities: Intersectionality as a (Self-)Critical Framework and Tool within Mental Health Care." *Philosophy, Ethics, and Humanities in Medicine* 18 (2023): 21. https://doi.org/10.1186/s13010-023-00144-6.

Gallup. "American Youth: A Research Overview." Accessed November 3, 2024. https://www.gallup.com/analytics/506663/american-youth-research.aspx.

"Global, regional, and national burden of 12 mental disorders in 204 countries and territories, 1990–2019: a systematic analysis for the Global Burden of Disease Study 2019."

The Lancet Psychiatry, Volume 9, Issue 2, 137-150. https://www.thelancet.com/action/showPdf?pii=S2215-0366%2821%2900395-3.

Goldberg, Simon B., Raymond P. Tucker, Preston A. Greene, Richard J. Davidson, Bruce E. Wampold, David J. Kearney, and Tracy L. Simpson. "Mindfulness-Based Interventions for Psychiatric Disorders: A Systematic Review and Meta-Analysis." *Clinical Psychology Review* 59 (2018): 52–60. https://doi.org/10.1016/j.cpr.2017.10.011.

Godman, Heidi. "Having a Hobby Tied to Happiness and Well-Being." Harvard Health Publishing. January 1, 2024. https://www.health.harvard.edu/mind-and-mood/having-a-hobby-tied-to-happiness-and-well-being.

Gregory, Sarah Youngblood. "The Mental Health Benefits of Nature: Spending Time Outdoors to Refresh Your Mind." Mayo Clinic. March 4, 2024. https://mcpress.mayoclinic.org/mental-health/the-mental-health -benefits-of-nature-spending-time-outdoors-to-refresh-your-mind/.

Grelle, Kaitlin, et al. "The Generation Gap Revisited: Generational Differences in Mental Health, Maladaptive Coping Behaviors, and Pandemic-Related Concerns During the Initial COVID-19 Pandemic." *Journal of Adult Development* (February 16, 2023): 1-12. https://doi.org/10.1007/s10804-023-09442-x.

Guzman-Ruiz, Yenny. "A Neglected Challenge of Mental Health." *Think Global Health*. July 5, 2023. https://www.thinkglobalhealth.org/article /neglected-challenge-mental-health.

Helliwell, John F., Richard Layard, and Jeffrey D. Sachs. "World Happiness, Trust, and Social Connections in Times of Crisis." In *World Happiness Report 2023*, 11th ed., Chapter 2. Sustainable Development Solutions Network, 2023.

Holt-Lunstad, Julianne, Timothy B. Smith, and JB Layton. "Social Relationships and Mortality Risk: A Meta-Analytic Review." *PLoS Medicine* 7, no. 7 (2010): e1000316. https://doi.org/10.1371/journal .pmed.1000316.

Hughes, Charlotte. "Mental Health: Focused on Diversity and Inclusion." American Society for Healthcare Human Resources Administration. *HR Pulse*, Summer 2021. https://ashhra.org/resources _library/mental-health-focused-on-diversity-and-inclusion/.

Huizen, Jennifer. "Mental Health Stigma in Latin America." Medically reviewed by C.C. Cassell, Psy.D. *Medical News Today*. Accessed November 3, 2024. https://www.medicalnewstoday.com/articles /mental-health-stigma-in-latin-america#in-latin-america.

InformedHealth.org. "In Brief: Cognitive Behavioral Therapy (CBT)." Cologne, Germany: Institute for Quality and Efficiency in Health Care (IQWiG), 2006. Updated June 2, 2022. https://www.ncbi.nlm.nih.gov /books/NBK279297/.

Jayman, Michelle, Jonathan Glazzard, and Anthea Rose. "Tipping Point: The Staff Wellbeing Crisis in Higher Education." *Frontiers in Education* 7 (2022). https://doi.org/10.3389/feduc.2022.929335.

Kaiser Family Foundation. "EHBS 2023: Summary of Findings." October 18, 2023. https://www.kff.org/report-section/ehbs-2023 -summary-of-findings/.

Kelly, Jack. "How Major Companies Are Addressing Mental Health in the Workplace." *Forbes*, March 14, 2024. https://www.forbes.com/sites/jackkelly/2024/03/14/ how-major-companies-are-addressing-mental-health-in-the-workplace/.

Kelly, Jack. "The Dark Side of Investment Banking: Stress, Pressure, and 100-Hour Workweeks." *Forbes*, May 30, 2024. https://www.forbes.com /sites/jackkelly/2024/05/30/the-dark-side-of-investment-banking-stress -pressure-and-100-hour-workweeks/.

Khayatzadeh-Mahani, A., et al. "Mental Health in the Workplace: A Review." *National Center for Biotechnology Information*. 2019. https://pmc.ncbi.nlm.nih.gov/articles/PMC6949012/.

Khoury, Bassam, Tania Lecomte, Guillaume Fortin, Marjolaine Masse, Phillip Therien, Vanessa Bouchard, Marie-Andrée Chapleau, Karine Paquin, and Stefan G. Hofmann. "Mindfulness-Based Therapy: A Comprehensive Meta-Analysis." *Clinical Psychology Review* 33, no. 6 (2013): 763–771. https://doi.org/10.1016/j.cpr.2013.05.005.

Komeilipoor, N. "Brain-Computer Interface (BCI) Technology Revolutionizing Healthcare with Brain-Controlled Technology." *MedPage Today*. February 2024. https://medcitynews.com/2024/02 /brain-computer-interface-bci-technology-revolutionizing-healthcare -with-brain-controlled-technology/.

Krill, Patrick R., Hannah M. Thomas, Meaghyn R. Kramer, Nikki Degeneffe, and Justin J. Anker. 2023. "Stressed, Lonely, and Overcommitted: Predictors of Lawyer Suicide Risk" Healthcare 11, no. 4: 536. https://doi.org/10.3390/healthcare11040536

Krpan, Katherine M., Ethan Kross, M. G. Berman, P. J. Deldin, M. K. Askren, and J. Jonides. "An Everyday Activity as a Treatment for Depression: The Benefits of Expressive Writing for People Diagnosed with Major Depressive Disorder." *Journal of Affective Disorders* 150, no. 3 (2013): 1148–1151. https://doi.org/10.1016/j.jad.2013.05.065.

Kyere, E., and S. Fukui. "Structural Racism, Workforce Diversity, and Mental Health Disparities: A Critical Review." *Journal of Racial and Ethnic Health Disparities* 10 (2023): 1985–1996. https://doi.org/10.1007 /s40615-022-01380-w.

Lachance, Laura, and Drew Ramsey. "Food, Mood, and Brain Health: Implications for the Modern Clinician." *Missouri Medicine* 112, no. 2 (2015): 111–115.

Lark Suite. "5-15 Report." December 19, 2023. https://www.larksuite .com/en_us/topics/productivity-glossary/5-15-report.

LG2. "The Biggest Conversation in the Country." Accessed November 3, 2024. https://lg2.com/en/our-work/the-biggest-conversation-in -the-country.

Luxton, Emma. "Workplace Anxiety Costs More Than You Think." *World Economic Forum.* August 3, 2016. https://www.weforum.org /agenda/2016/08/workplace-anxiety-costs-more-than-you-think/.

Lyubykh, Zhanna, and Duygu Biricik Gulseren. "How to Take Better Breaks at Work, According to Research." *Harvard Business Review,* May 31, 2023. https://hbr.org/2023/05/how-to-take-better-breaks-at-work -according-to-research.

Manufacturers Alliance. "Manufacturing — The impact of good mental health." Accessed November 3, 2024. https://www .manufacturersalliance.org/sites/default/files/2021-07/Cost%20of%20 Mental%20Health%20Report%20%E2%80%94%20Manufacturing.pdf.

Mayberry, Sean. "4 Facts About Mental Health in Africa." *World Economic Forum.* August 19, 2021. https://www.weforum.org /agenda/2021/08/4-facts-mental-health-africa/.

Mayo Clinic Staff. "Depression and Exercise." Mayo Clinic. Accessed November 3, 2024. https://www.mayoclinic.org/diseases-conditions /depression/in-depth/depression-and-exercise/art-20046495.

McCandless, Sean, Bruce McDonald, and Sara Rinfret. "Walking Faculty Back from the Cliff." *Inside Higher Ed.* August 21, 2023. https://www .insidehighered.com/opinion/views/2023/08/21/institutions-must -take-faculty-burnout-seriously-opinion.

McFarland, Dennis J., et al. "Therapeutic Applications of BCI Technologies." *Brain Computer Interfaces* 47, no. 1–2 (2017): 37–52. https://doi.org/10.1080/2326263X.2017.1307625.

Medaris, Anna. "Gen Z Adults and Younger Millennials Are 'Completely Overwhelmed' by Stress." American Psychological Association. November 1, 2023. https://www.apa.org/topics/stress/generation -z-millennials-young-adults-worries.

Mental Health America. "The Mental Health of Healthcare Workers During COVID-19." Accessed November 3, 2024. https://mhanational .org/mental-health-healthcare-workers-covid-19.

Mental Health America. "Workplace Mental Health Training." Accessed November 3, 2024. https://mhanational.org/workplace-mental-health -training.

Mental Health Europe. "Intersectionality." Accessed November 3, 2024. https://www.mentalhealtheurope.org/what-we-do/intersectionality/.

Mental Health Partners of Colorado. "Intersectionality and Mental Health." Accessed November 3, 2024. https://mhpcolorado.org/blog /intersectionality-mental-health.

Mostert, Cyprian M., et al. "Who Should Pay the Bill for the Mental Health Crisis in Africa?" *Public Health in Practice* (Oxford, England) 7 (December 15, 2023): 100458. https://doi.org/10.1016/j.puhip.2023 .100458.

Murthy, Vivek H. "Surgeon General: Why I'm Calling for a Warning Label on Social Media Platforms," *The New York Times,* June 17, 2024. https://www.nytimes.com/2024/06/17/opinion/social-media-health -warning.html.

National Alliance on Mental Illness NYC Metro. "Workplace Mental Health Trainings." Accessed November 3, 2024. https://naminycmetro .org/workplace-mental-health/trainings/.

National Cancer Institute, Division of Epidemiology and Genetics. "Neurodiversity." April 25, 2022. https://dceg.cancer.gov/about /diversity-inclusion/inclusivity-minute/2022/neurodiversity#.

National Conference of State Legislatures. "Mental Health Matters: Policy Framework on Workforce Mental Health." Updated September 7, 2023. https://www.ncsl.org/labor-and-employment/mental-health -matters-policy-framework-on-workforce-mental-health.

National Heart, Lung, and Blood Institute. "How Sleep Affects Your Health." Updated June 15, 2022. https://www.nhlbi.nih.gov/health /sleep-deprivation/health-effects#:~:text=Sleep%20helps%20your%20 brain%20work,lower%20grades%20and%20feel%20stressed.

National Institute on Alcohol Abuse and Alcoholism. "Alcohol Use Disorder (AUD) in the United States: Age Groups and Demographic Characteristics." Updated 2024. https://www.niaaa.nih.gov/alcohols -effects-health/alcohol-topics/alcohol-facts-and-statistics/alcohol -use-disorder-aud-united-states-age-groups-and-demographic -characteristics.

National Institutes of Health. "Prevalence of Any Mental Illness Among U.S. Adults." Updated September 2024. http://www.nimh.nih.gov/health /statistics/prevalence/any-mental-illness-ami-among-us-adults.shtml.

National Safety Council. "New Mental Health Cost Calculator Demonstrates Why." May 13, 2021. https://www.nsc.org/newsroom /new-mental-health-cost-calculator-demonstrates-why?srsltid=AfmBOo rWF0htZjx0mCj1OMRZ63qQIkMAWnn62_GDrBq72CWVDMDsnz6h.

Office of Juvenile Justice and Delinquency Prevention. "U.S. Surgeon General Issues Advisory on Social Media and Youth Mental Health." June 5, 2023. https://ojjdp.ojp.gov/news/juvjust/us-surgeon-general -issues-advisory-social-media-and-youth-mental-health.

Paige, Jessica. "Retailers Need to Focus on Employee Mental Health: Experts Weigh In." *Retail Insight Network.* May 14, 2021. https://www.retail-insight-network.com/features/retailers-need-to -focus-on-employee-mental-health-experts-weigh-in/?cf-view.

Pan American Health Organization. "Mental Health." Accessed November 3, 2024. https://www.paho.org/en/topics/mental-health.

Peterson, Cora, Aaron Sussell, Jia Li, Pamela K. Schumacher, Kristin Yeoman, and Deborah M. Stone. "Suicide Rates by Industry and Occupation — National Violent Death Reporting System, 32 States, 2016." *MMWR Morbidity and Mortality Weekly Report* 69 (2020): 57–62. https://doi.org/10.15585/mmwr.mm6903a1.

Pfeffer, Jeffrey, and Leanne Williams. "Mental Health in the Workplace: The Coming Revolution." *McKinsey Quarterly*. December 8, 2020. https://www.mckinsey.com/industries/healthcare/our-insights/mental-health-in-the-workplace-the-coming-revolution.

"Please Don't Quit: New Data from Zipline Show Declining Mental Health Among Retail Associates." *Zipline Blog*. February 10, 2022. https://getzipline.com/blog/please-dont-quit-new-data-from-zipline-show-declining-mental-health-among-retail-associates/.

PricewaterhouseCoopers. "Medical Cost Trend: Behind the numbers 2025." 2024. https://www.pwc.com/us/en/industries/health-industries/library/assets/pwc-behind-the-numbers-2025.pdf.

Rees, Amelia, Mark W. Wiggins, William S. Helton, Thomas Loveday, and David O'Hare. "The Impact of Breaks on Sustained Attention in a Simulated, Semi-Automated Train Control Task." *Applied Cognitive Psychology* 31 (2017): 351–359. https://doi.org/10.1002/acp.3334.

Roe, Dan. "Old-School Expectations Plague Young Lawyer Mental Health, but Not All Predecessors Are Sympathetic." *The American Lawyer*. May 17, 2024. https://www.law.com/americanlawyer/2024/05/17/old-school-expectations-plague-young-lawyer-mental-health-but-not-all-predecessors-are-sympathetic/.

Saha, Gautam. "Advocacy in Mental Health." *Indian Journal of Psychiatry* 63, no. 6 (2021): 523–526. https://doi.org/10.4103/indianjpsychiatry .indianjpsychiatry_901_21.

Sankoh, Osman, et al. "Mental Health in Africa." *The Lancet Global Health* 6, no. 9 (2018): e954–e955. https://doi.org/10.1016/S2214 -109X(18)30303-6.

SCA Health. "Exploring the Mind-Body Connection: Exercise and Mental Health." June 3, 2024. https://insights.sca.health/insight/article /exploring-the-mind-body-connection-exercise-and-mental-health.

Schawbel, Dan. "Leaders Championing Mental Health: A Work Movement." *LinkedIn Pulse*. November 25, 2019. https://www.linkedin .com/pulse/leaders-championing-mental-health-work-movement -dan-schawbel/.

ScienceDirect. "Brain-Computer Interface." Updated 2024. https://www.sciencedirect.com/topics/medicine-and-dentistry/brain -computer-interface.

Scott, Elizabeth. "Why You Should Take a Break." *Verywell Mind*. Updated November 8, 2023. https://www.verywellmind.com/why -you-should-take-a-break-3144576.

Selhub, Eva. "Nutritional Psychiatry: Your Brain on Food." Harvard Health Publishing. September 18, 2022. https://www.health.harvard. edu/blog/nutritional-psychiatry-your-brain-on-food-201511168626.

Shisana, Olive, Dan J. Stein, Nompumelelo P. Zungu, and Gustaaf Wolvaardt. "The Rationale for South Africa to Prioritize Mental Health Care as a Critical Aspect of Overall Health Care." *Comprehensive Psychiatry* 130 (2024): 152458. https://doi.org/10.1016/j.comppsych .2024.152458.

Shushansky, Larry. "Disparities Within Minority Mental Health Care." National Alliance on Mental Illness. July 31, 2017. https://www.nami .org/advocate/disparities-within-minority-mental-health-care/.

Smyth, Joshua M., et al. "Online Positive Affect Journaling in the Improvement of Mental Distress and Well-Being in General Medical Patients with Elevated Anxiety Symptoms: A Preliminary Randomized Controlled Trial." *JMIR Mental Health* 5, no. 4 (December 10, 2018): e11290. https://doi.org/10.2196/11290.

Sohal, Monika, Pavneet Singh, Bhupinder Singh Dhillon, and Harbir Singh Gill. "Efficacy of Journaling in the Management of Mental Illness: A Systematic Review and Meta-Analysis." *Family Medicine and Community Health* 10, no. 1 (March 2022): e001154. https://doi .org/10.1136/fmch-2021-001154.

Sloan, Karen. "Stress and Overwork Linked to Lawyers' Suicidal Thoughts, Study Says." *Reuters.* February 14, 2023. https://www.reuters. com/legal/litigation/stress-overwork-linked-lawyers-suicidal-thoughts -study-says-2023-02-13/.

Sorsdahl, K., I. Petersen, B. Myers, Z. Zingela, C. Lund, and C. van der Westhuizen. "A Reflection of the Current Status of the Mental Healthcare System in South Africa." *SSM—Mental Health* 4 (2023): 100247. https://doi.org/10.1016/j.ssmmh.2023.100247.

Spitalniak, Laura. "College Student Employee Mental Health Worsened, Survey Finds." *Higher Ed Dive.* January 18, 2024. https://www .highereddive.com/news/college-student-employee-mental-health -worsened-NASPA/640669/.

Substance Abuse and Mental Health Services Administration. "2020 National Survey on Drug Use and Health: Veteran Adults." U.S. Department of Health and Human Services. July 2022. https://www.samhsa.gov/data/sites/default/files/reports/rpt37926 /2020NSDUHVeteransSlides072222.pdf.

Sun, Jianmin, et al. "The Association between Digitalization and Mental Health: The Mediating Role of Wellbeing at Work." *Frontiers in Psychiatry* 13 (2022): 934357. https://doi.org/10.3389/fpsyt.2022 .934357.

Suni, Eric, and Alex Dimitriu. "Mental Health and Sleep." Sleep Foundation. March 26, 2024. https://www.sleepfoundation.org /mental-health.

Sutter Health. "Eating Well for Mental Health." 2024. https://www. sutterhealth.org/health/nutrition/eating-well-for-mental-health.

Thomson Reuters. "Today's Lawyers and Mental Health." *Thomson Reuters Legal.* May 16, 2024. https://legal.thomsonreuters.com/blog /todays-lawyers-and-mental-health/.

Trczinski, Arielle, Annalise Clayton, and Caleb Ewald. "Why Mental Health Needs to Be on Every Company's 2020 Agenda." Forrester Research. December 9, 2019. https://www.forrester.com/blogs/mental -healththe-not-so-widely-talked-about-problem-that-needs-to-be-on -every-companys-agenda-in-2020/.

UCLA Center for Health Policy Research. "Recent immigrants saw biggest spike in mental distress as anti-immigrant sentiment increased." December 18, 2023. https://healthpolicy.ucla.edu/newsroom/blog /californias-newest-immigrants-had-biggest-increase-serious -psychological-distress-between-2015-2021.

UNICEF, WHO. "Mental health a human right, but only 1 psychiatrist per 1,000,000 people in sub-Saharan Africa." October 10, 2023. https://www.unicef.org/esa/press-releases/mental-health-a-human-right.

U.S. Department of Veterans Affairs, Office of Mental Health and Suicide Prevention. "2022 National Veteran Suicide Prevention Annual Report." September 2022. https://www.mentalhealth.va.gov/docs/data -sheets/2022/2022-National-Veteran-Suicide-Prevention-Annual -Report-FINAL-508.pdf.

Utley, Tori. "How EY Is Tackling Stigma and Promoting Mental Health for Employees." *Forbes.* May 30, 2017. https://www.forbes.com/sites /toriutley/2017/05/30/how-one-company-normalized-mental-health -and-encouraged-employees-to-ask-for-help/.

Vos, Theo, et al. "Global Burden of 369 Diseases and Injuries in 204 Countries and Territories, 1990–2019: A Systematic Analysis for the Global Burden of Disease Study 2019." *The Lancet* 396, no. 10258 (2020): 1204–1222.

Wang, Y., et al. "Mental Health Outcomes of the COVID-19 Pandemic: A Comprehensive Review." *The Lancet Regional Health—Southeast Asia* 4 (2023). https://www.thelancet.com/journals/lansea/article/PIIS2772 -3682(23)00147-6/fulltext.

Wang, Yi, et al. "The Relationship Between Mindfulness and Mental Health: A Meta-Analysis." *PMC9902068.* 2022. https://www.ncbi.nlm .nih.gov/pmc/articles/PMC9902068/.

WebWire. "New Study Reveals Retail Workers' Mental Health Crisis." Accessed November 3, 2024. https://www.webwire.com/ViewPressRel .asp?aId=285120.

Weir, K. (2019, January 1). "Give me a break". *Monitor on Psychology*, 50(1). https://www.apa.org/monitor/2019/01/break.

Weiss, Debra Cassens. "17% of BigLaw lawyers and employees feel emotionally depleted by work, survey finds." *ABA Journal.* November 2, 2023. https://www.abajournal.com/news/article/biglaw-associates-at -higher-risk-of-burnout-than-colleagues-survey-says.

Wharton School of the University of Pennsylvania. "BlackRock's Diversity Expert: Employees Feel They Belong." Accessed November 3, 2024. https://knowledge.wharton.upenn.edu/article/blackrocks -diversity-expert-employees-feel-belong.

White, William, and David Sharar. "The Evolution of Employee Assistance: A Brief History and Trend Analysis." Chestnut Global Partners. Accessed November 3, 2024. https://www.chestnut.org /Resources/344a45f4-e241-41ef-8fa6-419accbcc6ff/2003EAPhistorytren dsEAPDigest.pdf.

Whitley, Rob. "Men's Mental Health: A Silent Crisis." *Psychology Today*, February 2017. https://www.psychologytoday.com/us/blog/talking-about -men/201702/mens-mental-health-silent-crisis.

Wondimagegn, D., C. Pain, N. Seifu, et al. "Reimagining Global Mental Health in Africa." *BMJ Global Health* 8 (2023): e013232.

Wong, Bernie, and Kelly Greenwood. "The Future of Mental Health at Work Is Safety, Community, and a Healthy Organizational Culture." *Harvard Business Review*. October 10, 2023. https://hbr.org/2023/10/the -future-of-mental-health-at-work-is-safety-community-and-a-healthy -organizational-culture.

World Health Organization. "Mental Health of Adolescents." Fact sheet. October 10, 2024. https://www.who.int/news-room/fact-sheets /detail/adolescent-mental-health.

World Health Organization. "Community-Based Mental Health Services Using a Rights-Based Approach." June 10, 2021. https://www.who.int/news-room/feature-stories/detail/community-based-mental-health-services-using-a-rights-based-approach.

World Health Organization. "Investing in Treatment for Depression and Anxiety Leads to Fourfold Return." April 13, 2016. https://www.who.int/news/item/13-04-2016-investing-in-treatment-for-depression-and-anxiety-leads-to-fourfold-return.

World Health Organization. *World Mental Health Report: Transforming Mental Health for All.* June 2022. https://www.who.int/publications/i/item/9789240049338.

World Health Organization. "Mental Health." Fact sheet. June 17, 2022. https://www.who.int/news-room/fact-sheets/detail/mental-health-strengthening-our-response.

World Health Organization. "Mental Health at Work." Fact sheet. September 2, 2024. https://www.who.int/news-room/fact-sheets/detail/mental-health-at-work.

World Health Organization, Regional Office for Africa. "Barriers to Mental Health Care in Africa." October 12, 2022. https://www.afro.who.int/news/barriers-mental-health-care-africa.

World Health Organization, Regional Office for Europe. "WHO/Europe Launches for Consultation Its New Quality Standards to Improve the Quality of Child and Adolescent Mental Health Care." July 2, 2024. https://www.who.int/europe/news-room/events/item/2024/07/02/default-calendar/who-europe-launches-for-consultation-its-new-quality-standards-to-improve-the-quality-of-child-and-adolescent-mental-health-care.

Wulsin, Lawson, Toni Alterman, P. Timothy Bushnell, Jia Li, and Rui Shen. "Prevalence Rates for Depression by Industry: A Claims Database Analysis." *Social Psychiatry and Psychiatric Epidemiology* 49, no. 11 (November 2014): 1805–21. https://doi.org/10.1007/s00127-014 -0891-3.

Yiengprugsawan, Vasoontara, Michelle Apostol, and Dinesh Arora. "Five Steps to Address Mental Health in Asia and the Pacific and Beyond." Asian Development Bank Blog. May 22, 2024. https://blogs.adb.org/blog /five-steps-address-mental-health-asia-and-pacific-and-beyond.

Zhao, SiNing. "Bridging the Mental Health Gap in Asia: Challenges and Opportunities." RGA. December 2023. https://www.rgare.com /knowledge-center/article/bridging-the-mental-health-gap-in-asia -challenges-and-opportunities.

ABOUT THE AUTHOR

Stephen Sokoler is an entrepreneur committed to helping people live happier, healthier, and less stressed lives. As the Founder and CEO of Journey, the leading proactive mental health solution for modern companies, Stephen is focused on changing how businesses care for their employees' mental health. Before starting Journey, he co-founded Altrum Honors, the global leader in helping organizations celebrate and inspire their employees. Stephen graduated from NYU's Stern School of Business and lives in New York City with his wife and son.